LEFT HOOKS AND DANGEROUS CROOKS

TEL CURRIE
Foreword by Roy Shaw

APEX PUBLISHING LTD

First published in 2009 by
Apex Publishing Ltd
PO Box 7086, Clacton on Sea, Essex, CO15 5WN

www.apexpublishing.co.uk

Copyright © 2009 by Tel Currie
The author has asserted his moral rights

**British Library Cataloguing-in-Publication Data
A catalogue record for this book
is available from the British Library**

**ISBN 1-906358-58-3
978-1-906358-58-7**

All rights reserved. This book is sold subject to the condition, that no part of this book is to be reproduced, in any shape or form. Or by way of trade, stored in a retrieval system or transmitted in any form or by any means, electronic, mechanical, photocopying, recording, be lent, re-sold, hired out or otherwise circulated in any form of binding or cover other than that in which it is published and without a similar condition, including this condition being imposed on the subsequent purchaser, without prior permission of the copyright holder.

Typeset in 11.5pt Baskerville Win95BT

Editor: Kim Kimber
Thanks must go to Steve Leonard

Production Manager: Chris Cowlin

Cover Design: Siobhan Smith
Main cover image: Sean Keating (P4P Event Photography)

Printed and bound in Great Britain by
the MPG Books Group, Bodmin and King's Lynn

*Publishers Note:
The views and opinions expressed in this publication are those of the author and are not necessarily those of Apex Publishing Ltd*

*Copyright:
Every attempt has been made to contact the relevant copyright holders, Apex Publishing Ltd would be grateful if the appropriate people contact us on:
01255 428500 or mail@apexpublishing.co.uk*

*This book is dedicated to my beloved father
Terry Currie senior 1938 - 2008*

Also, free Kevin Lane and Ian McAteer!

And for all the great men and women who have given and are still giving their bodies and minds for our country!

CONTENTS

	ACKNOWLEDGMENTS	v
	FOREWORD BY ROY SHAW	vii
	INTRODUCTION	ix
1.	LEANING ON A PASSING BULLET	1
2.	THE MOST DANGEROUS MAN WE HAVE EVER ATTEMPTED TO TREAT!	5
3.	BIGGS AND CUTTING THE GRASS!	10
4.	THE BOWELS OF THE EARTH ... BROADMOOR	14
5.	MURDER AND MAYHEM	19
6.	GYPSY KINGS AND BARE KNUCKLE KNIGHTS!	23
7.	UNLICENSED - HOW IT ALL BEGAN!	49
8.	PRETTY BOY ON THE RAMPAGE!	59
9.	UNLICENSED PEAKS!	67
10.	CLOSE ENCOUNTERS!	73
11.	FIELD OF BLOOD!	80
12.	THE SHOW GOES ON!	93
13.	CHANGES ALL AROUND	102
14.	WHERE ARE WE NOW?	107
15.	DIG THE NEW BREED	119
16.	WARRIORS	129
17.	DEBTS!	136
18.	WARRIORS 4	141
19.	GOODBYE TONY!	150
20.	A COUPLE MORE FIGHT NIGHTS!	155
21.	MASSIVE RIGHT HANDERS AND MASS MURDERERS!	165
22.	BIG NIGHT FOR THE 'BOSS'	175
23.	FUNERAL FOR THE DON	188
24.	JOEY PYLE SNR - FAREWELL TO A TRUE LEGEND	190
25.	BOUNCERS - A DYING TRADE?	193
26.	FOOTBALL AND TORTURE	196
27.	THEY DESERVE MORE RESPECT THAN THEY GET!	203
28.	EPILOGUE	208

ACKNOWLEDGMENTS

These are all good, staunch men who at some time or other have played a role in my life so far. However, the fact that I have friends who are villains does not make me one, just as I have friends who are bricklayers but I have never built a wall. These men also have a lot more skills than their reputations sometimes suggest. Some of my pals though, did not want to be mentioned and I have honoured that. If people took the time to learn rather than judge, they would find a great many gentlemen here.

Thank you, in no particular order to: My family, Chris Cowlin at Apex Publishing Ltd, Charlie Richardson (who I claim as my step dad and he claims me as his step son! Ha!), Chris Lambrianou, Freddie Foreman, Wilf Pine, Ronnie Knight, John Knight, Paul Knight, Ronnie Biggs, Howard Marks, Roy 'Pretty Boy' Shaw, Carlton Leach, 'Big' Albert Chapman, Johnny Nash, Vic Dark, Jimmy Tibbs, Bruce Reynolds, Greg Steen, 'Welsh' Bernie Davies, Charlie Bronson, Ronnie Field, Ronnie Easterbrook, Harry Roberts, Ricky English, Ray Mills, Bill Hicks, Anthony Thomas, Juggy, Stilks, Kenny Noye, Bertie Coster, Charlie Breaker, Jamie O'Keefe, Norman Parker, Kevin Lane and Ian McAteer (both innocent political prisoners) Gary Shaw, Liam and Yvette, Mike Gray, Jason Mariner, 'Nightmare', Joey Pyle jnr, Mitch Pyle, Alan Mortlock, Terry Sabini, Alfie Hutchinson, Brian Smyth, Steve Holdsworth, Mike Biggs, Paul Massey, Paul Ferris, Cass Pennant, Red Menzies, Greg Foreman, Jamie Foreman, 'Buddy' Bill Cooper, Micky Dunn, Cliff Field, Johnny Waldron, Phil Goodson, Brian Hall, Billy Cribb, Jimmy Lambrianou, Terry Smith, Razor Smith, 'Gypsy' Joe Smith, Jimmy 'On the Cobbles' Stockin, Wally Stockin, Billy Smith, Johnny 'King of the Gypsies' Frankham, Bobby Frankham, Les Stevens and all the decent gypsy lads, John Bleakney, Nosher Powell, Harry Starbuck, Terry Stone, DC, Max Lacovou, Mal Vango, the Bowers family, Mr T, Lee Richardson, Dennis Arif, Sean Scott, Tony Currie, Stan Bowles, Rodney Marsh and all at QPR, and the great Lennox Lewis.

And there are also a few ladies, apart from my family, who have been just as good friends I can assure you they are in an elite club of very special women: Veronica Richardson, Eira Peterson, Janice Foreman, Ann Leach, Helen and Wendy Lambrianou, Ros Pine, Lynda Nash, Christine Smith, Jemma (Razor's), Joanne Bleakney.

Finally, may these people of honour rest in peace: Tel Currie snr, Joey Pyle snr, Harry and Rosina Shaw, Ronnie and Danny Currie, my special mate Lee Richardson, Johnny Nash, Kevin Finnegan, Freddie Sansom, Tony Lambrianou, Ronnie, Reggie and Charlie Kray. Buster Edwards, Charlie Wilson, Ronnie Bender, Lenny McLean, Tiger and Edwin Thomas and George Best.

Just to lighten things up... Bertie Smalls is also dead ha ha!

FOREWORD
BY ROY SHAW

I have known Tel Currie for over 10 years and we have been extremely close and trusted friends ever since. This book hits harder than some of my opponents!

Telboy, as I call him, is like my right hand man and is respected by all the 'chaps'. He is also extremely close to Charlie Richardson, Ronnie & John Knight, Freddie Foreman, Carlton Leach, Alfie Hutchinson, Albert Chapman and loads of others. In fact, it would take all day to write all of his contacts, he is very well connected. He was also great friends with my best friend of all time, 'the main man' or 'Boss' Joey Pyle snr and you really had to come recommended to be in Joe's company let alone a trusted friend of the man, we all miss him. Me and Telboy also visit Ronnie Biggs together and what they are doing to him is disgusting, what do they want blood? Probably yes! Both me and Telboy keep in touch with a lot of the proper lads inside. I have no need to go into anything because it's all in this book.

I'm glad Telboy's written this book and can't see how it can fail, he has seen it all you know, things you would not believe!

Telboy is young, only in his 30s but he is definitely 'old school' and has the morals, principles and values of the older 'chaps'. He is not flash, he is polite, a gentleman (especially around ladies) and good company. One thing that shows how much I trust him is the fact that I would tell him anything and know it will go no further. This book is the complete truth and covers so many subjects. Telboy also goes well out of his way to help people and has in all the years I have known him. Problem is some people don't like being told the truth and Telboy is always honest with the 'chaps'. Some don't appreciate how much he has sacrificed himself for them and gets no thanks back! (I can think of two or three now!)

Most of the 'faces' will have a story where he helped them. He has trained fighters, worked the toughest doors, fought some tough men, put on his own boxing shows, brought people together, punched the wrong un's and if his temper snaps it's serious trouble!

He is tolerant and never looks for a fight, in fact he would rather avoid one but if you do get him to breaking point, he can be very brutal!

This is one of the last books out there worth reading. I don't read much but loved this book and so will you. I'm not one for writing loads so be lucky, enjoy the book and welcome to our world!

Good Luck!
Roy Shaw

INTRODUCTION

To most people, unlicensed boxing and bare knuckle fighting are full of mystery. Many think unlicensed boxing is illegal and only takes place in far out well hidden places. That's the case in bare knuckle or 'on the cobbles', but unlicensed is 100% legal with rules and regulations including gloves.

Men like Roy 'Pretty Boy' Shaw and Lenny McLean are now well known, thanks in no small part to their best selling autobiographies. But the myths, rumours and complete lies that surround their stories are plentiful!

Lenny McLean, for example, claims an unbeaten record but actually lost six of the unlicensed fights he took part in, including being stopped brutally by Shaw in three rounds and knocked out cold four times! I will say now, what I write in this book is the 100% truth!

This book is mostly about the start, and golden age, of unlicensed boxing and takes us right up to date. The end chapters are about some of my own naughty antics and those of the 'chaps'. I am not, and have never claimed to be, the hardest man on the planet, I'm not into this 'Dis me and I will chase you all over the world!' business, I am, who I am.

If you have only read *The Guv'nor* you will be in for a shock, so much for the unbeaten myth of the self proclaimed Guv'nor. This is just one example of the myths and self propaganda that surround the unlicensed fighters. Much more of those later on. This book may put a few noses out of joint but at least, for the first time, we have the complete truth. Just as many people still think that the Krays ruled London, many think that the likes of Lenny McLean ruled the fight world. This is not the case.

A man named Cliff Field knocked Lenny spark out twice, so did Johnny Waldron a light heavyweight who knocked McLean out twice both in the first round! So if Lenny was the Guv'nor, what does that make those two?

This book deals in the truth only as it happened, I am not into myth building, there has been far too much of that. It examines the top fighters and gangsters (many I know personally) and studies the relationship between the fight game and the underworld over the years. Unlicensed boxing was started by Joey Pyle snr, Roy 'Pretty Boy' Shaw' and Alex Steene, this book will chart their rise to the top.

It's important to realise this book is not anti anyone, it's not about ruining reputations, what it is about is the truth! So what makes him think he knows the truth? I hear you say.

Well, it's not just me, all of us who have been around the 'chaps' for a long time know the truth. It's the same in any business. Footballers are going to know more about dressing room flare ups than tabloid readers - it's obvious.

We will also reveal the fighter the warriors themselves pick as the real Guv'nor and those that carry the most respect in the underworld past and present.

Many of the accounts in this book are first hand from men like Roy Shaw, Charlie Richardson, Ronnie Knight, Cliff Field, Johnny Nash and more, too many to count. Other accounts are drawn from my own direct experiences of being with the 'chaps', putting on four unlicensed boxing shows of my own and the often violent happenings that came with it. There are no third and fourth hand accounts here, it's all true. I know this world inside out; the underworld is not a foreign land to me. I'm not a highly educated journalist trying to get interviews with men that don't trust me. You get the picture. If I have a question for any of the 'chaps' I just ring them up or meet up with them. This is not showing off, just proving that this is all first hand and real!

However, being a trusted friend of the 'chaps' doesn't automatically make you a criminal. Problem is, how you see yourself is not always how others see you. This is the one book that will take you into every corner of the fight game with a little stop off in the underworld. The real 'faces', the fakes, famous and otherwise, the mugs, the best, the worst, men you really don't want to annoy and those who are a joke even though their reputation says otherwise, the grasses, those we have lost and the man I (any many others) considered to be 'The Boss'.

Also, importantly, Kevin Lane and Ian McAteer ARE INNOCENT. Do your research, it's barbaric and it's happening NOW!

Welcome to my world, read on ... you will love to read it, not to live it!

1
LEANING ON A PASSING BULLET

The Nash family were one of, if not the most, respected families in the whole of London. Even today they carry an aura that very few have, especially Johnny Nash who was truly one of the late, great Joey Pyle senior's closest friends for around 50 years. Even Ronnie and Reggie Kray, who were well known for listening to nobody except their mother, always paid attention when it came to the Nash family and it's well known that given the choice of being in trouble with the Nashes or in trouble with the Krays most people would rather have had the twins after them!

The Nash family and Freddie Foreman were two of the very few in the '60s who could, and would, go to any part of London and not care, Joey Pyle was another. They still go wherever they want to go. The Nash family come from North London and Freddie from South London. I have witnessed Fred get extremely angry when the media have written that he was a 'Kray henchman from the East End'.

Joey Pyle was very much part of the Nash firm and together they fronted the famous 'Colony Club' in Mayfair for Hollywood legend George Raft (whose infamous friends included Benjamin 'Bugsy' Seigal). This was the kind of up-market establishment in the West End of London that the Nash family and Joey were trusted to look after.

The Pen Club, in Duval Street in London's East End got its tongue-in-cheek name because it had been financed by a robbery at the Parker pen company. It was owned by a man named Billy Ambrose. On 7th February 1960, Jimmy Nash, Joey Pyle, John Read and Jimmy Nash's girlfriend, Doreen Masters, entered the

Pen club. What happened next went down in gangland folklore.

A row started and Ambrose tried to calm things down but got in the way and was shot. The gunman's target was a man from Yorkshire called Selwyn Cooney who worked for notorious 'King of the underworld' Billy Hill.

Billy Hill was no plastic gangster, that is certain. Selwyn Cooney was shot twice in the head and died. Why was he shot? The most common theory is that Cooney had been in a car accident with blonde Vicky James, the girlfriend of Jimmy's brother, Ronnie Nash. Cooney sent her a bill for the damage and came to blows about the matter with Ronnie in a club. The Pen Club fracas was revenge for Ronnie by brother Jimmy. Jimmy is reported to have said: "That's what you get for picking on little girls." But that could easily be what used to be called 'verballing' (where the police would add or take away what they wanted from statements).

Joe claims a different version of events. Unbeknown to Cooney, because he didn't know Jimmy, Joe and John Read were in the club, Cooney could be heard in a loud voice saying: "Fuck Ronnie Nash, fuck all the Nashes. If Ronnie or any of the Nash brothers want it, they can have it anytime."

Jimmy then tapped him on the shoulder and said: "My name is Jimmy Nash and you're talking about my brothers."

"I don't give a fuck what your name is," Cooney responded. So Jimmy broke his nose and all hell broke loose.

In those days, the lads could have hung but after much complication and legal jargon (out of the scope of this book - read Joey Pyle's *Notorious*), Jimmy Nash instead received five years and Joe and John Read each received eighteen months.

Joey Pyle once told me: "We were worried Tel, wouldn't you fucking be? We were 100% convinced that we were going to hang, sure of it, and crazy Jim didn't help keep getting shoelaces, styling them into the shape of nooses and slipping them under my fucking door or putting them in magazines!"

The thing is that Jimmy, Joe and John Read never said a thing to incriminate one another, none of them told on the other. Can you imagine that now? Whoever pulled the trigger would still be inside, even if those who grassed didn't actually see who did it! But Joe always said, it doesn't make you special just because you didn't grass!

Whenever we were out, if anyone asked Joe who pulled the trigger in the Pen Club (a bloody stupid question if ever there was one!), Joe would always say, "I don't know. The fella just leaned on a passing bullet!"

While Joe was banged up in the Scrubs, he became close to another inmate, Roy Shaw, and the two men became the closest of friends. Both men were pro fighters and had met before when they were boxers. They had great respect for each other and a life long friendship was sealed. Joe was always extremely loyal to his friends and continued to visit Roy right up until Roy got out.

While on the run, Roy changed his surname to West when he was fighting pro. He remembers his toughest unlicensed fight as being against Ron Stander and not Lenny McLean (Lenny never fought amateur or pro) as people might think, but he claims his best and toughest pro fight to be against a guy named Dennis Wingrove at Wembley Town Hall on 29th November, 1956.

Reports of the day record a classic bout, with both men nearly going down, and it was a real blood filled battle with Roy West (Shaw) winning a six rounds points decision. 'Nobbins' (cash for the fighters in appreciation for a great fight) were thrown into the ring, a common fight night practice. The alternative for a 'stinker' was receiving boos, with coins and beer being thrown into the ring at you and the prospect of few bookings in future. You would think that most of the 'chaps' became friends because of villainy, but a lot of the lads actually met when they were young through boxing and the crime came much later. When a young Joe and Roy first met as teenagers, they wanted to make a name in the ring not robbing banks! But things took a different course, a very common story among villains.

Freddie Foreman, for instance, had a reputation with his fists in the ring and on the cobbles long before he made a reputation for himself with tools and, subsequently, guns. Freddie had a fearless, awesome reputation in a street battle. He may have used weapons later as things became more violent, but he has never been the type to hide behind them. They are known as 'weapons merchants' and that's not Freddie!

Freddie is as solid as a pit bull and can still have an extremely brutal fight if somebody takes a liberty with him or his family. In those days, every pro fighter was a good one and British title fights were bigger than world title fights today. British champions were household names, whereas today, only the fanatic knows the world champions. Ronnie, Reggie and Charlie Kray, The Richardsons, most of the Nashes, Freddie Foreman, Roy Shaw, Alfie Hutchinson, Bertie Coster, Joey Pyle snr, Jimmy Stockin and Wally Stockin, Bill 'The Bomb' Williams, Fred 'The Head', Vic Dark, Charlie Bronson, the Knight brothers ... how many of those guys would have been champion boxers if they had stayed out of crime? Imagine if Roy Shaw had just boxed and not become involved in crime? I was also told by a few people that Joey Pyle snr had an enormous amount of boxing talent, more than the Krays ... we can only wonder!

One thing was for certain, the name Joey Pyle was becoming known. And he had another little project up his sleeve. He would reinvent boxing ... as you do!

2
THE MOST DANGEROUS MAN WE HAVE EVER ATTEMPTED TO TREAT!

Unlike Joey and the Nash brothers, Roy Shaw was not what the media would refer to as a 'gangster'. He was an armed robber or 'on the pavement' and although he would go to work in a team, he was a loner and hard to get near. Roy was also violent - extremely violent. He was one of the most dangerous men to pass through the prison system, which included a stint in Broadmoor, a hospital for the criminally insane. Roy's life inside prison heavily reflected those of 'Mad' Frankie Fraser and Scottish hard man Jimmy Boyle.

Before crime and prison, in 1954, Roy was conscripted into the army. Roy was actually looking forward to the training but, as usual, authority and small men in uniforms bellowing orders and abuse stopped Roy and many other young lads from being good soldiers. If you had what it took to be a decent soldier but were also a rebel you had no chance. The pointless idea of National Service was to break the youngster's spirit and then replace it with the army's own type of robot programming.

Lads like Roy, of course, would not take this and were not scared to protest with extreme violence. Within the first six weeks of training Private Roy Shaw was already a walking time bomb and it didn't take long for the first sergeant major to be knocked spark out! He certainly wasn't the last and Roy kept knocking them out on a regular basis. He soon found himself sent to a nut house in Germany where he was based. For the first time, Roy was 'treated' with electric shock treatment or electroconvulsive therapy better known as ECT. It was no use. Eventually, he was given a dishonourable discharge and pronounced mad. Roy would be considered mad many more times through the years.

Ironically, the boy who would become Britain's most violent man, as a child was constantly bullied at school. "There's Shaw, get him," was something that he heard every day and it wasn't a few pushes, he was really set upon. The one thing Roy did look forward to in his life was going to speedway races on the back of his Dad's motorbike. One day, Roy wanted to go but on this occasion, Roy's Dad was taking a pal instead. The young Roy pleaded and sulked but to no avail. Later that night, Roy heard a piercing scream from his mother downstairs and he rushed to see what was wrong. The police had been there to say that there had been a terrible accident on the way home from the speedway track. Roy's Mum went to the hospital and Roy was left with his older sisters. Upon her return with puffy eyes and trembling voice, she told them, "Daddy's dead."

Roy was ten years old. Recently I lost my own father and as Roy comforted me, he was crying too, all these years later, Roy is nowhere near getting over the loss of his Dad. The bullying and loss of his father at a young age changed Roy beyond belief. At the funeral, Roy threw himself into the grave and hung on to the coffin. His uncles had to pull him off by his legs. Three days later, a very different Roy Shaw returned to his nightmare school. But this new version of Roy was about to discover a lethal talent he never knew he had, if he had it before at all. A talent that would make him feared, respected, infamous and ultimately rich - a punch as powerful as a sledgehammer!

This would be the last time he would ever be picked on. Eight bullies were waiting for Roy as usual. Flashbacks of his beloved Dad flashed through his mind. The laughing, the rides on the bike, Christmas, birthdays and diving on to his Dad's coffin. As the images of the man he had lost zoomed through his head, a sensation like an electric current surged from his feet right up through his body giving him the strength of ten men. The first coward hit the deck, then another, and another, and another until all eight were lying at his feet. Where had this come from? This unstoppable rage and power?

It taught Roy that bullies are cowards. And whenever I have

been out with him and he has knocked someone out (I have never seen anyone get up so far!), he has always gone straight for the bully and helped the underdog. I remember a terrified woman come up to me and Roy in a club in Essex a couple of years back. This woman was shaking like a leaf. She approached Roy and said: "Mr Shaw, do you mind if I stand with you for a little while?"

Roy replied, "Sure darling, what's the problem?"

"That man who just came in, he is my ex and he used to beat me up and hurt me very badly. If he sees me in here he will start on me, he doesn't normally come in this place. that's why I am here."

Roy ground his teeth and he said: "Really, he sounds a lovely man. You stay with me, he won't touch you tonight."

After a while Roy left the girl in the company of a couple of our pals. "I'm just going to the toilet darling, these are my pals, you will be fine." Both Roy and I had spotted this mongrel heading for the toilet and (I know everyone says it but he was a big lump, huge!! Remember, Roy is NOT a huge man). I followed Roy to watch his back but, as ever, he seemed to actually grow to twice his size the more wound up he got. We waited for the last person bar him to leave the loo, then we went in. I lent on the door to stop anyone else from entering and Roy stood right next to this big mongrel.

Roy said: "'Ello mate."

The bloke replied "'Ello Roy, how are you?"

"I'm fine cunt, hit any small women lately?"

With that, it was "I don't kkkknow what you mean Roy really." Never one to argue, Roy threw a left hook to this slag's jaw, then an uppercut. Before this big lump's shoes touched the floor he threw another uppercut and the bloke shot up in the air and landed on his feet, out cold but still standing!

I have never seen anyone out for the count standing up before. After a few seconds, he just fell like one of those big trees 'TIMBER!' But from where we stood next to him I could actually see his veins bulging, then he went red. Roy's famous eyes started to glaze over. That's the electric current sensation Roy discovered the last time he was bullied, and it's a sight to behold, trust me.

That's just one example of what Roy Shaw found in himself that day as a ten year old and I can assure you, Roy's power has not diminished with age. Unlike many unlicensed fighters like Lenny McLean, Cliff Field and Kevin Paddock (the only opponent both Lenny and Roy fought. Lenny lost, Roy won in the final fight of his career). Roy was a career criminal. Between the fights and supplementing his income by working on the doors, he was an armed robber and ran protection rackets.

1963 saw Roy's biggest ever haul a record breaking robbery (the amount is thought to be a round 80k ... a lot for the time), although the record didn't stand for long because a little piece of work called 'The Great Train Robbery' came along in the same year.

Roy and a small team (a very small team for that kind of job) robbed a security van in Kent. One young man of 21 was brought up to be charged for the same robbery. Roy mouthed: "Who the fuck are you?"

The lad's name was William Curbishley and Roy had never seen him in his life. He had not been on the robbery that's for sure but he drew 15 years anyway, a real injustice!

Bill Curbishley later went on to become the manager of one of the greatest bands of all time, The Who, and still is, good luck to him, he is class. Roy says of him: "It was a long time ago and I have no reason to lie. I will tell you straight, Bill Curbishley had fuck all to do with that robbery. But Bill is a proper man and never rolled over on the rest of us which many would of done, especially today, and he never even complained. He is an unbelievable man and has my highest respect. Could you do 15 years, let alone 15 days for something you never did?"

Now, Roy had a wife and two young children Gary and Chatina. His son Gary went on to become an extremely good unlicensed fighter himself. He is a friend, I have worked his corner and he fought on my shows. Gary Shaw is a fantastic, top bloke and Chatina is a lovely lady. It is through Chatina that I first became close friends with Roy. They are both diamonds and I will always be there for them.

That's a lot for any man's mind to wrestle with, it's Hell on earth! Roy could not see the end of it and was incapable of settling down and being a good prisoner, like Frankie Fraser he simply did not know how to behave like that. Unlike Fraser, Shaw was an extremely powerful, trained fighting machine. Roy remains to this day one of the most dangerous men ever to walk through prison gates.

But Roy Shaw's inner pain never turned to self pity or depression, It turned to raw, sore, pure, undiluted anger and no limits rage. It's a miracle (like Jimmy Boyle) that he came out alive. Shaw, Boyle and Fraser had one thing in common, the only reason they survived each day was their burning hatred of the screws, that was the fuel that kept them going.

The prison system was about to find out that they had incarcerated an extremely dangerous man.

3
BIGGS AND CUTTING THE GRASS!

Roy was sent to Wandsworth (known as the hate factory) and made a friend who wasn't planning on staying around too long. Roy's new pal was train robber Ronnie Biggs and the two found themselves sewing mail bags together. Ronnie told Roy he was planning on going over the wall and said did Roy want to join him, it would cost ten thousand pounds for a life of freedom?

Ronnie really wanted Roy to go with him and Roy was sorely tempted. The decision not to go was not one Roy made easily, in fact it took him a whole week to arrive at staying put. When Ronnie went over the wall, Roy was left to wonder if he had made the right decision.

In 2002, myself, our close friend Mike Grey and Roy visited a very unwell Ronnie Biggs for the first of many times in HMP Belmarsh known as 'Hellmarsh'!

Ronnie had by now had a number of strokes, was being fed through a tube in his stomach and could not talk. Ronnie communicated through a word board. He would point at letters and one of us would write the letters down on paper forming a word and eventually a sentence. We would then answer Ron back. This was our first visit to Ronnie Biggs and, although we actually had a laugh (Ronnie has lost none of his humour), both myself and Roy were heartbroken and close to tears. You can't comment on our feelings unless you have seen up close what this cowardly, faceless system is doing to this old, sick man.

We had much the same feeling when Roy and I visited the once mighty king of the unlicensed ring, Cliff Field, after he had been sectioned. Cliff had lost an eye when a pack of cowards (they would never have done it one on one or even two on one!) took his eye out with a bottle while he was working the door some years before. Cliff, who was a full blooded heavyweight who knocked Lenny McLean spark out twice, was now painfully thin and a heavy drinker. We visited Cliff with our close friend Richard 'Red' Menzies. Red has been a diamond where Cliff is concerned and looked after him, I mean REALLY looked after Cliff for years. He didn't get paid, it was out of pure friendship and respect and, even though Red had a wife and children to look after, he would be straight to Cliff's side if he was in trouble whatever the time of day or night. Red has even taken a couple of clumps off Cliff when Cliff was confused and Red was trying to get him out of somewhere ... a clump off Cliff Field is not a cheery event for anyone!

Men like Mike Grey, Mal Vango who runs Dave Courtney's website and Red Menzies are the silent heroes of our world and firm friends of both myself and Roy, they have our respect. I also got on the phone to the 'King of the Gypsies', the great Johnny Frankham, the former British light heavyweight champion and awesome cobble fighter. He and Cliff had been close friends and travelled the world as sparring partners. I told him about Cliff and just like the gentleman he is, John went to see Cliff a day or two later. Red told me Cliff was over the moon because John's visit was a complete surprise and, of course, it gave me satisfaction to be able to do that.

Roy and I were silently upset after that visit as well. You see, despite his deserved reputation as one of Britain's toughest men, Roy Shaw is also a man with feelings and can get emotional like everyone else. So, the question whether or not Roy should have gone with Ronnie Biggs on the escape was answered on that visit. There was Ronnie, ill and unable to speak and stuck in maximum security Belmarsh prison while Roy Shaw, now a very successful businessman with plenty of property had driven us to Belmarsh in his new Bentley. Roy had made the right decision in seeing his time through, even if it was far from smooth.

I don't spend all my time arranging reunions for the 'chaps' but one that I did organise was fantastic. Roy mentioned that he hadn't seen Ronnie Knight for years and as I speak to Ronnie

Knight almost every week, I arranged for me and Roy to meet up with Ronnie on his manor. We had a great meal and a real laugh and I loved just listening to the two rascals going over the old times. It was a great day and Ronnie Knight is always the cheeky, cockney, rascal you expect, full of wit, mischief and charm with a twinkle in his eyes. I have all the time in the world for Ronnie Knight and his brother John (who masterminded the Security Express Robbery), and Ronnie knows I will always be there for him.

A while ago, the press wrote a story about Ronnie and where he lives and made out he was almost down and out. Well, nothing can be further from the truth and I have been to Ronnie's home a few times. It's a lovely, tidy, welcoming place and his car is no banger either. This can happen with the press; they simply run out of robberies!

They had bled the Kent Robbery dry and run out of stories. So they make the usual move of dragging up the 'chaps' from the old days just for something to write about. I remember, shortly after that robbery they had a centre page spread of Ronnie Knight with Barbara Windsor, a 40 year old photo of Biggsy and Buster Edwards and one I think of Bruce Reynolds. Why?

Ronnie was also carrying some old folks shopping and giving them a lift. Well, that's the sort of thing Ronnie would do, he's a gentleman, and he doesn't drive a 'banger'. Even if he did, he's had all the supercars any man can dream of and the Spanish Villa to go with it! Ronnie living off charity and old mates is complete bollocks! Trust me. I refuse to lie about anything in this book because you will always get found out.

One day, an old pal of Roy, Albert Rainbird, arrived at Parkhurst, but he was a friend no longer. Through the tight underworld grapevine, Roy had learned that Rainbird had become the lowest of the low and become a grass!

Roy was also convinced that Carolina, the mother of his two children was seeing someone else. All in all, Roy Shaw's mind was not in a good place. Roy smashed his hair cream bottle and sharpened it on stone until it was like a razor. He went up behind Rainbird, yanked his hair back and cut his throat screaming: "My face is the last thing you will ever see on earth!" The doctors saved him ... just.

I asked Roy about this and he told me he felt nothing, no nerves, no excitement, just numb, completely numb. This wasn't a human, this was a grass and that attitude has not mellowed down the years with the REAL 'chaps'.

Roy, Freddie Foreman, Wilf Pine, Frankie Fraser all despise grasses and see them as subhuman ... and too right as well! I have witnessed grasses being done and done properly (not by any of the names mentioned above I hasten to add) and I felt complete joy. In my opinion grasses and nonces are the scum of the earth!

Roy also did something that has never been repeated and is not likely to be done again. On two occasions, he actually smashed his way out of his locked cell door from the inside! Think about that for a second, those things are solid iron and he smashed himself free when the thing was locked from the inside, that's got to be near supernatural.

But Roy was now too violent for the system to handle and there was only one place left he could go. He was the most violent prisoner in the system. Many of Frank Mitchell's antics were funny (Frank was a bit backward) but Roy Shaw's were born out of raw evil and hate. He was like a wild animal and Britain's human zoo is called Broadmoor.

4
THE BOWELS OF THE EARTH ... BROADMOOR

While the Krays were doing their thing in the East End, the Nash Brothers in the North of London, the Richardsons in the South and Teddy 'Ginger' Dennis and guys like Jimmy Smith (The Paddington Puncher) in the West (it was actually 'Ginger' Dennis that slashed Jack Spot NOT Frankie Fraser but Frank takes the credit), Roy Shaw was out of the game and locked inside Broadmoor Hospital for the criminally insane.

If Roy had been free to join one of these 'firms' which was how things were now being run, it's easy to think that he would have joined the Kray Twins because he was a cockney and so were they. (I'm shocked by the number of people who think that cockney just means from London. No, to be a cockney you must have been born within earshot of Bow bells, if you can't hear the bells of Bow from where you were born, you are NOT a cockney. Both Roy and the twins were true cockneys!)

I think he would of gravitated toward the Nash family because of his friendship with Joey Pyle. Roy may well have stayed a loner working with fellow loners but the Rainbird issue may have convinced him it was always better to stay with the tried, tested and loyal like Freddie Foreman always did.

Fred had a small trusted team around him who always kept their cards very close to their chests and never had the desire to tell everyone when they had a result. If Fred's gang had done something big, people may assume, but they would NEVER actually know, if Fred was involved or not and it's not the type of thing you ask, that rule still stands. But (if it were possible) Roy was becoming more and more violent. He was now being given the 'liquid cosh' (an injection of various drugs to knock him out) and he was turning into a zombie.

Roy had heard that Carolina was seeing a plumber from Romford. On one of his regular visits to Broadmoor, Roy asked Joey Pyle if he would take care of things. Joe of course agreed but then something came up and Joe had to put the favour on hold for a little while. About a week later Ronnie Kray made a visit to Roy in Broadmoor. Roy was shocked by this because he had done one of their 'firm', Willy Malone, and he was prepared for a show down with the colonel. Roy was even more taken aback when Ronnie Kray, in those hushed tones, almost a whisper, asked "is there anything we can do for you Roy?"

It has been suggested that Ronnie had his own agenda for this. He knew of Roy's reputation for startling, brutal violence and wanted to court Roy so he joined the Kray 'firm' when he got out, perhaps to counterbalance the threat of 'Mad' Frankie Fraser who was of course with the Richardsons. But because Roy was so violent his sentence went on and on and in the end a plan B was brought in. The name of plan B was Frank 'the mad axeman' Mitchell' and it was one of the worst mistakes the twins ever made ... and they made a few!

Roy replied: "Yes Ron, there is actually," and proceeded to tell Ronnie Kray all about the plumber. Roy then contacted Joey Pyle and told him not to worry about the favour he had mentioned as Ronnie Kray was sorting it out.

Only a few days later Ronnie Kray returned and said in a whisper: "It's sorted Roy."

Roy was over the moon, it made his year, he had not felt happy for years.

But it wasn't sorted at all. Ronnie Kray had sent what turned out to be the two biggest grasses in his own trial a few years later, the twins' cousin Ronnie Hart and the first 'supergrass' Albert Donoghue. They did nothing, just lied to the twins and no doubt took their money as well!

The plumber was in more danger from his own screwdriver than this pair of mongrels. Roy never found out until years later, but Joey Pyle smelt a rat (well two actually) straight away.

Roy may have been satisfied that the plumber had been ironed out but his violent outbursts were still on the increase. Screws were being brutally beaten and Roy even jumped over the Governor's desk and broke his cheekbone!

There was now only one place left for Roy Shaw to be sent, the punishment blocks known as the 'dungeons', so called because they are below the main building and have the aura of the Tower of London hundreds of years ago!

It's simply the bowels of the earth!

When Roy's neck was being squeezed to make him pass out, he said he managed to snarl at all the screws and say: "I'm gonna do every last one of ya."

Then the dungeon door slammed shut. He claimed he was injected every four hours with a drug called serenade of all things, and he was hallucinating so horribly that a simple fly looked like a giant monster!

This is where the real nuts were sent. His food was shoved through a flap and the drugs kept coming. The night air was filled with insane screams from real loons, it was like medieval times, Hell on earth.

If you ask Roy Shaw who has saved his life on more than one occasion, without hesitation the answer will be Joey Pyle. Without Joe, Roy will tell you that he would have been left to die in Broadmoor. Joe, even in the '60s was one of the most connected men in Britain and remained that way until his sad death.

But Roy had other supporters. One of the greatest boxing champions the world has ever seen is the late Joe Louis, former heavyweight world champion and more famous than Tyson in his day. In the '30s when Adolf Hitler thought the Arian man was the perfect man, Hitler's darling and hero of the Reich, Max Schmelling was knocked spark out in one round by Joe Louis, a black man, imagine the fuss that caused! Also with Joe and Roy was our own Middleweight world champion Terry Downes. Both Joe Louis and Terry Downes called for a big cheers for their good friend ... Roy Shaw!

The Governor and screws were stunned! The Governor was so over the moon that these two world champions had been to his nick, that he took Joe out that night. The Governor didn't know Joe was a gangster and thought he had done it for the prison -

idiot!

Joe asked after Roy and was told: "If he carries on, he will be dead within months."

The purpose of the Louis and Downes visit was to bring his name up as a friend so he wouldn't be forgotten and allowed to rot in the dungeons. As I said, 'The Boss' - Joe, was a clever man.

You may at this point be thinking, 'I thought this book was about fighting not prison', but unless you know where the inventors of unlicensed boxing came from, you will never know the complete story. I promise, we will cover the whole story from day one right up to the present, so read on. It also proves that Roy Shaw and Joey Pyle were real villains, Lenny McLean and others who will pop up later were not. In fact, some were not heard of at all but we will go into that later in the book.

At this time, most of the Great Train Robbers were in prison (three were NEVER caught!) and the police were taking a great interest in the Richardson and Kray 'firms' but they had their fingers burnt by the Nash brothers and Joe Pyle when they walked after the Pen Club shooting. Roy Shaw was in a different world, oblivious to everything outside the dungeon, but Joey Pyle was not going to let it stay that way. When you hear what Roy went through in prison, it's amazing he didn't come out a cabbage let alone the first ever Guv'nor!

One experiment Roy will never forget is when he was held down while a needle was forced through his cheek, up behind his eyeball and finally into his brain at which point he passed out. This was to test 'the movement and function of his brain' and when you consider that this was only 40 years ago it really is chilling. The visit from Joe Louis and Terry Downes had made sure people could not forget Roy but there was still a long way to go yet. Many in Broadmooor never see the light of day again, especially if located in the dungeons. This was a place where the tea was served by the world famous poisoner Graham Young!

Later, Ronnie Kray would end up here and end his days as a Broadmoor patient. 'Mad' Frankie Fraser and Charlie Bronson would also do a spell in the main part of the 'Hospital'.

After what Joey Pyle had been told by the governor, he had to get someone Roy trusted in quick to talk to him, Joe was too high profile so he looked elsewhere. He decided on a mutual friend called Sulky who owned the Astor Club. Sulky was shocked to see the state his old pal was in and Roy was shocked at how much trouble he was in, he had no idea these drugs could kill him in months, not to mention the good old fashioned and frequent beatings he was made to take by eight or more screws. Sulky begged Roy to stop doing the screws because he would never win and could be dead very soon. Roy's will to beat the system had not let him think like this before but now he took note.

The next morning Roy promised he would not hurt any more screws as long as he was left alone to do his bird. For a fortnight Roy was polite to the screws proving a vital point, he was NOT mad and WAS in control of his actions. The fact was that his war with authority had become his natural way of behaving and surviving, again there are echoes of Jimmy Boyle here. Eventually Roy was let into the solitary ward and his medication decreased, a big step. Soon he was back in his old cell, he had by now done five years in Broadmoor. Some people can't stay there for five minutes - and they are visitors!

Roy managed to bribe someone to get hold of his prison record, he was shocked. The doctor at Grendon had written, 'Shaw is the most powerful and dangerous man I have attempted to treat'. That said it all.

Roy was desperate and attempted a rooftop protest after giving guards the slip, he hurled slates down while he was up there. Somehow, something worked because soon Roy was out of Broadmoor and on his way to Parkhurst on the Isle of Wight.

5
MURDER AND MAYHEM

Joey Pyle had his card marked that he and Johnny Nash were about to be nicked. The real targets were the Krays but the police needed as many of the twins' friends off the street as possible, so when it came to the big event that the Kray trial of course would be, there was nobody left to intimidate the jury. The very next day, Joey and John, as shrewd as ever, left for Spain.

Joey Pyle snr told me personally that he had always been disgusted with the way Jack 'The Hat' Mcvitie had been killed with sycophants jumping all over him. Ronnie Kray got the blame for pinning Jack's arms back so Reg could stab him but Tony Lambrianou, who was there, told me it was actually Ronnie Hart, the twins' own cousin. The same Ronnie Hart that never shot the plumber for Roy as promised and was in the dock giving evidence against the twins at the trial. Apart from three or four staunch men, the twins really were not very good judges of character because the others rolled over like dogs!

Joey told me, "Jack (or Mac) as Joe called him died like a grass, like a slag, he never deserved that."

Roy was friends with two Kray victims, Jack Mcvitie and Frank Mitchell, and he admired them both. Roy and Jack would actually stand side by side and dive into the screws together. Mcvitie was not the coward he was portrayed as in the film or the twins' books. But he was taking too many pills and drinking too much by now. Joey had warned him what would happen if he kept up the insults, unlike Roy, Jack took no notice and became a Reggie Kray victim.

The three murders the twins were charged for; Cornell, Mitchell and Mcvitie were completely pointless.

Most of the Richardson gang had been arrested a couple of days before the Cornell killing and Charlie Richardson was arrested on the very day England won the World Cup. The question is, if the twins hated the Richardsons so much, why did they wait until the minute the others were out of the way before they shot Cornell?

Cornell was an East Ender but had gone south to be with his wife, Olive, and had joined the Richardsons. They could have killed him anytime in the past twenty years but Ronnie waited until the others were safely out of the way. Why?

And why, if they ruled London as people have tried to claim, didn't they shoot Charlie, Eddie or Frankie Fraser? The fact is, the Richardsons were a lot stronger firm and Cornell was the only one left. In all those years, there was only a bridge between them, they knew where to find the Richardsons. It doesn't work the other way round because the Richardsons were unconcerned about the twins, they didn't see them as a threat and waiting for that moment to shoot Cornell proves it. If you read a book by the twins, especially Ronnie, you can see that he was obsessed by the Richardsons. If you read anything by the Richardsons or watch the film *Charlie*, the twins are hardly mentioned! More about Charlie Richardson later ...

Earlier in the decade, a man called Tommy 'Ginger' Marks was killed and vanished, a slag called Jimmy Evans was supposed to go with him but hid under a lorry. Much later, Freddie Foreman admitted to these shootings as both these men were involved in shooting Fred's brother George in his own home - something you do not do. Fred also admitted to shooting Frank Mitchell as a favour to the twins (never for money as has been wrongly reported) along with Alf Gerrard and disposing of the body of Jack 'The Hat' Mcvitie. Now, you can see why he is called 'Brown Bread Fred' but Fred is actually a real gentleman just like all the real 'chaps'. The growling bullies are found much further down the scale and are not tolerated for very long by the elite.

While in Parkhurst, after a football match, Roy Shaw also found himself on a murder charge along with Bertie Coster, a decent boxer. A man known as Mr Brown was having a grudge match with Bertie Coster on the pitch. On the way up the stone steps, Mr Brown was really slagging off LGs (London Gangsters). A tussle took place and Brown flew down the stone steps and walloped his head at the bottom, he was out cold.

Two days after the scuffle, that most had forgotten about, Roy was told that Mr Brown was dead! No prizes for guessing who got Roy the best solicitor money can buy? Yep, Joey Pyle. Witnesses had been scared off and only two remained. As the first, extremely camp witness took the stand Roy screamed: "Tell the truth you fucking poof!"

The witness replied: "Er ... I just saw Roy helping Brown up from the steps."

With just one witness left, Roy did the same: "Now tell the fucking truth!"

Again, he replied "I just saw Shaw helping him up."

The solicitor pointed out that Mr Shaw now had no case to answer. He didn't and Roy was acquitted. Bertie Coster got another nine months on his sentence.

Roy was shipped to Gartree to finish his sentence, but moved around the system. In Wakefield, Roy trained and sparred with a full blooded heavyweight and violent nutter, Paul Sykes. Sykes went on to fight for the British heavyweight title and could really have a row. I asked Roy about it and he didn't think much of Paul Sykes, not as a boxer or a man, and always managed to get under his guard, stay in close and batter the body, the classic Shaw style that would later bring down many a giant. Roy only has short arms so he couldn't out jab a heavyweight but this 'raging bull' style was usually a winner. Later, when the unlicensed game had taken off Paul Sykes was due to fight Lenny McLean. Now THAT would have been a smash up if Sykes went for the kill. A good unlicensed fighter will rarely outbox a pro but in a tear up who knows?

Unfortunately, as ever, Sykes couldn't go out without having a good scrap but this time he got injured fighting a load of bouncers and the fight was off, a shame for every fight fan.

Roy always trained (except when in the dungeon of course) and trained with heavyweights. He trained often with Reggie Kray who was also very strong for a small man. Roy blew up from a middleweight when he was a pro to fifteen and a half stone of pure muscle! As Roy is five feet eight and a half inches, that's some width!

At last, the prison sentence of Roy Shaw was over. He had made it through hell with the help of men like Joey Pyle, Sulky, Ray Mills, Alfie Hutchinson and Bertie Coster. It had been an extremely violent decade in gangland and I sometimes wonder what Roy would have done if he was out while all this was going on.

Anyway, he was now free! Next stop Essex.

6
GYPSY KINGS AND BARE KNUCKLE KNIGHTS!

Bare knuckle, on the cobbles or street fighting has been around since the year dot but is most commonly associated with the gypsy community. Of course, not all cobble fighters are of travelling stock but travellers have settled financial and domestic disputes in this noble way for centuries. The top man in the unlicensed game has long been known as the Guv'nor where the travellers hail him the 'King of the Gypsies'.

The most common method is what is known as a 'straightener' where no kicking or butting are permitted and a mutually agreed 'fair play man' acts as a referee. 'The fair play man' is usually somebody who has been a fighter themselves and has respect from everyone involved. No gloves are worn on the cobbles and commonly the fight continues until one side calls 'best' (gives in) or is simply unconscious. The 'all in' is even more savage and has no rules at all. 'All in' fights have been known to be fought to the death!

It goes without saying, that the 'all in' is the most brutal, savage form of organised street combat and is mostly saved for family verses other family disputes where pure hatred or revenge is the motivation. Bare knuckle fighting is illegal, unlicensed is not and here some get confused. I have worked on the doors for many years and some doormen count a punch up with a drunk or simply slinging one out as a street fight. If you have witnessed a real organised bare knuckle fight you will realise that this is not true. This is the only explanation for some of the ridiculous tallies of street fights some doormen claim. Lenny McLean claimed around 30,000 bare knuckle fights! (Depending on the interview). Sorry, but unless you are counting every drunk you turn away, that's impossible!

Also, so much money is staked on these fights that with that many clean wins, McLean would have owned his own island! Trust me, 20 to 30 organised bare knuckle fights is a lot, even in a lifetime. Lenny's unlicensed record was 15 fights, six losses, knocked-out four times, stopped once in three rounds and outpointed once. That would mean he won thousands of fights against raw hard knuckle but was knocked spark out with gloves on, it doesn't add up. None of this takes away from the respect I have for these men, but when writing the truth and dispelling myths, you can only deal in fact ... and some people love their myths. I find it amazing that many people need these things pointed out to them. It's also a difficult thing to do when the person in question has passed away, but again, there are no insults here just plain fact. Everyone of us must pass away at some point, that does not give us the right to be regarded as perfect and it has to be said that some of what Lenny McLean said was far from the truth. This has now even been admitted by McLean fans, like my good friend Tony Thomas, whose book *The GUV'NOR: Through the Eyes of Others* is a classic read. But some of these books are just so obviously made up. Unlike pro boxing, you can't just look up fighters' records in unlicensed or bare knuckle, so you are simply taking the author's word.

I am fortunate enough to have lots of gypsy friends who are staunch, respected people including good families like the Frankhams, Stockins, Smiths, Frenches, Brazils and men like 'Gypsy' Joe Carrington ... all good solid families. These are proud people and don't leave their crap everywhere, some of the caravans are like palaces.

There are some great bare knuckle gypsy names that run down the years including ... Tucker Dunn, the Gaskins, Mark Ripley, Hughie Burton, Uriah Burton (Known as Big Just), John-John Stanley, boxer Tom Taylor, Dan Rooney, John Rooney, Ernie McGinley, Henry 'The dentist' Arab, Henry 'The outlaw' Francis, Eli Frankham, Joe-Boy Botton, Bobby Frankham, Johnny Love, Joe Smith and, one of the best fighters I have witnessed, Louis Welch from Darlington who may well be the modern day 'King of the Gypsies'. Mark Ripley from Kent is a man with an awesome reputation. Joey Pyle's son Joe jnr, a man who of course was brought up surrounded by the fight game, calls Mark 'one hell of a tasty bastard'. Joe jnr has seen it all and is not easily impressed. When you add that to the equation, Mark really is a bit special.

One man who you really wouldn't want to fight on the cobbles is former British Light Middleweight champion Andy Till. He is simply ferocious! He is no longer a light middleweight but he is one of the hardest men I have met and I know most of them!

When Andy was British Champion, he was also a milkman. He wasn't my milkman but Greenford/Hanwell where I am from is next door to Andy's manor of Northolt. He would do his roadwork at around 3am then go on his round, that would kill most people for a start off! He was a good man and took his Lonsdale belt to his kids' school to show all the other children. Andy was a warrior in the ring, one of those you would have to near kill to beat.

On his milk round one day, he knocked on the door of a family with a bit of a reputation, to collect the bill. For some reason, a row broke out. Then three big lumps who were brothers all sprinted halfway down the stairs and took flying leaps at Andy. Andy clumped each one right on the button while they were in mid-air. Each of the brothers thumped to the ground fast asleep after being knocked spark out. Another member of the family, then went to fetch the milk bill money. If only they had done that in the first place!

Andy had some rowdy, loyal supporters as well. During a fight with a guy named Robert McCracken from Watford, the crowd tried to kill each other in one of the worst boxing crowd bust ups ever seen. But if you want to see Andy at his best, get hold of the two fights against Wally Swift, a highly rated boxer also from Watford and you will see how hard Andy Till is. I think Andy could have been pretty untouchable on the unlicensed circuit but, although he came to mine and a few other shows, I don't know if he was interested in doing it. Andy had been fighting since a very young age, so he may have fancied a well earned rest by then. But he's certainly not someone to take liberties with!

Without doubt one of, if not the hardest man in a street fight, is not a gypsy either but on the top rung of the 'chaps' - his name is

Vic Dark. Vic is a soft spoken, polite, gentleman from the East End and now lives in Essex. Young Vic Dark was a member of the notorious West Ham I.C.F. (Inter City Firm). A lot of hard men started in the I.C.F., Like Carlton Leach, Cass Pennant, Steve Guy and of course Billy Gardner. Add Vic Dark, and just those few are positively lethal!

Vic is a black belt in a number of martial arts and a heavy weight lifter. But Vic doesn't use Karate or whatever, he mixes everything together into one awesome street fighting technique so that I really don't think anyone would get near him on the street. He is also extremely respected by the top so called gangsters. He was a pallbearer along with young Joe Pyle, Roy Shaw, Jamie Foremen (movie star son of Freddie), Freddie himself and Ronnie Nash at the funeral of the 'Boss of Bosses' Joey Pyle snr. That's how highly Vic is thought of. He was also one of Reg Kray's trusted inner circle in the nick.

Vic is someone I see as ideal. There's no shouting and roaring, he's a gentleman. He would rather have a laugh with his trusted mates than go fighting all over the place but take a liberty and God help you!

A couple of years ago, they tried to get Vic put away for life after a contract killing. Every day he went to court there were guns, vans and helicopters everywhere. I wrote to Vic and gave him my support while he was on remand. When he got a not guilty (quite right too!) he phoned me and sent me a message of thanks for the support. I will always support Vic Dark. A man among men!

One man from America, who has been called the 'hardest man in the world', is Randy Couture, a mixed martial arts fighter who I'm sure we will hear a lot more of in the future. Perhaps a fight against Kimbo Slice? But then again, my cage fighting and mixed martial arts knowledge is pretty crap!

As I said earlier, the man who has been considered as 'King of the Gypsies' for many years now is 'gypsy' Johnny Frankham. Johnny was not only a thrilling cobble fighter, he was British light heavyweight champion and had three blistering fights with Chris Finnegan at a packed Royal Albert Hall when the crowd and chairs became as much a part of the fight as Frankham and Finnegan. Johnny was usually asked to be 'fair play man' in local fights because he had the respect of everyone and still does. As a ring fighter, he was extremely hard to hit, a bit like Kevin Paddock but, with respect to Kevin, of a lot higher calibre than the unlicensed fighters.

"Frankham, You are as slippery as an eel!" Finnegan called to Johnny at ringside in jest at one night out. On the cobbles, he was the complete reverse. Another gypsy warrior who commands great respect is Les Stevens from Reading who was also a pro and took the great John Conteh the full distance which took some doing in those days. John Conteh was one of the most underrated fighters this country has produced. I spent a couple of great fight nights in the company of these two legends. The real deals are always gentlemen, it's the wannabes that are prats!

Bartley Gorman claims: "I challenged Johnny to a bare knuckle fight a couple of times at Doncaster Races. I was heavier than him but he was quick and experienced. I would liked to have tested my boxing skills against his." I related this story to Johnny Frankham who nearly choked on his beer laughing! I know a hell of a lot of good gypsies as Joe Smith and Jimmy Stockin will confirm for you and nobody had heard about these challenges!

Bartley also claims with confidence: "If Mike Tyson and Lennox Lewis were fighting in one field and I (Bartley) was fighting in the next field, all the gypsies would come and watch me." What do you think?

One ex bare knuckle fighter stands out for various reasons, he was a decent fighter but far from the best and certainly not the worst. He was also a safe blower, that great occupation pioneered by men like George 'Tatters' Chatham and wartime double agent Eddie Chapman, in the same era as the Irish Charmer Peter Scott was stealing Sophia Loren's jewels and breaking into any Mayfair pad that took his Raffles-influenced fancy. But this young cobble fighter from Sunderland turned desperately to the cobbles and gelignite just to make ends meet. As he fought and felt the pain, there was no way he could have known that one day he would buy Darlington football club and clear their five million plus debt in one swoop. He is worth £300 million, he went from a four year prison sentence to the *Sunday Times* rich list from selling chipboard and worktops. He is of course George Reynolds.

My Geordie friends do make me laugh, I love them to death and they are most funny when they are being serious. It doesn't matter what you have, if you are from Sunderland they refuse to be impressed. I remember asking my late friend Harry Marsden and John 'Mario' Cunningham, founders of the original 'Geordie Mafia' and extremely dangerous men in their day, about George Reynolds. I said: "This guy was one of your own. He's now worth three hundred million and has a football club, yacht, helicopter and Christ knows what!"

They both fixed me with a stare that blurted out MISTAKE! MISTAKE!

Harry said: "Tel Man, wayya mean one of oors? He's a dirty fucking mackem man!" It was a gem. Then he started on about them calling 'us' monkey hangers and other stuff that completely lost me. Harry wound himself up and started to punch things. Then 'Mario', a man who had once escaped from Durham prison before everything was tightened up after the John McVicar escape, piped up ... I never mentioned Sunderland again and I still don't know what a 'mackem' is.

One of the most famous bare knuckle fights took place between two Irishmen Dan Rooney and Ernie McGinley for the championship of Ireland. It turns up on every unlicensed and bare knuckle video in circulation. There are masses of spectators all over the place, a swarm of people even sitting on their roofs for a better look. It was a bitter, brutal battle. The crowd actually became uncontrollable and the fight was a draw but it would appear Dan Rooney had the upper hand at that point.

Of the new breed, one of the best bare knuckle fighters is an East End gypsy called Matt Attrell. A lot of people talk about Matt and it's all good. It would seem if you want to be known as a man who has fought everyone on the cobbles now, you must beat Matt Attrell who has never ducked anyone. Danny Woolard tells how he and Matt were put in hospital after a fight in a Chinese restaurant but they took twelve of the enemy to hospital with them, the foe were full of stitches and one had lost his eye!

Danny Woolard is another man who was more than tasty on the cobbles, he has a book out and it's worth a read. In the Chinese restaurant encounter a meat cleaver was put through Woolard's head and he carried on fighting. To the Chinese's credit they made no statements (it goes without saying that Woolard and Attrell didn't). So many people have claimed to have been a close friend of Reg Kray in prison but Danny was, I know that for a fact, plus Reggie gives Danny Woolard a mention in his last book *A way of life*.

One gypsy cobble fighter who I had the pleasure of training and preparing for the unlicensed ring was 'Gypsy' Joe Smith from West London. Joe was a brutal and fear free cobble fighter but just needed to brush up on boxing ring craft. I taught Joe the value of working from behind a solid jab, cutting off the ring and footwork, as well as getting him into prime fitness. We had a full gym at our disposal, as I worked in one at the time, and we would sweat it out every day. Joe's cousins Billy Smith and Jimmy Stockin also came along to a specialised boxercise circuit I set up and for some sparring after. Sometimes I needed to calm them down as these boys loved nothing more than a claret filled tear up. They were, and still are, extremely hard men. Joe, Jimmy and brother Wally Stockin were also extremely close, as I was, to Joey Pyle snr and we would always catch up at parties. Myself and a few of the lads also did a fair bit of hair raising debt collecting for a very well known East End 'face' and other bits and pieces.

With Joe, the first thing to sort out in training, as well as fitness, was controlling his aggression. He was used to the cobbles where fights only last about 10-20 minutes tops and are often personal so hatred plays a large part. The boxing ring is not like that. You have to keep things under control and relax, not get wound up. You might start as first on the bill and end up last, while your opponent sits in traffic, but you must just let it ride. Getting angry was asking for defeat - why do you think Ali used to wind his opponents up so much?

At one of Joe's early unlicensed fights, when he hadn't mastered the mental side and was still thinking like a cobble fighter, it all blew up in proper gangland fashion. It was like Eddie Richardson and Frankie Fraser at Mr Smith's club all over again. Now, it seems funny. Actually, even then it seemed funny!

I was in Joe's corner with his older brother Aaron and younger brother John. As will become clear, I have not given details of venues although I can say that this one took place near London. We were due to be second on the bill. A lot of preparation is needed on fight night; getting your man kitted out, hands bandaged up, keeping him warm on the pads and greasing him up around his eyes and face. Every time our fight slot changed, Joe had to be cooled down again, made to relax and brought back to normal thinking. Then we got a call via the promoter to say our opponent was in traffic, so we would be on fourth. Now, for some reason, nobody liked this guy we were supposed to be fighting. There were twelve fights on the bill so just how long were we going to be kept waiting was anybody's guess.

Roy Shaw, as guest of honour, had taken his place at the ringside and the place was packed. So we warmed up again. While on the pads and getting a light sweat on, another call came in, we were now on sixth. It was stand down time again and Joe was starting to get very heated. "If this mush is not here soon, any one of 'em will do." I told him that this was normal routine in amateur, unlicensed and even pro events. So off we went again, another call and we were due on eighth but he still wasn't there, then ninth!

By now Joe's eyes were glazed over and he was pacing and staring at people. The ever reliable Steve Holdsworth of Eurosport came in the dressing room to calm him down. But now I had the old cobble fighter on my hands and I could tell not many double jabs were going to be thrown, it was going to be a smash up!

Then the guy arrives, gets weighed in with Joe in his face, gets changed and waits in the passage near us, not a clever move. Every time Joe saw him another vein popped up in his temple. Joe walked up to him and said something that I doubt was 'lovely weather' and the guy, a big, tall gangly bloke looked stunned.

Finally, we warmed up and were on our way to the ring. A slight touch of gloves and ding! The bell goes. But this guy did not want to punch, he wanted to come in with both arms and smother his opponent. We had been told this and had prepared for it, practicing stepping under the guard as it came down and smashing an uppercut into the unguarded chin. But Joe had lost it and the guy was like an octopus all over him. Then it happened; frustrated, Joe leans back and cracked his head right in the guy's face. So then the guy tried wrestling for his life and both ended up on the canvas, rolling around, kicking and punching lumps out of each other.

In the packed crowd half were for the other guy and half were hard arsed gypsies. The crowd turned on each other with fists and chairs flying. Joe was still punching his opponent on the deck screaming, "Get these poxy gloves off me." When he got up his hand was raised because of his opponent's persistent holding and refusing to punch. As we looked back, the referee was rolling around the canvas with this bloke and had taken over where Joe left off! We all howled with laughter as fighter and ref had it out and all we could hear from the referee was: "I never liked you, you fucker!"

As a chair landed in the ring, we turned our attention to the crowd. Security had made a passageway for us through the gypsy's supporters to get us out of there and we had a few limos lined up. Then we heard, what sounded like fire crackers, until one of the security guys shouted: "Fuck me! They're firing shooters." There were firecracker bangs and pings all over the place. A few of the other firm tried to punch us on the way out and we actually stopped and smashed them in the face with chairs!

There were a few strangers lined up with hands in pockets outside, so we made straight for the limos and drove off, pissing ourselves laughing as we went. When things had calmed down a little, Joe spluttered: "That fucking curry house I booked better still be open, I'm starving now."

They opened the restaurant as we arrived mob handed in different limos and checking for holes in ourselves almost in their foyer! That kind of night, never puts you in the mood for a jobs worth. Our waiter refused to sell beer until, that is, Aaron and 'Big' John who is about 6ft 7" and 20 odd stone, stood up and asked him if he wanted to be put on the next day's menu - beer was served!

It was the thought of the referee battering a boxer that really got me though and I just couldn't get this strange picture out of my head. Joe came to my club the next day and we told everyone that we won the fight, I think we went with an easy points win. That battle is still talked about today but there were others ... surprise,

surprise! But back to bare knuckle.

One man who hardly gets a mention but could look after himself was a man named Mark Owens (No, not the Take That bloke!). He knocked 'Mad' Frankie Fraser out cold when they were in Parkhurst, this was when Frank was at his most feared. Mark Owens obviously didn't give a toss for reputations. I think Mark and Frank became pals in the end. Also, my close friend Chris Lambrianou clumped Ian Brady and a slag called Don Barrett who turned supergrass - twice! Chris served up a nonce and a grass, instant knighthood surely! But more about Chris later.

One famous gypsy story took place In1994. A whole army of Irish travellers about 150 trailers in all, headed north causing real problems for northern English gypsies who called on their Scottish allies the Macphee family for help. It was like a military invasion and the best of the Macphees travelled to meet the Irish. Both groups produced a fighter. If the Macphees won, the Irish would have to turn back but if the Irish won, the take over of Scotland would proceed. It was like the Jacobite wars and Bonny Prince Charlie.

The fight kicked off and the chosen Macphee was on the brink of success when suddenly the Irishman's pals joined in. No 'fair play' man would have been able to handle this lot! Eventually, order was restored and the fight continued but the Scottish Macphee was now so seething with rage, he laid into the Irishman, got hold of his head, bit his nose clean off and in front of both clans ... swallowed it!

For some reason, a month or so later the Irish tried to invade again with fresh troops, but the Scottish Macphees were ready for them and the Irish were forced to put up a fighting retreat. The domination of the northern English and their main prize, domination of the Scottish gypsies had failed badly. No such huge 'invasion' has happened since. It was like Culloden all over again but this time the Scots won!

One day, in about 1995 I met up with a few of my close mates just outside a huge roundabout called Milton Keynes (never ask for directions in Milton Keynes!). I didn't know exactly where we were going but I assumed we were off to watch and wager on a 'straightener' so I guessed it would be open air somewhere. For some reason a 'straightener' usually takes place in the open but as we carried on, we turned into an industrial estate, tooted the horn three times and this huge metal warehouse door opened. I knew then, it was going to be an 'all in' because they usually take place in built up areas, mostly inside with the door firmly bolted. Again, it's just the way it is. There were only about 20-30 of us there, not a lot for the size of the place but 'all ins' of course are top secret as they are illegal.

One fighter was a huge Yorkshire man and the other a much smaller bloke from West London, whom of course was the man we were supporting. The other guy was so pumped up with steroids he looked like he was about to burst and he certainly had more than a minor dose of 'roid rage'. As he kicked, punched and head butted everything metal in sight of his corner, we all tried not to burst out laughing including his opponent who I shall call 'Mark'.

Now Mark was one of those guys people came unstuck with especially when he worked the doors. He was one of the smallest guys on the door but most of the hardest and respected men have been small men. People like Roy Shaw, Freddie Foreman, Frankie Fraser and even the Krays were not big men. Small, sinewy blokes with tons of bottle are by far the worst.

Somebody kicked a gas cylinder and the two were at each other. Hands round each other's necks and trying to butt each other. Then, there was a loud bang on the door. We all scattered and put T shirts back on the fighters as it could only be Old Bill.

One of the lads moved the door slightly ajar and in strutted, like the king of the world, Lenny McLean or 'the Guv'nor' as he liked to be called. He sat on an old pallet and growled, "carry on boys". I assume he had staked his money somewhere else and was popping in to check on his investment. I don't know who he had his money on but the fact was that Lenny was heavily into the steroid scene himself and used to jack up all the time, I'm afraid, unlike the myth, he was also a brutal bully (check with anyone who knew him who wasn't above him, i.e. normal people, and they will tell you what he was like). My guess was that he was backing 'Mr pumped up and roaring'.

Even Lenny's own cousin and promoter Frank Warren, did a magazine interview in which he described Lenny as 'the very worse type of bully'. He also stated that 'his book was a joke, all those bare knuckle fights and claiming to be unbeaten in the unlicensed ring. Roy Shaw stopped him early and Cliff Field and Johnny Waldron knocked him out cold twice each. He was also beaten by a guy called Kevin Paddock. How he got away with that book I will never know, I guess people believe what they want to believe'.

And that was his own family!

Bob Mee, author of *Bare Fists* wrote: 'The marketing of Lenny McLean's book was undeniably a success as it produced a bestseller. However, the startling claim of the first sentence of the fly-sheet - "Lenny McLean is the deadliest bare-knuckle fighter Britain has ever seen" - is laughably wide of the mark'. He added, 'McLean was a tough man but had little ability outside rage, borne out of personal misery' and that McLean 'could not box'.

I spoke to so many people who knew, or had crossed swords with Lenny McLean, but I only left in the comments from men who would have said them whether Lenny was alive or dead, if he was standing in front of them or not. Those who didn't give a shit for his reputation. I chose not to use their names, they never asked me not to. The comments from those I know would have been 'Lenny me old mate, great to see you!' I have left out! The same applies to the twins, in fact the same applies to everyone.

A famous incident I have been told by about six different people, was when a 16-year-old Roy Shaw fan said "bad luck Len" after Shaw had stopped him. McLean's response was to beat the kid senseless with a chair leg!

Trust me, not the sort of thing you make up. I have seen him bully people with my own eyes and then slobber when a well known north London 'face' has walked in the club with his brother. As I say, it's impossible to tell the truth AND keep everyone happy.

Lenny's trademark on the doors was to spread-eagle a guy's legs and punch him as hard as he could right up the groin - these were just everyday bank clerks and the like, not hard men. The idea was that the guy would wake up with huge, swollen testicles. This can now be proven, as to milk the cow even further, a book called *The Guv'nor Tapes* was released. This contained everything that was too much for the original book and Lenny talks about this method with glee to Peter Gerrard his ghostwriter.

Now, Mark and the other lump were back at each other. Mark suddenly grabbed the guy's ears, nutted him three or four times then lifted his knee in a blur of about a dozen times into the genitals. (The difference of course between this and the McLean story is that these two were fighters who had agreed this was an 'all in' and NOT a plumber's mate!) As he did this at dazzling speed, Mark sank his teeth into the big guy's face, there was a ripping sound and a lump of meat that resembled a nose and some other bits were in Mark's mouth, he then spat them out and forced all his finger nails into the claret filled hole of goo, blood and snot. He then ripped out yet more flesh and the bone could now easily be seen. Just before calling 'best' (surrender).

Lenny McLean dipped his head, turned away like he was about to retch, went a bit green and said, "See ya boys, that's enough for Lenny for one day."

So I assumed he had lost his money and had got used to the gloved life. Dave Courtney who worked with Lenny for ages says in his book *Heroes and Villains* that Lenny couldn't handle the celebrity when it came and was responsible for being 'a bit of a bully'. I have sparred with Roy a few times and moved around with the likes of Jimmy Stockin but they were taking it VERY easy with me ... ha!

Lenny just would not have been able to do that, he would have had to knock you all over the ring, gain a victory, roar and basically taken a liberty (although he would not have seen it that way). On one occasion, an unlicensed legend (who never fought unlicensed but was heavily involved), who was actually a pro, battered Lenny all over the ring and the guy must have been in his 60s by then!

He let me use his name for this book but I won't bring his name up, if you don't believe me then tough shit, I really have nothing to gain by lying. Actually, it doesn't take much working out. This man who was a very big heavyweight and would have beaten all the unlicensed fighters in his day just jabbed Lenny's head off, with Lenny getting more and more wound up throwing punches at thin air. He had also sparred with Roy and found him in a far superior class, there was also a lot more mutual respect. This man had been all over the world with Joe Louis and took shit off nobody ... including the Kray Twins.

Talking of the Krays and rubbish stories, it is said that the infamous Scottish gangster Arthur Thompson, came to the East End to find the twins. He found them in a club, pulled out a gun and forced one twin to kiss the other twin's arse. Bullshit! As if! The Scots can't believe we fell for that story and I don't think the twins ever heard it.

A lot of London 'faces' used to have respect for Arthur Thompson but how many of them knew that Arthur (who put money into McLean) gave evidence against Paul Ferris at his trial and actually pointed him out? I know that 'Mad' Frankie Fraser now knows (Frank was one of those who thought Arthur was a great man) because Paul pulled Frank aside and politely told him exactly what happened in that court room. Whether Frank believed him is another matter, it is a bit of a shocker but a true shocker.

Of course, this happened years after Thompson's dealings with Lenny McLean took place and McLean would never have known about his mentor's real methods. Arthur did offer McLean the contract to kill Paul Ferris but Lenny died before moves were made. Anyway, if Joey Pyle had got wind of it, it would have finished there and then. I know for a fact the huge amount of respect Joe had for Paul Ferris and every other man of respect. I really don't think Lenny would have used a gun anyway, he admitted himself he hated them.

The story that the twins were also chased out of Newcastle is also bullshit!

Not to say it couldn't have happened, they can have a ruck, those Geordie boys, it just didn't happen.

Now, I have been out with Roy Shaw more times than I or anyone else can remember and he always had time for everyone, an autograph here, a photo there, nobody was, or is, turned away. Throughout the realms of the 'chaps' I was always known as 'Roy Shaw's man' and apart from a couple of bumps in the road, that's how I was seen. A man like Dave Courtney would tell you that if you ever asked him. It was that way for about eight years, now I'm sometimes known as 'Charlie Richardson's man', 'Ronnie Knight's man' or 'Carlton Leach's' man. I think I have been associated with them all in different people's minds. Again, that doesn't mean this book is biased towards Roy, everything I am writing can be proved or has already been said in a different way with different experiences as examples. And I never saw Lenny in Charlie, Ronnie or Roy's league I'm afraid. Well, he wasn't ... end of!

There's no point writing a book that crumbles under examination and that's exactly what Lenny's and a couple of other books have done ... crumbled.

Another bare knuckle fighter in the nineties was called Joe Savage who claimed he was British bare knuckle champion (how many of them have there been?). He claimed 41 wins on the trot and no losses (nowhere near Lenny McLean's 30,000 or 20,000 or 40,000 etc. Tut, tut!). He was meant to take part in a fight festival in America in 1993. The fighters fighting for a grand cash prize included former heavyweights Tony Tubbs, 'Bonecrusher' Smith who had handed Frank Bruno his first defeat, Tyrell Biggs and 'Smokin' Bert Cooper who replaced Mike Tyson in a fight against the Warrior himself, Evander Holyfield, in 1991. Tyson claimed damaged ribs, while some say he didn't want the fight because he knew he did not have the heart, mental power or fitness of Evander. Whatever the reason, Burt Cooper was a late replacement.

In the first round, Holyfield v Cooper, the unthinkable happened. Cooper caught Evander with a left hook that nearly made the arena crumble and fall to the ground! If Evander was not near the ropes, he would not have got up, nobody would of. Evander grabbed the ropes, his legs going in different directions, Tyson must have been kicking himself but the Warrior cleared his head and, God knows how, stopped Cooper in seven explosive rounds. After watching these guys going at each other in sparring, the undefeated bare knuckle champion of Britain Joe Savage pulled out with a hand injury!

Talking of Tyson, one of his genuine friends (because he has a lot of 'yes' men around) is 'Big' Joe Egan from Birmingham via Ireland. The tongue in cheek title of his book is *The Hardest White Man in the World*. Joe was a very tasty boxer who admires Roy

Shaw. I met Joe at a Dave Courtney party (that's about the only bit I remember!) and I took a photo of Joe and Roy together. As a real fighting man, Joe is a gent and great company who can really have a proper row and by that I mean 80 wins by the age of 24, a Golden Gloves Champion, who went the distance with Lennox Lewis and beat Bruce Seldon. That's how good. Joe did a prison sentence and Roy's book *Pretty Boy* helped get him through it. He is a top bloke. Good on ya Joe!

Back to Joe Savage, after that April 1994, Savage challenged who he thought was a 'shot' (burned out) Bert Cooper. He certainly didn't fancy going toe to toe with 'Bone crusher', 'Tyrell Biggs' or Tony Tubbs with or without gloves, after witnessing the other former champions' claret filled sparring sessions. Every top pro I have ever met has been keen to tell me that fighting is their full time job. Tim Witherspoon, a gentle giant told me he would train sometimes six to eight hours a day, six to seven days a week. They hire the best sparring partners available, top dieticians and physical conditioners. They get loads of sleep, prepare well mentally and study videos of their opponents; in short, they eat, sleep and breathe boxing. Most unlicensed fighters, unless you happen to be Roy Shaw, have full time jobs!

So even a 'shot' top fighter will nearly always beat an unlicensed or cobble fighter. As I said, the key is, if you can brawl on the cobbles, brawl in the ring, box in the ring and be a good defensive fighter in the ring, like Johnny Frankham and now Joe Smith. So even against a 'shot' Bert Cooper, Joe Savage was way out of his depth and he knew it. Britain's undefeated bare knuckle champion was knocked spark out in 65 seconds and in that time hit the deck twice. The bare knuckle champion retired after this fight.

One of the youngest bare knuckle champions ever was just 14 when he was crowned Romany champion, he was from Galway, Ireland and his name was Billy Heaney. He won bare fist titles again at 16, 21 and 24. Not bad at all. There are a lot of real champions out there who don't do the celebrity thing, but they are the real deal.

Our great friend 'Welsh' Bernie Davies is an extremely hard man! Human beings are supposed to be made out of flesh and bone but Bernie is made out of pure muscle fibre. He is currently (November 2008) in prison on a fire arms charge but we communicate often by letter. He is one of Wales' toughest men with his bare fists and has an 'old school' manner, which means he's not a big mouth who offends people. Bernie is a friend of all the 'chaps' and we all hope the powers that be have some compassion for Bernie whose wife is extremely ill. Bernie though, is too big a trophy for them and since when did the law have compassion?

But Bernie won't be forgotten and his brutal battles in the Welsh Valleys shall never be forgotten either. Talking of Wales, if you think you're hard, give it large in any pub in Merthyr Tydfil and see if they are in the mood to give you your limbs back!

Lately, America has gone mad for a 6ft 2", 34 year old block of muscle called Kimbo Slice. His real name is Kimbo Ferguson, but, after a nasty cut over the right eye he gave an opponent called Big D Ferguson, (obviously, no relation) he acquired the nickname Kimbo 'Slice'. Kimbo built his reputation on bare knuckle brawls, or, as they say in America, 'underground' fights. After an awesome reputation built in fields, barns and warehouses with his bare fists, Kimbo got bored of knocking huge men spark out on the cobbles and trained for the mixed martial arts circuit and fighting in the octagon. Recently he fought a former WBO boxing champion (famous for annihilating Tommy 'The Duke' Morrison, star of *Rocky V* and having a chin of iron!) and beat him in under three minutes.

Kimbo has become an Internet legend where sites like You Tube showing his fights, receive thousands of hits. He has become a phenomenon and now has his own website where his bare knuckle fights can be seen. I think it's hard to know whether Kimbo Slice is a true and brutal bare knuckle warrior or a piece of American novelty and money spinner, the latter of course being what the Americans are so good at. Everything has to be a brand and business with a slogan or two and Kimbo is being made into a star. Kimbo can certainly have a fight, but is a touch wild and plodding. I'm not sure if he could do the business against Britain's top knuckle men or men like Ian Freeman. Ian is a good friend and the problem when a boxer fights a man like Ian is that, once a boxer's legs are taken away, it's game over!

Another American who has been called 'the hardest man in the world' is a guy called Randy Couture, who is a mixed martial arts fighter - will these two get it on?

But if you can box and grapple, choke and hold, you are in the driving seat. Have a look at a busy street anywhere on a Saturday night at those who are drunk and get into a fight, 90% will end up on the pavement. So if you are strongly trained in fighting on the floor, the fight is yours. I have rarely seen two guys come out of a club or pub for a fight and both men stay on their feet like a real cobble fighter.

In fact in 1990, when I was 18, two friends of ours came out of a club near Ealing called the Top Hat, along with about 20 of us. The two lads looked good as they were both boxers and looked slick, not like these idiots who have a few drinks and suddenly think they are Reg Kray and start flailing their arms like a windmill. (How many blokes do that? You almost expect their Dad to come and put their hand on the guys head as if they were a kid!) They were moving around well, when one slag ran past and with full force, he swivelled and plunged a carving knife straight between our mate's ribs. You could actually hear it enter, crack and then a squishing sound. The knife was a kitchen knife and he must have been trying to kill our pal but he was gone! This was when very few places had CCTV. When the paramedics (or Ambulance men as we called them before Britain became America's 51st state!) arrived you could see a huge hole opening and closing like it was breathing! Our pal was in intensive care for two months, he only just made it.

We knew that the prick who stabbed him was one of the 'firm' we were fighting and after a bit of research to find him (like torturing his mates) he spent three months in intensive care!

There are always two sides to every story. Like the rivalry between Henry 'The Outlaw' Francis and Jimmy Stockin, two top gypsy knuckle men. My first book was called *Bouncers* and was written with my close, trusted Welsh pal Julian Davies or 'Juggy' as we call him. 'Juggy' is no slouch himself. Before our collaboration, Julian wrote a book called *Streetfighters*, a fantastic read. In it, he presented Henry's version of this spiky old rivalry, so I feel I should write Jimmy's to balance things out.

Jimmy Stockin fought 180 amateur fights, that's some going. One day at Peterborough fair, Jimmy had been on the ale all day and he was well pissed. He was well aware that his arch rival, a man called Henry Francis was at the fair. Jimmy bumped into Henry, drunk and stumbling, not in an aggressive way but just drunk. Jimmy wasn't out for starting a fight but Henry thought he was and threw a few punches at Jimmy cutting his face. Henry was hardly affected by drink at all, unlike Jimmy, so Jim knew this was not the time. They made arrangements to fight in the morning but Henry had gone. He had left the site and gone back up north. Jimmy said a man called out: "Henry didn't know it was you Jim."

"Too bad, I'm coming after him!"

The next meeting would be the Doncaster St Leger, right on Henry's doorstep. About 30 travellers from West London went along because you have to prepare for the worst. This was a bold move, this was really northerners only and a London 'face' was on his way looking to fight. As they pulled up, Henry's father and brother were there but said again: "He didn't know it was you Jim."

They were sure that Henry's mob would be in the pub and burst in through both doors to keep everyone in but once again, no Henry Francis! They waited around for a few hours but he didn't show, so they went back south. And that was that. Now, when Henry hit Jimmy a few times, Jimmy would have been well pissed. I have seen Jimmy after a few 'sherbets' many times and if he hadn't been leaning on the bar, you could push him over with your index finger. It's a very different story when Jimmy is sober though.

Jimmy Stockin and his brother Wally (another good fighter and one of the 'firm'), Joe Smith, Johnny and Bobby Frankham are certainly not bullies but I think Henry Francis was trying to make them look like a pack of wild men.

Unlike my experience of Lenny McLean, everybody has informed me that Bartley Gorman was a complete gentleman and family man. The problem again is that he was not the unbeaten superman he made out and was never 'King of the Gypsies'.

Here's an example. Gorman claims that he challenged Roy

Shaw, Lenny McLean, Bobby and Johnny Frankham and everyone was too scared to fight him! Now, a lot of the Gypsies had not even heard of Bartley before his book came out but, of course, had heard of all these men who were supposed to be dodging him. I personally asked Roy Shaw, Joey Pyle, Les Stevens and Johnny Frankham about Bartley Gorman and no one knew who he was. If you see his book, there is not one single photo in the whole book of him fighting. Not one!

All we have is one photo of Gorman in a crowd, with his 'fight' being broken up by the police and himself very neatly covered in dust. He says that he challenged Roy Shaw and Lenny McLean, so why didn't he get in the ring and offer the challenge as is the custom and certainly was during the 1970s. If a challenge was made, Joey Pyle who was Roy's promoter, would have known but he didn't. There is one photo of Bartley posing with the caption 'Taken in 1974 when I challenged Roy "Pretty Boy" Shaw'. Well, Roy wasn't that well known until he knocked out Donny 'The Bull' Adams and that was December 1975. And Roy wasn't released from prison until 1975! So how could Roy have been challenged in 1974 when he was not released from Lartin until a year later?

Bartley says he was at the Shaw v Adams fight, so why didn't he challenge Roy in the ring? Why didn't he do it at any of Roy's fights? Lenny McLean, Roy Shaw, Cliff Field, Kevin Paddock, Johnny Waldron, Lew Yates, Columbo Richards at some point, all got in the ring and challenged who they wanted to fight, this is how fights were made. Why didn't Gorman ever get in the ring and challenge Roy and the other one, who was supposedly too scared of him, Lenny?

Bartley's book makes the 'King of the Gypsies' sound like a well organised, official body. It's not, and just like 'the Guv'nor', it's a very loose term. You don't fight for the title of 'Guv'nor', then defend, lose, or get stripped of it, if you don't fight so and so, and it's not an ongoing event. It's not like a pro world champion who has to first win a world title and then defend it. In London, we call everyone Guv'nor!

'King of the Gypsies' is the same. It's not an official title as Bartley Gorman makes it sound. That's why, after all these years, John Frankham is still thought of as 'King of the Gypsies' because it's to do with the type of man you are, it's more a lifetime achievement award. Otherwise, Joe Smith could lay a claim because he had nine unlicensed fights and no losses but Joe has never claimed it because even to him, the title belongs to Johnny. It's like Ali being called the 'greatest'. When Frazier and Norton beat him, they didn't become the 'greatest' did they?

I remember the first time Roy Shaw ever laid eyes on Bartley Gorman and it wasn't in a field or warehouse, it was at Reggie Kray's graveside. Roy shook his hand like he has with millions of strangers everywhere. When I told Roy it was Bartley Gorman he looked at me as if to say 'who's that'? My mate Liam, who knows every 'face' because he films them all the time, can be heard on the video asking Bartley, "And who are you mate?"

Bartley looked a bit put out and mumbled, "Bartley Gorman."

Sometime later, I showed Roy, Bartley's book. When he read the bit about him being challenged Roy went completely mental and he said: "Why the fuck is everyone lying about me just to get a gee up; it's lies and always about me just to make these slags look like something when they are nothing!" He then said: "Tel, you know every fucker there is to know, find this bloke and tell him I will fight him now! fucking NOW!"

Those instructions were pretty clear, so I rang Joe Smith as a starting point. Joe was with his cousin Billy, he mumbled something to him as if he was checking something, then said to me: "Telboy, tell the Guv'nor to calm down. Bartley Gorman died a couple of months ago."

"How?" I asked.

"Cancer I think mate."

I mumbled, "God rest him," and thanked Joe.

I told Roy the news. He was still in a rage but as soon as I told him he said: "That's terrible for his family, did he have kids? Perhaps we should send flowers?" I respected Roy for that because the family man and the fighting man meant two different things to him. He could have said something really nasty but instead he was respectful.

A few weeks later, Roy and Joey Pyle looked through Bartley's book. They looked at the photos to try and picture him and jog their memories. Along with coppers, it's obvious that a gangster or villain has to remember names and faces, you wouldn't get very far without that skill. Neither Joe or Roy could place Bartley Gorman. When Bartley challenged Bobby Frankham, it was clearly a publicity stunt that Bartley would not have gone through with and none of Bobby's team were contacted. Bobby himself thought it was a publicity joke and, remember, Bobby had assaulted a referee in a pro fight and lost his license. He was still in his early twenties and his number one priority was to get his pro licensed back. An illegal bare knuckle fight on a boat was not the way to get his pro license back - that's obvious!

As I said before, it's hard to write about the dead. I have full respect for the way Bartley conducted his life, he was a true man, this is purely about his claims to fights. The man commonly regarded as the 'King of the Gypsies', and was when Bartley claims to have been, is 'Gypsy' Johnny Frankham, that's a fact.

It's also a fact that gypsies (mostly English) and 'tinkers' (mostly Irish) for the most part hate each other. I know a place where one side of the street is gypsy and the other is tinker with the road being no man's land. A lot of gypsies don't even travel, they stay on a site. And I have had countless punch ups with idiots who claim to 'hate pikeys'. If they went into a real gypsy home, they would be in awe especially Johnny Frankham's (I wouldn't get any ideas about trying to rob it though. Ha!).

As I have said, never underestimate a man just because he is not huge with bulging biceps. Billy Cribb (author of *Tarmac Warrior*) is also rather a small man but has the heart of a lion. Most people think that the bigger the muscles in your arms, the harder you will punch, that if you pump iron like a maniac, the size of the muscle will increase and therefore your strength. It doesn't happen like that. What you are given naturally in terms of power is pretty much where you will stay. I used to tell people this in the gym but it usually fell on deaf ears.

Say, for example, you are doing bicep curls with heavy weights, yes, your strength will improve but ONLY on bicep curls! If you are pumping out leg extensions you will get stronger but ONLY on leg extensions. In other words, bicep curls will not make you punch harder. In fact, if you don't stretch the muscle enough after the workout (which 99.9% of people do not!) you will actually decrease your power by losing range and making you more open to injury because you are so tight. Look at Ali's body or Sugar Ray Robinson or Joe Louis, they are loose and supple which means they can throw punches from every angle.

The key is to keep the muscles lengthened and well stretched, and to have perfect timing and accuracy, Arnie type biceps are no substitute for a shot of speed and timing that your opponent never saw coming and carries the element of surprise. Weights DO NOT make you punch harder, they only improve the weight you can lift on the exercise you are actually performing. Remember heavyweight flop Bruce Seldon? He should have been able to knock a barn door off with the muscle he carried and so should Frank Bruno but it doesn't work that way. Evander Hollyfield, my particular hero, may spend an hour training his arms but he would make sure he spent an hour and a half stretching them back out again.

About seven years ago, I was pure muscle because in my free time I worked out in the gym. But I was as stiff as a board and my restricted movement actually decreased my punch power! I have seen many a good fighter lose a fight before it started because he has seen the size of his opponents biceps!

I have sparred with countless people and don't think I have ever been in trouble with a body builder sort. The most painful are the tall, sinewy, snappy, natural punchers.

But you can't put muscles on your chin. Bruce Seldon had huge built up arms but no heart, it's like a lovely looking car with no engine. So never underestimate a man by his muscle or general size, it's a recipe for disaster. A man like Freddie Foreman is not a huge muscle bound lump but he has the heart of five lions! If you want to beat him, you really would have to kill him. Now, that's a lot more useful on your firm than a steroid filled lump who in truth is only doing that to himself to try and cover some sort of insecurity in the first place. Why else would you want to take steroids, get to mammoth size and oil your muscles? It's because you are trying to hide something or make up for the lack of something. The heart of men like Foreman cannot be trained into you, it is something you are born with.

Richy Horsley from Hartlepool fought on one of my shows and

displayed all the attributes that a real fighter needs. In his second unlicensed fight he showed power, movement, mental strength and raw primitive courage. That's pure fighting instinct, it's not thinking just sheer, raw, cave man type survival. Richy has had many street fights and I can imagine has done some real damage. Richy and I didn't see eye to eye all the time but my respect for him as a modern day fighting man is 100%. I could have left Richy out of this book, on the grounds of our little falling out, but he is included because my respect for a real fighter outweighs the playground stuff and I still wrote a foreword for his book *Born to Fight* and got Roy to do one as well. There's such a very small circle of respected, staunch men left who could be so strong together and make some real money, that I do actually find it upsetting when people in such a small trusted group fall out. It's a tragedy because you can't just replace them, they are tried and tested and it's usually misinformation or something stupid that screws up what should be a team!

On this occasion, Richy had accused me of things that must have been planted in his head because it came out of the blue and I honestly could not make sense of it. I was accused of getting him beaten on purpose. Well, only the fighter can win or lose not the promoter, plus the fight was a classic and he lost - just! If I had wanted him beaten, I would not have put someone in who was going to struggle!

I wouldn't have put him top of the bill just to have him beaten as top of the bill means 'we have plans'. The idea was for him to fight Charlie Bronson and, as Richy knows, that would have made all of us. So why would I want him beaten in his second fight? It doesn't make sense does it, well it didn't to me that's for sure. I was pretty hurt that he thought I would do that, as we had been friends before and his opponent wasn't even one of my fighters!

So I gained nothing from a Horsley defeat. But it takes a lot to lose a respect for a fighter of courage and my respect for him as a fighter is still high. I hope Richy now knows the truth and that I really needed him to win! It's a shame but Richy and I have never spoken since that incident but his book is well worth a read.

At the time of Horsley's fight on my show, my fighter Joe Smith was unbeaten and remains so. A lot of people asked me who would win between those two and could I arrange a fight. I could have set it up but at that time Joe was in full flight, fully fit, full of confidence and hungry and time was on his side. Richy was still easing into the game after a very long lay off, so it would be unfair to compare them at that time. And Joe, being a very well liked gypsy with a huge following would of had crowd advantage at that time. Then again, with Horsley's heart, it may not have mattered.

But there was a grand plan involved in getting Richy on my shows. It looked for a little while like the infamous prisoner Charlie Bronson would be released within two or three years, this info came straight from his legal team. Richy Horsley is the man Bronson wanted to fight. I don't recall whether Bronson hated Richy or not but I know he was picked due to 'disrespect' so at this time they were not the best of friends. You can also see that it was in my interest for Richy to win.

It may sound stupid making plans for Charlie Bronson but he had an appeal at the Bailey coming up, he had not been in trouble for ages, he hadn't killed or attempted to kill and the staff at Wakefield, to a man, couldn't understand why Charlie was still in there. We knew he wouldn't get out straight away but a three to four year programme that saw him with another chance of release if he stayed out of trouble was all we needed. And knowing Charlie, if he had the fight to focus on he would have concentrated on that and stayed out of trouble. We wanted a couple of warm up fights and then a big venue showdown with Richy. Harry Marsden, our dear pal from Newcastle, would prepare Charlie and Richy already had a capable team around him. Now it seems like light years ago but at the time it was more real and, for once, the powers that be showed signs of giving Charlie some leeway on his sentence. From then on, every letter I got from Charlie had a section about how he would destroy Richy. I remember on a visit he asked: "How is he going to deal with 30 years of rage, hurt and anger flying at him?"

Would the whole build up and atmosphere get to him so that he would crumble like Frank Bruno used to? Who knew? That would have been the problem for Richy, there was bound to be an early storm - could he weather it? We were now ahead of ourselves and talking like it was really on but we had to, for now.

If he did ride it, the logical tactic would have been to let Charlie, then anger and rage himself, out then open up. A Stupid idea to some, an interesting pick 'em fight for others whose minds could avoid the fact that it was Charlie Bronson. If it came off, we would be the ones laughing. It would certainly eclipse Roy Shaw v Donny Adams in 1975.

Richy would certainly have to train and get strong, Richy is not a lover of training (a problem I encountered before with him) but I think he would have enough motivation for this one, he would have to. Charlie of course had been on the weights since his sentence started and he was as strong as an ox. It would be more difficult to guess his fitness in jail than his strength because, of course, there was not a great deal of scope for road work in Wakefield's concrete coffin. Then, a few weeks later myself, Joey Pyle snr, Charlie Breaker and a few others made our way to the Old Bailey to hear Charlie Bronson's appeal.

On the second day, the place was full of more police with dogs and riot gear than I have ever seen in my life! By that, we knew that Charlie had been turned down on appeal. I admit, we all shed a few tears for Charlie (we had honestly forgotten about boxing in the drama of that court room). Charlie acted with amazing dignity and pride. His head held high, he thanked Judge Rose who insisted on saying: "I would say to the parole board, that this is a very different man than the one who started this sentence." He didn't have to say anything but he felt compelled to tell the world that Charlie had changed. But how much longer must one man do? More about Charlie later.

Flashing back to the 1970s, Roy Shaw was about to start off a chain of events that would produce a new sport - unlicensed boxing and all the infamous names that went with it.

7
UNLICENSED - HOW IT ALL BEGAN!

Upon his release from jail in 1975, Roy like most just turned ex cons, needed money and needed it fast. But all Roy was special at was fighting, how was he going to make a living through fighting now? He was 42 years old and had a record of violence that was second to none, he had even been to Broadmoor!

He hadn't discovered any other hidden talents in prison. He couldn't sculpt like Jimmy Boyle or Hugh Collins and couldn't produce art like Charlie Bronson or Eddie Richardson did in later years. He was too old to get his professional boxing license back and, with his reputation as a villain, he wouldn't have got it anyway ... he was stuck!

Then one fateful day, one of Roy's pals, named Ronnie Smith suggested Barnet Fare. Ronnie had a well known cousin called Levi Smith, both men were gypsies and Levi Smith was a real fighting man who, as far as I know, has never lost a row. Roy was building a house and needed a cash injection but wasn't interested in Barnet until Peter suggested the money that changed hands there - for fighting!

Both men knew this would be like taking candy from a baby. Roy was used to ten handed screws with riot sticks beating down on him, a one on one fight would be a joke. And so it proved. Although not a joke exactly, for a man like Roy Shaw and what he had suffered, this was easy work for good money. The fight area as always was crowded with gypsies and they came in increasing numbers as this 'gorger' (Romany term for a non-gypsy) knocked out more and more travellers with bare fists.

Roy was in heaven, loving every minute. Their best fighter was put up and he was also knocked spark out. Those of you who have met Roy in recent years would have found a very different Roy in the 1970s. He was like a wild animal and quite capable of killing anyone who had wronged him. His reputation grew and grew until even the Americans had heard of him. In one afternoon, Roy made three grand, imagine that in the mid 1970s.

It's a small world they say and in the crowd was a man Roy had met in prison, they didn't really like each other and it's a miracle nothing happened in jail between them. The man's name was Donny 'The Bull' Adams. He claimed to be the 'King of the Gypsies' but, as we have seen, a few people considered themselves to be the king when it's really what everyone else thinks that's important. It's doubtful that Donny was even a gypsy at all but one thing was known, his awesome reputation for a street fight. It had been reported that he had had 48 street fights and as many wins. He was no boxer, but as Joey Pyle put it, he was 'a non smoking, teetotal, hard faced mauler'.

Someone whispered to Roy: "There is only one man for you and that's Donny Adams."

"Anytime," replied Roy. Adams just observed that day but nobody not even Adams and Shaw could imagine that within months they would be in a packed circus tent ready to do battle in the very first unlicensed fight and give birth to an old sport in a brand new guise.

Joey Pyle and the late great Alex Steen took control of the business side. From finding a venue to getting tickets printed, Joey and Alex were on to it. But there was a major problem. This was going to be a bare knuckle fight, moreover as agreed between Shaw and Adams it was to be a bare knuckle fight till the 'end' or to the death in other words!

Both men agreed to a fight till the death, it was even printed on the tickets. It was no show, if it had to go that far both fighters agreed that that's how far it would go. To the winner a huge chunk of money, to the loser, very possibly, a grave!

The original bare knuckle fight was supposed to take place on 19th October 1975 at Holborn stud farm, Wormley, Herts at midday. The original ticket (Roy gave me one of these precious pieces of memorabilia when he found a few of the tickets whilst cleaning out his Mum's loft after her sad passing. It's a gangster cliche but Roy loved both his parents to bits. May they rest in peace ... together forever), read 'The fight of the century. Bare knuckle contest - fight to the finish!'

This was how it was going to be. A violent, brutal, blood filled slug fest until one man, or even both, drop! The demand was overwhelming but there was a problem.

Of course, a bare knuckle fight was illegal and there was no way around it. So how do you pack out a large venue and make as many people as possible aware of it without the Old Bill finding out? It's impossible. Shaw and Adams ended up in court and were bound over to keep the peace for a year. A compromise was reached and the fighters agreed to wear lightweight gloves that wouldn't make much difference but at least they would be wearing gloves so the fight was legal.

Two whole lots of tickets had been printed and all had been sold. There was no way this one was going to get away. Joey Pyle was originally going to fill the first few rows with the 'chaps' which would be normal anyway. Then, as soon as the bell went Shaw and Adams corners were going to cut the gloves off at lightning speed, then the two fighters would fly at each other while all the 'chaps' blocked the ring from the police so they couldn't get in to stop the fight. If they did get in there, chances are the fight would already be over because bare knuckle fights only last a few minutes.

It was a plan that was settled on for a long time until Joe and Alex thought better of it. It might have presented too good a chance for some of the over excited rascals just to batter Old Bill and then a riot would ensue. Then there would be a hell of a financial and legal mess to clear up. There was no way around using the gloves but the gloves would be as close to bag mitts as possible. The gloves were agreed and the fight was moved to 1st December 1975.

Roy was getting in some good sparring with a rough, tough fighter called Brian Hall, a real hard man and perfect for a decent workout. Both fighters trained like demons for this showdown. Roy was visited by a film producer who came to watch him spar with the idea of making a film of the whole event and after leaving Roy's camp he went to have a look at Adams. Roy rang him to ask how Adams was looking in training. It's always great to hear 'he looks rubbish', 'his timings well out' or 'he seems to be carrying an injury' but not a bit of it, Adams he reported, looked fantastic in training, fit, strong, aggressive with good timing. Roy suddenly realised that perhaps Adams was in a higher league to him and upped his training even more.

For some reason, journalists were giving all their attention to Adams and Roy was getting the hump with it. He told Joe he was getting fed up with playing second fiddle and to sort something out. Joe thought it might simply be the fact that Adams had a good nickname 'The Bull' and people were attracted by that, while Roy was still plain Roy Shaw. Joe happened to be talking to a journalist who thought Roy was very handsome. When Roy opened the next day's paper, there it was in big bold headline writing Donny 'The Bull' Adams v Roy 'Pretty Boy' Shaw!

Needless to say, Roy went nuts! who the hell was he going to scare called 'Pretty Boy'? Doubtless, Joe and Alex Steen were giggling their heads off somewhere and then pretending to be furious about it when Roy was around. That would have been a very Joe thing to do, he did love a laugh. In fact, he's one of the very few 'gangsters' who are usually smiling or laughing in photos. For Joey Pyle, life was for living and boy did he live it!

Alex Steen was one of those rare men who got on with everyone. He was close to the Krays and Richardsons the same as Joe, and that was extremely rare. I'm pretty sure that Alex had no enemies, he was a lovely man and Joe never got over his death. One night, we were having one of Joe's amazing barbeques in his back garden. There was a band playing and plenty of laughter, it was about 2004 or 2005 (that's how good the parties were ... I can't even remember what year it was!).

Everyone was there. Freddie Foreman, Johnny Nash, Jamie Foreman, Bruce Reynolds Charlie Richardson, Big H, Jimmy and Wally Stockin, Dave Courtney, Alan Minter, John H Stracey - to name but a few! I always loved Joe's dos.

Joe was in the early stages of his illness and asked me if I would get his favourite drink for him, Jameson's and coke, because now things were becoming an effort for him. When I returned with the Boss's drink, despite the fact that he was completely surrounded by people, he looked totally alone. He was looking up at the night sky like he was in a trance. I said: "Are you OK Boss?"

"Yeah, Telboy," he replied. "I'm fine. I was just thinking about Alex and hoping when I go I will be with him ... I think about him every day you know. I loved that man."

It was a very sincere and moving moment because, although all of us were doing everything we could to raise money to fight his illness, we all knew it had started to take a hold. Joe has lost many friends over the years but it was Alex he was thinking of.

Back to 1975 and Roy gradually got used to being called 'Pretty Boy' and his only obsession was Donny Adams. He was taking vitamins and a couple of ginseng capsules to boost his energy. Adams too was training like a Spartan.

Venues had been offered on loan from all over Britain but when Billy Smart offered his big top circus tent, all other considerations went out the window. The big fight in the big top and the circus would be packed, it was a complete sell out three times over!

Finally, it was fight night - 1st December 1975, at Billy Smarts big top and unlicensed (Joey Pyle and Alex Steen always preferred the word 'unaffiliated'). Roy and Donny were introduced by former top heavyweight Nosher Powell. An opportunist, who had clearly got his bravery from a bottle, climbed in the ring to try to challenge Shaw and Adams. But it was not 100% clear what he was trying to do and both Shaw and Adams grabbed him and sent him flying over the top rope and back into the packed out audience. Adams was more relaxed than Roy who looked like an atom bomb about to hit Nagasaki!

Minutes away from the bell and Joe faced a major problem, the referee he had booked had not turned up! Without a referee the fight would be illegal and would be stopped before it had even started by the Old Bill. Luckily, Joe saw an old friend making his way to his £30 seat and shouted from the ring, "Ray, get in here. I need you to be the ref!"

Ray was stunned but with some Pyle persuasion got in the ring and saved the fight. So the first ever unlicensed fight nearly never happened. Ray's instructions were pretty simple as he brought the two fighters to the centre of the ring. "No kicking, no biting, otherwise please yourselves."

As the bell rang, Roy was facing away from Adams. As Adams charged, Roy span round and threw a straight right that caught Adams flush on the button. Adams hit the deck and skidded along the canvas. The Bull got up quick but another left, right combination on the jaw and Adam's hit the deck again with a crash. Roy was getting frustrated with the lack of violence so he picked Adams up, and crashed a right onto his jaw. Adams hit the deck again, this times Adams was out and his eyes were closed. Roy picked him up twice more and sent him thundering to the canvas again while proceeding to stamp on Adams head twice.

The ref can be heard screaming: "He's dead Roy, he's dead, Roy, he's dead!"

So Roy hurled the ref out of the way and jumped fully on Adams' unconscious head. Joe Carrington and the rest of Roy's corner jumped in to try and calm the wild man down.

Adams corner man was Tommy 'The Bear' Brown. Tommy was one of the original Kray gang. He had known them since they were kids and always looked out for them. It's commonly agreed that when the twins went over the top with violence and pointless murder, they lost men of the calibre of Tommy and Bobby Ramsey and replaced them with mongrels like Ronnie Hart and that was the beginning of the end for the Kray firm. Tommy remained a very respected man. Tommy 'The Bear' picked up the 'Bull' and sat him on a stool.

Roy was celebrating. It's almost impossible now to understand the full impact this fight made. Now, unless you follow it, you wouldn't know the fighters names or anything about unlicensed boxing. Then though, it was all over the national press. 'The Guv'nor' screamed out one national headline, 'Pretty Boy dumps The Bull' said the back page of another and 'Pretty Boy wins underworld punch up!'

All the papers including broadsheets, magazines and television were full of the fight, it was nothing short of a phenomenon! People now don't realise how well known 'Pretty Boy' Shaw was in the 1970s, he was a genuine star. Unlicensed boxing no longer produces national stars. Although he was truly a real celebrity, Roy stayed among his own, the people he trusted, the 'chaps'.

It was supposed to have been just the one fight, a one off show piece but demand was so high, Joe and Alex had to rethink. There was far too much money to be made to pack up now and Roy was receiving challenges from all over the place, everybody now wanted to get the dream chance of fighting Roy Shaw and being the 'Guv'nor'!

Some thought Roy's fight against Adams was a fluke ... but they were everyday, normal folk and only had those few seconds with the Bull to go on. They didn't know his history in prison and Broadmoor and his reputation for brutal violence. The only people who really knew about Roy were the underworld, he had been a gangland legend for years, long before he became a bare knuckle and unlicensed legend. The 'chaps' knew exactly what Roy was and God help all the Friday night gangsters who got in his way thinking Adams was a one off. He could have easily killed Donny and men in the know like Joe and Alex and Tommy 'the Bear' knew it. Tommy already knew that Roy had smashed up a member of the Kray gang and got away with it.

For 'Pretty Boy', 1975 was some year. He had started it penniless and in prison and ended it as a celebrity. All the newspapers wanted a piece of him, he had plenty of money, started building his dream home and was known as 'the Guv'nor', and he had no problems attracting women either.

Yep, it was a hell of a year alright and credit must also go to Joey Pyle snr, Alex Steen, Sulky of the Astor club and, indeed, Ronnie Smith whose idea it was for Roy to fight for money in the first place. Even though he had boxed as a pro under Mickey Duff (Changing his surname to West on occasions) and had ten fights and won them all, six by knockout, it was nowhere near the money unlicensed could bring in.

In a 1981 article in *Time Out* magazine, that even had Roy on the cover with the main story titled 'The last prize fighter' Mickey Duff even said: "Roy Shaw was a bloody good prospect, he was colourful, he had a spectacular style and could punch. He looked like a young Rocky Graziano, and I had great hopes for him. He was the most exciting thing that had happened to me at that time." So much for those who claim that Mickey Duff knew nothing about Roy Shaw! I would say that puts the lid on that one wouldn't you? Many people have asked why Roy's pro record can't be found. I would say that the British Boxing Board of Control (who basically monopolise boxing in Britain with an iron fist) wiped it from their records because make no mistake, unlicensed really pissed them off!

So why is Cliff Fields record available? Because Roy was the first, he was the ringleader of the gang, it was all his fault because by now unlicensed was getting as much attention as the BBC's 'My lords, ladies and gentlemen' version. They are a very old fashioned and very powerful force and are very easily upset if that power is threatened which it was, and still is, but more so then. In those days, a British title fight gained more attention than a world title fight does today. So why does Mickey Duff deny it?

In the book *Bare Fist*, it claims that Roy only had one pro fight? Even if that was the case, he should still have a record.

Let's also remember who was in charge of the British Boxing Board through these and many more years. A man named Leonard 'Nipper' Read. Might it be the small fact that, while inside, Roy had become good friends of the Kray twins!

If you were a bigwig at the BBC, would you have Roy Shaw on your record sheet? The man who is overshadowing us with this unlicensed nonsense used to hold one of our official licenses. A man who was also a big time robber, and Britain's most violent man, who was sent to Broadmoor, faced a murder charge, smashed up every screw he could lay his fists on including Governors and has only recently been released ... would you put him on your records ... of course you wouldn't!

Cliffy Fields and Johnny Waldron, two ex pros who turned to unlicensed were not violent villains! I think the answer lies in there, don't you? You have to remember what a very real threat unlicensed was to the Board of Control in the 1970s, it was threatening to become more popular. Mickey Duff by the way, is not a popular man in many circles for certain reasons.

So how did you get a fight with the Guv'nor? Well, if you could put the money in the pot that the promoter was asking or if you could assure ticket sales you would usually get your fight. These days we do it differently. In my shows, you could only fight if you could sell the amount of tickets I gave you. Basically, you could be a great unlicensed fighter but if you had no mates to sell the tickets to you were no use. Some of those who fought on mine, and others, unlicensed shows were pretty awful fighters but they had 200 mates who would follow them anywhere. So it wasn't about being good, if you had lots of mates who would buy tickets to see you, you could definitely be an unlicensed fighter. Trust me!

It was all about ticket sales. I had one guy who could of been pro, he was that good. The problem was, he was a 'Billy no mates' so he didn't get to fight. On the same show, I had a guy who would swing for the heavy bag and miss but he had loads of friends and always sold tons of tickets ... he got to fight!

The fighters were paid a percentage of the tickets they sold. And because there was no ranking system (something I wanted to bring in) it didn't matter if you got knocked out, you could still fight again next month. In the '70s it was slightly different. The champion's camp might put three grand in the pot and the challenger's camp would then have to match it and also put in three grand. Then, in a lot of the fights (i.e. the first Shaw v McLean fight) the winner would take all six grand, the loser would get nothing except a battering.

These days we rely more on the ticket sale method, a good idea in theory but it's a learning curve for promoters to pick out the reliable fighters from the blaggers i.e. the ones who swear they can sell 100 tickets and come the night of the fight, they give you a couple of quid and 95 unsold tickets back ... that's when the promoters turn into violent beasts!

Luckily, I had good people around me for my shows and always took their advice, hence avoiding a lot of common learning mistakes. Men like Joey Pyle snr, Alan Mortlock, Joey Pyle jnr, Steve Holdsworth and Dave Courtney were all an incredible help and I would like to thank every one of them sincerely. You can buy the Warriors shows from my pal Liam at gangstervideos.co.uk as well as loads of other good stuff. The Warriors shows had lasers, big screens and even pyrotechnics. These were all straight from the imagination of Dave Courtney who's flare for show bizz is second to none ... cheers Dave!

I put on my Warriors' shows with a guy named Steve Hough, who I used to train along with Andy 'pit bull' Hunter, who became a regular attraction on the fight bills. Andy started very overweight and diabetic. I trained him like a Spartan, he lost a hell of a lot of flab, became extremely fit, the diabetes went and he became one of the most exciting and hard hitting fighters on the unlicensed circuit. It was incredible how Andy changed from what he was to what he became, he built up his own fan club of people he didn't know who used to lap up the tickets to see the 'pit bull' in action. I sparred with him often and he was one of those awkward creations called south paws. But I also taught him how to switch to orthodox because I knew his opponents would be training for a south paw. He was also one of those guys who was impossible to dislike, he wasn't a pit bull at all, everyone loved Andy.

One thing that surprised me was how entertaining a fight between two bad fighters could be. A fight between two guys who couldn't really fight, where with every single punch they tried to take the other guy's head off could be fantastic to watch, often better than seeing two technical pro boxers who just cancel each other out for twelve rounds in what are called 'stinkers'. You would often get two doormen who had a grudge or even better, a doorman and a tasty bastard the doorman had thrown out. The grudge matches were great. I always wanted to get one of the 'chaps' in against a copper ha! Can you imagine?

I never did get that one off the ground.

8
PRETTY BOY ON THE RAMPAGE!

After the total destruction of Donny Adams, Roy accepted a challenge from an Irishman called 'Mad Dog' Mullins. Mullins was billed as a top tinker fighter who was feared throughout the Emerald Isle. In fact, on the night, nobody seemed scared accept Mullins. For once, Roy was fighting a smaller opponent, a rare thing indeed. When Roy entered the ring Mullins was in Shaw's corner. Roy shoved Mullins out of the way sending him sprawling into his own corner. Nosher Powell, as always, introduced the fighters and they were off. Straight away, 'Mad Dog' took some awesome thuds straight in his ribs and doubled over, sliding along the ropes. He was then so desperate and so short of ideas, he grabbed Roy's legs in a rugby tackle and both men hit the deck. This annoyed Roy and he pummelled Mullins into submission. It was all over and Mullins had only moved about three yards in the fight. Another win for the Guv'nor. After the fight, Mullins went into Roy's dressing room and told him: "Be Jaysus Roy, I must be the first Irishman to be knocked over the moon!"

Next was a man Roy hated, his name was Mickey Gluckstead. In the book *Pretty Boy* Roy calls him 'a mongrel'. Roy told me he was a well known bully and deeply unpopular. Nicky Gerard (son of Alfie, Freddie Foreman's closest ally) had opened Gluckstead's face cutting him from ear to nose, shot him twice and kicked him about the head. Gerard was cleared of attempted murder but still received seven years. At one point, John Knight's name (Ronnie's brother) was related to the attack but he was quickly acquitted. Gerard and Ronnie Knight had also been acquitted for the killing of 'Italian' Tony Zomparelli who Ronnie believed had killed his young brother David. Zomparelli was shot dead while playing pinball in the Golden Goose arcade in Soho. Ronnie stood accused of paying Gerard for the revenge attack. It's a miracle Gluckstead survived.

He was also sent down for a crime I refuse to repeat in this book, because if everything I have heard about it is true, it's one of the worst things I have ever heard and I am doing Mickey Gluckstead a favour by not repeating it here. But at the time they fought, Roy hated him because he was a 'a big mouth, liberty taking bully'.

Gluckstead was stopped in three rounds. But as became the habit with almost all Roy Shaw's opponents, Gluckstead claims he actually won, Roy was out on his feet. There are about five opponents who have written exactly the same thing. Terry Hollingsworth was next. A tall, former ABA champion with a long reach. Again, Roy attacked the body to bring his height down and then unloaded on the chin. It was goodnight again in one round.

Next was a guy neither Joey Pyle or Alex Steene had ever heard of but he matched the stake money and agreed to fight on a winner take all basis. He was unheard of but he was also massive ... his name was Lenny McLean. Roy had heard of the name before because he had phone calls from club owners he was protecting saying McLean was causing trouble or wouldn't leave at closing time. The phone calls were becoming more and more frequent and Roy was getting the hump. He turned up at one of the clubs looking for Lenny but he wasn't there. McLean had also seen a poster advertising Shaw v Adams and had said: "I could do both of them at the same time."

After starting on the barman, who was a pal of Roys, the word was out. Roy Shaw was looking for Lenny McLean and McLean wanted a fight with Shaw. In the underworld, things like that don't stay secret for long. With the help of Ronnie Nash, one of the much respected Nash family, the word got to Roy that Lenny wanted to challenge him.

The size, aggression and aura of Lenny McLean had put the fear of God into many a landlord or club owner and his name and reputation were getting bigger all the time in London, especially his manor of Hoxton in the East End. Strangely enough considering their differences, Roy and Lenny had a few things in common. Both had lost their beloved fathers at a young age and, although Roy wasn't abused by a step father like Lenny was, they both carried that pain and Roy still does. They both adored their loving mothers and both found their gift in their fists.

The honest truth is, Roy never liked Lenny McLean. It was nothing to do with the fights, it began when Lenny started taking liberties in clubs and pubs Roy was looking after. Roy also knew Lenny had a terrible reputation as a brutal bully and that's what really caused the problem. Roy despised bullies and loved punishing them, he would always fight for the underdog. Lenny McLean and Mickey Gluckstead are the only two fighters Roy actually disliked to the point of hatred, long before fighting either of them. But Lenny matched Joey Pyle and Alex Steen's stake with Lenny's cousin Frank Warren taking care of the business side of things.

At the time, I had been flooded by stories of Lenny being a bully and, contrary to what some have written, these were not all from people who had a grudge against Lenny, some thought he was OK. Lenny had even got pissed and assaulted one of his greatest friends. Jimmy Briggs bumped into Lenny in the East End and as Jimmy was down on his luck, Lenny insisted he went out for a drink with him to cheer him up. Both men ended up pissed and got into a row over a woman Jimmy had just met. The two men started arguing, Jimmy was no match for Lenny especially pissed, but McLean lost his temper and went to work on his old 'friend'. He ended up in St Mary's hospital. His jaw was broken in five places, his nose and a few ribs were broken and his skull was fractured!

Jimmy actually died on the trolley, that's how much damage was done, luckily for all, the doctors brought him round ... just. So much for the cheer up drink! I was told rightly or wrongly, I don't know, that Lenny was boasting about the assault and said to one 'face', I shall call Pat, that Lenny had said: "What a cunt, I nearly had my button their Pat!" (Button is a word used by the Mafia for killing someone!) I don't think it includes killing your mate in a pissed up brawl though. It may have been a misjudged joke by Lenny but it added weight to the notion that he was a bit of a sadist.

The fight would take place at Cinatra's club in Croydon on Monday 23rd May1977. The undercard included regulars at the world famous Thomas a Becket gym like Steve (Columbo) Richards, Patsy Gutteridge and Danny Chippendale all well known on the unlicensed circuit. Columbo had actually trained and helped Lenny prepare for this fight. Ringside seats were £12.50, a lot of money in 1977, but every ticket went.

Lenny McLean claims in his book that he wasn't expecting to wear gloves (impossible as he had been to see Roy and others fight already, he knew exactly what was involved in unlicensed, he also knew bare knuckle was illegal!).

He also claims that Joey Pyle gave him gloves that kept springing open every time he made a fist. So why weren't Ron Stander, Donny Adams or any of the others given dodgy gloves? There was more at stake with the Adams fight because it was supposed to be a one off, a very big money one off! So why didn't Adams get dodgy gloves?

Ron Stander was a full blooded heavyweight world title contender who fought Joe Frazier for the heavyweight championship of the world. A man that could have done Roy (a natural middleweight) some serious damage. Why wasn't he given dodgy gloves? Why didn't ANY of Roy Shaw's other opponents complain that their gloves were doctored? No, it had to be Lenny didn't it. Why didn't his corner say 'hang on, you have given us gloves that spring open!' Wouldn't you if you were a trainer or fighter for that matter?

The truth is this. When Joey Pyle gave him his gloves (which he knew he had to wear), they were too small and a bit tight but they were the same size as Roy's. To appease Lenny, Joe did something that a promoter would never usually do. He let Lenny's corner man go to their locker and get a pair of their own (which again proves he knew he had to wear gloves otherwise he wouldn't have carried a spare pair would he?).

So, Lenny McLean actually wore his own gloves in his first fight with Roy Shaw NOT Joey Pyle's. And trust me, there's easier ways of swinging a fight in your favour than designing some spring adjusted popping open contraption in a leather glove!

Joe had nothing to gain by lying about the gloves, it was twenty years before I spoke to him about it. Trust me, if I had a money making fighter who was facing someone so good that we had to doctor his gloves to stop my bloke losing badly, we would just fight someone else ... simple isn't it?

The 'doctored glove system' was only invented years later for Lenny's book and instead of trying to come up with another five stitch ups for his other five losses he just left the opponents out of the book completely. And when you look at the many websites saying what a great man Lenny was, none of those who have posted messages even knew him. In fact most of them didn't even know he existed until the book came out, then they were unlicensed and Lenny experts! The Guv'nor was never beaten even in 30,000 bare knuckle fights, or by the Mafia or IRA! Give me strength! Does that clear things up a bit? or are we still going for the dodgy glove story? I bet there's loads that will ... bless 'em!

Nosher introduced the fighters and as soon as the bell went, the two men flew at each other. Lenny started to showboat for the crowd but was caught by a crippling body punch that sent McLean reeling backwards into the ropes. Roy paced after him, with his head on McLean's chest, hammering at his body. Lenny lifted his head and shouted to the crowd "look, he can't hurt me."

So Roy threw a thundering hook to the jaw and McLean stopped talking. Roy knew things Lenny didn't (yet). For example, he knew how to cut the ring off and keep Lenny pinned in the corner.

Second round, and Roy forced Lenny back into the corner where he was pinned to the ropes, taking brutal body shots that knocked the wind out of him. Lenny's back was covered in rope burns but he was not throwing anything back. By now both men were knackered.

Round three, McLean's legs were rubbery and Roy was breathing hard but again he bulldozed Lenny to the ropes, opened up on the body, then switched to the head. A huge straight right from Roy and Lenny struggled to get the sentence out: "Tell him to stop it Roy, I'm done."

Roy motioned the ref over and landed another left hook and McLean was half leaning sideways into the ropes, the place he had spent 99% of the fight. One more right smashed into McLean's face and the ref jumped in and raised Roy's hand.

He was still unbeaten and seemingly unbeatable. Let's not forget some very important facts. Lenny McLean was a foot taller, four or five stone heavier and 13 years younger than Roy Shaw who was a natural middleweight. Think about the disadvantages Roy had to overcome just to be on equal terms let alone win!

In a pro fight of course, it wouldn't be allowed to happen, it would be like Nigel Benn v Lennox Lewis. And imagine the shock if Benn stopped Lewis in three rounds! The two shouldn't have been in the same ring let alone Roy Shaw winning. It's true that Lenny won the next two fights but isn't it amazing that Shaw overcame all those disadvantages to win at all? And most of his fights were like that, I think Mullins and Adams were the only fighters who were not 18 - 22 stone who Roy beat!

Some people may consider Lenny McLean the best there ever was, fair enough. If that's the case though how much respect does Roy Shaw deserve for beating him even once against those odds? Think about it. It was real David v Goliath stuff and I don't think people really appreciate the achievement that beating and even stopping a man of that size is. By the same token, a lot of respect must go to McLean. Lenny McLean got in the ring with a man who had done some real damage to big men all his life, a man who was considered by some to be a blood thirsty lunatic who simply loved violence. Of course that perception of Roy was wrong but that was the reputation he had built for himself. How many men do you know who would want to fight the hardest man in London, money or no money? I bet there's not many!

Lenny McLean did and he went in to win, it was winner takes all, so there was no point holding on for dear life, not throwing a punch trying to get the money and bugger off ... doing a Henry Akinwande special!

No McLean went in to win and deserves respect for that. I think he would have retained more respect if he had just held his hands up and admitted defeat, rather than blaming a pair of James Bond style gloves, but he deserves respect all the same.

By this time, Roy Shaw was seriously considering retirement. His mind was turning more and more towards the good life he would enjoy without the hassle of fighting. Little did he know that all through his life some chancer in some club or pub would take a pop at him, usually when he'd had a heavy night drinking with the lads and could barely walk. Most blokes do it all the time and don't expect someone to challenge them when they have had a skin full and just want a cab home.

To this day, Roy Shaw gets these idiots trying to make a name for themselves and part of him is always on guard or his friends are watching out for him. I have clocked loads of these 'Billy the Kids' while sitting with Roy and the 'chaps', I think every one of us has. And we try and keep the trouble away from the 'chaps' because some scum bags, believe it or not, try and wind them up just so they can call Old Bill and have them nicked! Can you believe it?

These sick freaks get a kick out of getting a 'face' nicked ... and it's not just a few, it happens all the time, unreal. One thing you will have noticed about Roy Shaw and indeed all the 'faces' is if you treat them with respect you WILL get it back, that's for certain. But if you take a liberty with someone who is 'connected' you cannot win ... simple!

Why? Because you may win that night. Maybe they are just not in the mood for the stupidity on that occasion and you may even win a little battle if they are alone, BUT there are so many dangerous men in the chain and these men won't accept one of their pals having liberties taken with them, they WILL find who did it!

You may think I'm talking shit gangster talk but my advice is free, they are not called 'connected' for nothing. I know men with over 400 dangerous phone numbers, that's some going. So when you take that liberty when a man just wants a night out and has done nothing to you, unless you kill the underworld you will NOT win, even if you have a little firm of your own, that's just more people hurt. I say this because I see it happen so many times.

Why not show some respect and get some back? I know men who can't fight for toffee BUT if you take a liberty, they WILL find you, torture you and make you vanish. And it may be three years down the line when you have no idea why this is happening to you. That's why they are who they are, if you make them look stupid one night, they will NOT and I mean WILL NOT forget it! It will be the only thing on their minds for perhaps years! Would you drunkenly convince yourself you could beat Tiger Woods at golf and challenge him?

Come to think of it, there's bound to be someone out there!

9
UNLICENSED PEAKS!

By now, unlicensed was massive and more and more fighters were joining the scene. Fighters like Steve 'Columbo' Richards, Patsy Gutteridge, Danny Chippendale, Ron Redrupp, Paul Sykes, Micky May, Tommy Adams, Johnny Waldron, Harry Starbuck (who was backed by Eddie Richardson) and Danny Woods were all now unlicensed fighters. Most of them were on the undercard for the big boys Shaw, McLean and Cliff Field, an ex pro who was beating everyone in sight. A few years down the line, names like Dave Courtney and Charles Bronson would join the unlicensed gang. It was big business and everyone wanted in.

The great thing about unlicensed boxing is that lads can train and stay disciplined and make some good money. If you can sell tickets, you're laughing. Not everyone is good enough to turn pro, so it provides an opportunity for lads whose only other option is probably crime then the nick to make some money. If you have a decent promoter, you can fight on every show and that's good money. I can't begin to even guess the amount of men unlicensed has kept out of the nick. If unlicensed is banned where are these lads going to make their money? It's easy to work out.

By the late 1970s, unlicensed was a huge movement! Roy Shaw had said in many interviews that he would retire for definite after his next fight. And according to Roy, his next fight would be the toughest of his life. Ron 'The Butcher' Stander was an American pro heavyweight contender who had fought 'Smokin' Joe Frazier for the heavyweight championship of the world and had knocked out Ernie Shavers in five rounds. Ernie Shavers is still the hardest punching boxer of all time and had such greats as Larry Holmes on the deck, Ernie also went fifteen rounds with Ali. Stander had untouchable pedigree for an unlicensed fighter, he was also a very big lump with a solid chin. A lot of people warned Roy that he may be going a bit out of his league. "Bollocks" said the 'Guv'nor'.

The truth is, Stander didn't train or take the fight seriously. He assumed he would walk through the Brit with no bother. While he was in the gym, Stander started to mess about kicking the heavy bag, he slipped and cracked his ribs on the ring post but kept it silent. Nosher Powell, as ever, gave his famous 'bring on the lions' introduction and the fighters were on their way. The cracked ribs were kept secret and there were a lot of worried Roy Shaw friends and fans in the audience that night. Roy was determined to look good in his last fight and had trained like mad. This was no 'Mad Dog' Mullins in the ring tonight!

When the bell went, instead of flying at Stander, Roy used his jab and held his guard high showing Stander respect. When he had created the openings, he moved in and opened up. Ron Stander must be the only unlicensed fighter to take a full, clean Roy Shaw shot and not move. There is nothing more disheartening than connecting with your very best and sweetest punch and the bloke just looks at you as if to say 'is that it'?

Roy kept punching and kept connecting but nothing! Through his gum shield, Stander spat with contempt at Roy: "That's it boy, keep it up!" Every punch that landed: "Come on boy, let's see what you got! Is that it boy?"

The bell went and Roy returned to his corner totally baffled, a brick wall would have fallen under the barrage he put Stander under. Back in the corner, Joe Carrington said: "You're doing well Roy."

"Well!" Roy replied, "I'm landing my best punches and he's laughing!"

Joe's answer was, "try the body Roy".

Roy carried on with head shots and, at the end of the round, switched and threw some solid shots to the body, Stander groaned. At last, a breakthrough!

Round two was better than round one and Roy's confidence was boosted, he had found the weak spot. Round three and Roy threw some head shots to get Stander's hands up and then backed him up against the ropes. Then Roy got stuck into the ribs and Stander started slowly sagging, more hooks to the body and like a giant oak

Stander slowly hit the canvas.

Stander did not make the count. Eventually, Ron Stander got to his feet holding his ribs. Roy's honesty is refreshing, he says: "If he hadn't have done his ribs, he would of mullered me!"

Whether that would of been the case or not, we will never know. In the ring the usual challenges started and in jumped Lenny McLean, and an ever bigger looking McLean than from their first fight. Lenny was mad with desperation to get a return match but Roy had set his mind on retiring.

The challenges from Lenny kept coming. Finally, Roy agreed and the Shaw v McLean rollercoaster was back on track. Roy had nothing to prove anymore, he had beaten every man put in front of him, usually much bigger than him, and had even stopped a true heavyweight who was good enough to fight for the world title, even with the rib injury it was some feat. He had easily beaten Lenny McLean in three rounds who had consistently taken between 10 and 20 unanswered punches and whose back was covered in burns where he couldn't get off the ropes. Why fight again? The answer was money!

Roy had a desire to build his dream home and the 14 grand he would get for defending his unofficial British championship would help greatly, but not as much as his next tactic. To the general public, Roy Shaw has only told the TRUE story about Shaw v McLean II twice and that was to author Jon Hotten in 1998 and on the Gary Bushell show, although it was common knowledge in the fight game. In any big business whether it be music, film, TV or sport there is what the public know and what you want the public to know and then there is what the people within that business know. I was involved with unlicensed long before I put on my own shows, even before I trained unlicensed fighters. It is a small but tight circle and that's were the truth and the things we don't want the public to know about lives.

Actually, here's a strange one. Most of Lenny McLean's wins can be found somewhere on video rather easily but not one of his six losses. Roy has been looking desperately for a tape of his first fight with Lenny and is offering good money to anyone who finds it (if anyone does have it, please write and leave your details with Apex publishing). I thought it was just Roy's win you couldn't get until we spoke to Cliffy Field and Johnny Waldron and realised that they don't have a copy of their victories over McLean either, neither did Kevin Paddock!

Did the Lenny McLean camp simply destroy all evidence of his losses? I tried everyone from the gypsies to the underworld. Nothing!

In his books and interviews, Lenny always claimed that he was never beaten on the street or in the ring, so the everyday Joe who was not connected thought he really was unbeaten and unbeatable.

So here's the true story of the last two fights in the Roy Shaw v Lenny McLean saga. The rematch was set for 10th April, 1978 again at Cinatra's Club in Croyden. Now, Lenny was a huge underdog. Roy had not even looked like losing since he started, he was unbeaten and many thought him unbeatable. He had even beaten a heavyweight contender who had actually wobbled the great Joe Frazier. So who the hell is going to put money on Lenny McLean, who would be that stupid?

Well, a bloke called Roy 'Pretty Boy' Shaw put most of his growing fortune on Lenny McLean ... and it wasn't stupid, think of the odds!

If Roy had known that in 20 odd years, people like McLean would be making up 'biographies' and it would become a craze that everyone wanted to know about, he probably wouldn't of done it. But then, it was big but still very much an underworld sport and you don't think 20 years ahead when you are getting 24 grand for falling over! And how much would that 24 grand be worth now?

As for Lenny, he knew he had underestimated Roy and he was to repeat the mistake with other fighters in the near future. But he was persuaded to train like a boxer not a street fighter because street fights last two to ten minutes max, so he trained with the respected British middleweight Kevin Finnegan, whose brother Chris had those legendary fights in a packed Albert Hall with 'King of the Gypsies' Johnny Frankham, and clocked up the miles round Victoria Park. Roy's plan required minimum training as you may have guessed by now. Cinatra's was packed out with fans and underworld 'faces' ready to watch Lenny get another hiding but Roy knew, on this occasion, they would all get a shock.

As the bell rung, Lenny showed what he had learned from his time with Finnegan by taking the centre of the ring and using his jab. He knew laying on the ropes against Roy Shaw was no place to be and Lenny looked a lot bigger than he had a year ago. Roy was not powering forward in his usual style just winging big hooks from way out of range. Suddenly, Roy took a right hook followed by a three or four punch combination. Shaw fell back against the ropes, another Lenny combination and Roy hit the deck. Lenny McLean was actually boxing, he was not street fighting, but boxing. The sessions with Kevin Finnegan had paid off. That is until McLean fell to his knees and hit Roy in the face while on the floor and attempted to stamp on his face. Then the corner men were in, for a moment it looked like the fight was going to switch to Lenny v Joe Carrington!

Carrington wasn't scared of anyone and was screaming abuse at Lenny. The officials had to jump in to stop another fight breaking out. When the ring cleared they went at it again. Roy, of course, was torn between fighter's pride and the money but it was too late to change plans now, he was just waiting for a convincing time to go over. He had a reputation as a man who could take anything, so he couldn't just fall over with a jab. Somehow, Roy ended up facing the corner post and Lenny smacked him in the back of the head a few times. In the first fight, Lenny had desperately said to Shaw: "I'm done Roy, tell them to stop it!"

At that point, Roy had waved his glove at the ref to stop the fight. There was an enormous amount of anger in the crowd that McLean was not showing Roy the same respect that Roy had shown him and McLean jumped on every chance. Roy was punched three times in the back of the head and he went over again but didn't think the punches were hard enough to be convincing so he got back up.

McLean was also holding Shaw's head down every time he hooked him but he still couldn't put him away. When you consider again that McLean was probably six stone heavier, nearly a foot taller and 13 years younger plus he hadn't been involved in all the prison wars that Roy had, McLean really should have finished the fight sooner. Considering he had hit Roy every time he hit the floor, on the back of the head and tried stamping on his face, Lenny really should have had the fight wrapped up. As Roy's head was being held down once again, the ref ended the round.

Round two, and Roy threw a medium powered jab that actually shook Lenny but, remembering what he was in there for, Roy backed off. At last a big combination by Lenny and Roy went through the second and third rope onto the timekeeper's table. Roy was counted out and went back to his corner. The Guv'nor was 'beaten' ... But very, very rich. Lenny celebrated that night but so did Roy. He got showered, put on a suit and he, Joey Pyle, Alex Steen and a few of the 'chaps' went for a champagne piss up in the West End!

I have heard countless people ask Roy, "What was your hardest fight? Who punched you the hardest?" His answer to both questions is Ron Stander. "What about Lenny McLean," they ask.

"McLean was not a big puncher, I was getting bored waiting for him to knock me out but he simply didn't punch hard enough. Being big doesn't give you that natural power of punch; only God does, you're born with it and it's not something you can learn."

10
CLOSE ENCOUNTERS!

After the Roy Shaw fight, Lenny McLean took an easy fight against a bloke called Soli Francis at the Rainbow theatre and knocked him straight out. He wanted to show everyone he was the best. After the fight, Lenny accepted a challenge from ex pro Cliff Field. It turned out to be a big mistake but first the third and final fight with Roy Shaw was set up for 11th September 1978 at the Rainbow in Finsbury Park. Both fighters trained 100% this time. Roy had made his money in fight two and now it was time to regain the crown he gave away for 24 grand. It was a perfect plan. Roy wins the first fight easily, makes himself rich in fight two and wins the title back in fight three. But like all good plans, they often turn to crap!

This fight was the biggest in unlicensed history and was billed as 'Close encounter for a third time'. Both men were confident. Roy knew he had beaten Lenny before and why he 'lost' the second fight. Lenny, of course, thought he had battered Roy in fight two. It was a strange set up. All the usual suspects like Micky May and Columbo were on the undercard. This one would be the real decider.

Roy had always taken vitamins and ginseng capsules while in training and ginseng also before a fight. Ginseng is a natural Chinese or Korean root that can be used as an energy boost. As usual Roy stopped at a herbalists on the way to the fight and ask for ginseng but the guy brought out a bottle of liquid with a ginseng root in it. "What the hell's that?" asked Roy. The shop owner said it was liquid ginseng and it was more potent than capsules. "But I want capsules, I always have capsules you know that," said Roy.

"Sorry Roy, we are right out of capsules but it's the same stuff." One guy who was with the Shaw camp said the shop owner started to sweat and tremble, he knew only too well who Shaw was. Roy was agitated, and getting angry. He had psyched himself up for the fight and didn't need this.

"Right, give me the bleedin' bottle."

Back in the car, Roy didn't bother with the instructions and wolfed down half the bottle! You are supposed to take a small cap full. After half an hour Roy was expecting to explode with aggression, instead he nearly passed out in the car on the way to the Rainbow. Roy was extremely hyperactive before fights and this was not him, he was nodding off in the car!

Everyone knew he had only taken ginseng but this liquid stuff did not agree with him. Ten minutes before the fight and the effects had still not worn off. It is actually on video. Most tapes show Roy flying around like a lunatic, the tape of the third fight shows him sitting alone on a chair, staring vacantly, not moving and covered in sweat. Now for the first time in his unlicensed career Roy had to enter the ring first. Roy had a knee injury which was heavily bandaged. The referee for this fight was none other than Cliff Fields who would be fighting the winner.

Roy's music blared out and more ploddingly than usual he made his way to the ring. A huge cheer went up when Roy entered the ring. Then, Lenny's music 'Daddy Cool' started up and Lenny came running into the ring, giving a little display for the crowd. Roy knew that he was in no state to box and that something was very wrong. So he threw haymakers to try and get the fight over fast!

Lenny too was not going for points and haymakers started flying from both men. Lenny resorted to the trick he used in fight two, holding Roy's head down and belting him. Cliff said nothing. Lenny pulled Roy towards him by the neck so Shaw could get no leverage behind his punches. In a pro ring, Lenny would have been thrown out for these tactics but this was unlicensed and Roy has done his fair share of 'naughties' in the past. Roy was throwing punches that were completely missing McLean, it was like Roy was seeing double.

Joey Pyle snr who was sitting ringside with pals like Johnny Nash had realised something was very wrong and can't hide the fact that he is worried. Roy was getting a beating and was blinking like his vision was affected. Most men would have hit the deck by now but not Roy Shaw, he threw haymakers back that totally missed and tried to charge Lenny into the corner. Roy was fighting on instinct and holding on to Lenny to try and clear his head. Then Lenny lined Roy up with a jab and opened up, with great speed for a big man, with the hardest punch he could throw. Roy's head snapped back and he was hit full on by (about 20 stone of McLean knuckle!). Roy slowly got closer to the canvas with each punch until a one two and a thud was heard around the arena as Roy hit the deck.

The crowd were going nuts because it's the end of the fight ... but no ... Shaw had got back up and indicated to Fields that he wanted more. Not even McLean's camp could believe it and short applause echoed round the ring at Shaw's sheer guts. Roy's legs had been like jelly from the start and now he really was wobbling. Roy nodded at Cliff and on they went but no other fighter (especially considering the weight, height, reach and age difference) would have fought on. These two men were certainly hard bastards and we had our very own Ali v Frazier type trilogy ... maybe with less double jabs and shuffles!

Roy caught a few big hooks again but was still there. Lenny then gambled on a final onslaught, he knew that even a robot couldn't take that for much longer (if Lenny had not cut down on the smoking and let himself be convinced into hard cardio work, I really don't know if he would have had that final rally in him). Fact is, he did ... left right, left right, left right, left right snapping Roy's head back. Roy had become target practice, not knowing where he was; one two, left right, left right. Roy's head spun and snapped. The fight should have been stopped but Cliff seemed as stunned as everyone else. Finally, after over 20 unanswered head punches 'THUMP!' Roy hit the deck for the last time. It was an amazing show by both men. Lenny jumped on the ropes and shouted to the crowd "Who's the Guv'nor?"

There was no going out on the piss that night for Roy like in fight two when he won all that money. The crowd were clapping both men, nobody had seen a round like it. The best pro round in my opinion was the first round of Marvin Hagler v Tommy Hearns in 1985, but even that couldn't touch this. Nobody who knew the state Roy was in before the fight could believe he would produce that. OK, it was one round and he lost, but talk about losing with pride.

It's important to remember, that these were NOT equally matched fighters. Roy Shaw is only 5ft 8½ inches tall. His arms are very short, which means he had to go into the danger zone and into range every time he wanted to throw a punch!

Lenny McLean had listened to what his advisors had told him. You can be the best boxer in the world, carry the hardest punch and have the best chin but if your heart and lungs are only trained for one minute's work, it's goodnight, a lesson he learned in the first fight. Both men had shown amazing mental strength. Roy showed it on the night and Lenny showed it by the fact that when he lost and lost bad, being knocked spark out, the first thing he wanted was to fight again! There was no 'Well, I shall talk to my camp and my family before I make a decision'. He told the promoters just after he was beaten 'I want him again!'

So that's what happened. Roy is now a wealthy man. Well, now you know how he got hold of the capital to set him up in property, it kick started a second career as a very successful property businessman.

In Roy's classic book *Pretty Boy* by Kate Kray, it mentions only two fights. I can only say that there was a misunderstanding at the publishers and they took the second fight to be the last fight. It wouldn't be Roy trying to insult people's intelligence by trying to convince then it was one win each ha! He just wouldn't do it. Lenny's book came out first and, of course, he talks about all three fights, so people knew.

Both Roy and Lenny had been on countless TV programmes talking about three fights. After the third fight, it's true that Roy desperately wanted Lenny to fight him again. I have on tape from a few years later, Roy on the Gary Bushell TV show challenging Lenny McLean. He said to Lenny: "You reckon you're the Guv'nor? You're not. If you are, fight me and prove it." In the interview with Gary, Roy immaculate as ever in his tailor made blue/grey suit told TV viewers for the first time that the second McLean fight was a dive. Roy said: "I'd already beaten him easily in three rounds, no one was going to put their money on Lenny.

So I put all my purse money on him and just went over."

Gary looked half stunned and half happy. Stunned that Roy was being so open and was obviously telling the truth (either that or a better actor than Brando!) and happy because he had scored such a big coup.

Gary, who is a good man, and a valued friend of all the 'chaps' asked Roy outright "How many fights did you have with Lenny?" Roy replied "Three."

And, as I say, you simply can't beat a man so easily in three rounds then get knocked out in seconds in the two following fights! Points decisions going against you, of course but first round knockouts ... no way!

Gangster Danny Woolard, who witnessed all these fights and was a fighter himself, knew all the fighters of the that era. He wasn't biased towards Roy because he was a very close friend of Mickey Gluckstead, but even he said: "Something was wrong with Shaw in both those fights. You simply cannot knockout Roy Shaw with one punch. It just can't be done, it's impossible! In the third fight, Lenny McLean may have won but the real Roy Shaw was not there at all. Lenny only beat a shadow of the real man, Roy was fighting like he was in a dream!"

Danny Woolard, who was a genuine friend of Reg Kray when they were in Wayland together and is mentioned in Reg's book *Way of Life*, rated Roy as one of the hardest men he has ever seen. And Woolard also says the only time Roy came unstuck was when he was paralytic and could hardly walk.

He also claims that Gluckstead knocked out Lenny McLean in a street fight. I don't know if that's true or not. It's also claimed that Mickey Gluckstead had a bare knuckle fight with Donny 'The Bull' Adams and Adams was knocked spark out in about ten minutes, it would have been in the '60s because the man seeing fair play was none other than Ronnie Kray with Reggie looking on as well. Either Donny Adams was hit with some lethal punches, he had a glass jaw or both!

Danny Woolard knocked out a bloke called Frankie Salmon. I remember when he got nicked, it was a big thing around the late '80s, 1989 I think, because he was running protection rackets and all the headlines said nothing had been seen like it since the days of the Krays and the Richardsons. But he certainly didn't have the cunning of Charlie and Eddie Richardson, he was basically a bully and like all bullies, their time runs out!

Salmon thought he was in the Richardson/Nash/Kray league but he was shot dead in a pub in Plaistow. As I say, bullies run out of time sooner or later.

Fights two and three were back to back and I can only say, there was a bit of confusion at the publishers. I don't know but Roy NEVER said there was two. I even had it on his website when I was running it, that he had three fights. You can't lie about things like that, thousands of people saw them!

Roy is very approachable despite his reputation and if you ask him something straight, he will answer you. My pal Julian Davies or 'Juggy' who used to run the first and best website called *Unlicensed* (it really was the bollocks that site!), used to have a message board on there and it became a standing joke. If anyone asked me a question on there. Juggy would add to it "But how many fights did Roy and Lenny have?"

At first, I didn't know it was him and I had answered it about six times until I lost it and wrote 'It's three, three, three FUCKING three!' Ha! ha! Juggy rung me after laughing and said: "Tel, I really need your help."

He's a good pal so I replied: "What is it mate? Of course I will help."

"Did Roy and Lenny have two or three fights?" he asked. I think he left the phone and had to run to the toilet, he was laughing that much. I do love my Welsh pals like Juggy, Tony Thomas, Bernie Davies and of course Howard Marks, their humour just cripples me every time and to a man they are staunch and loyal.

So the trilogy was over. There never was a fourth fight. But when both men ended up at the same functions, Roy would always go for Lenny McLean and try and get him to fight out the back there and then. Don't forget the system Roy had fought and come through, he really didn't have any fear. This happened four or five times. Johnny Saebini, who was one of Roy's corner men recalls: "We were all in the Royal Tottenham one night and McLean was in there. Roy spotted him and headed for his table and, I promise you, McLean ran straight out of the club! And that was after the three fights! Roy was always trying to get him to fight on the cobbles."

But in 1978, Lenny McLean was king of the unlicensed ring and his young cousin Frank Warren had taken over the business side from Joey and Alex. Roy Shaw didn't want to retire in that way, he was a proud man. Roy had signed a comeback fight with a well know doorman Harry 'The Buck' Starbuck. Harry was managed by Eddie Richardson who had been released from his time for the so called 'Torture Trial' (more about that later!). Roy was now being promoted by Joe Carrington.

And Lenny wouldn't be the Guv'nor for long. In his next fight, against good advice, he took on a full blooded pro called Cliff 'Iron Man' Field ... A new unlicensed star was about to be unleashed!

11
FIELD OF BLOOD!

Cliff Field known as 'The Iron Man' was born on 3rd June 1943. He boxed as a child then joined the navy at 15 years old. While in the Navy he became the Navy boxing champion with little effort. When Cliff left the navy he went back to boxing and eventually turned pro. He fought Richard Dunn who had fought Ali but suffered from the famous British boxers' affliction - cuts!

In Cliff's case, he would cut very badly around the eyes. So much so, that his license was revoked for receiving cuts to the eyebrow area in 1977. So Cliff turned to the unlicensed circuit to make ends meet. His corner man is a great friend of myself, Red Menzies and Chris Lambrianou called Bill Cooper, a true gent who knows his stuff. Cliff, of course, went down a storm on the unlicensed circuit.

Lenny McLean, confident after his third fight with Roy Shaw, accepted Cliff's challenge and the fight was set for 4th December 1978 at the Rainbow Theatre, Finsbury Park. The ref was Danny Fontalio another ex boxer. You had to have someone who could handle themselves to keep these two giants under control. On the night Lenny ran down the aisle to 'Daddy Cool' and Cliff entered to 'Jungle Rock'.

At the bell, Lenny seemed to abandon the boxing he learned from Kevin Finnegan and tried to take Cliff's head off. Cliff just tucked up and left no openings. Cliff looked good, connecting with three to four punch combinations, crisp, clean, one twos with a left hook to follow. Lenny was already wobbling. About a minute from the end of round one, Cliff opened up with big, fast punches and Lenny held on for dear life. Bobby Warren rang the bell. He had shortened the round. It even reads in the report of the fight in the Dunstable papers (where Cliff is from) that 'Round one was made deliberately short', there was no denying that one.

Bill Cooper and the rest of Cliff's camp went mad at the ref while Lenny wobbled back to his corner and slumped on his stool. In fact, it made no difference. Lenny tried storming Cliff again but ran straight into a poleaxe jab, a four punch combination at a lightweight's speed and Lenny McLean was out cold on the canvas. He was out for about ten minutes before coming round, not knowing the fight had finished. At one point, he even raised his hands thinking he had won. Cliff looked as calm as a man who had just finished watching TV and strolled back to the dressing room. Shouting 'who's the Guv'nor?' was not Cliff's style, he wanted to make the pub before closing. Lenny went into Cliff's dressing room after the fight and said "Well done. But I will get you next time."

Cliff just said: "OK."

Another thing had Lenny feeling a bit off colour after the fight with Cliff. Lenny's team had encouraged him to back himself to the tune of 15 grand! Now, he was in the bankruptcy court. Lenny said he 'felt sick after his first defeat' but not half as sick as his bank manager who had put money on Lenny. In an interview, Lenny said: "He came into my changing room after the fight looking like he had swallowed my gum shield. He croaked, Len what happened, what will you do about the money?" Lenny appeared at the London bankruptcy court on the following Monday over debts of £18,530. The bank manager retired!

Cliff Field had hurt Lenny in every possible way. He knocked him clean out physically, mentally and financially. The whole thing was a complete disaster and left Lenny McLean with nothing, even if he still insisted on calling himself the 'Guv'nor'. Cliff had won easily and there was nobody in the unlicensed ranks to come near him. Cliffy was the REAL Guv'nor!

It seems Lenny was telling porkies about his defeats even then, telling the reporter that was his first loss, a habit he would keep up all his life. In fact he worked backwards until he got to zero defeats, only amazing wins! the quote that Lenny 'felt really sick' after his first defeat (this was 1982!) would join a long line of similar quotes during his career including bare knuckle.

Before the fight with Cliff, Lenny had planned to fight for the

Mr New York title in America. One of the previous holders was none other than Mr T from *The A-Team* and *Rocky III* fame. When Mr T won the title, 32 year old Lenny had challenged him to fight in London for 20 grand, winner take all. Mr T declined the challenge, but you obviously never knew with a Lenny story! A film script about Lenny was also being kicked about even then. In 2008, it still had not come off and a massive scam was found to be taking place while getting people money to put money in. A text message scam was also rumoured - who knows?

Lenny then fought Steve 'Columbo' Richards at Finsbury Park. But the pair were good friends and this was to be just an exhibition. Columbo was known for his madcap antics and he and Lenny gave the crowd a great laugh in good spirits. They weren't going for knock outs so it went the distance. The referee, with a grin, raised Columbo's hand in victory and both fighters and the crowd laughed their heads off at the decision, It was a fun night and great for boxing. Of course, it was just an exhibition and wouldn't go on either man's record, everyone enjoyed it though.

Lenny agreed to fight Paul Sykes again at Finsbury Park in November 1979. Two days before the fight, Sykes who was a troublemaker and bully who had sparred with Roy Shaw in Wakefield prison, pulled out. Sykes' Dad was a retired screw in Wakefield and supposedly bullied Sykes as a kid. Sykes said: "If screws ruled the world, we would not have found the bloody Isle of Man yet, screws give their brains in at birth, they are useless and I love winding them up, they are all scared of me."

It's not surprising, Sykes was a psychopath and the young offenders avoided him at all costs. "I want to serve my time with proper people. I have served with all the train robbers, Roy Shaw, the Lambrianous, Eddie Richardson, Fred the head, Frankie Fraser and that's what I want. I don't want to serve my time with drips and cornflakes!"

Sykes got into a fight with some bouncers just before the fight with Lenny and sustained a nasty cut ... the fight was off. A real shame because I think that would have been a classic. As a pro, Sykes had beaten an American called Dave Wilson to an inch of his life and put him in intensive care and on life support, luckily Wilson pulled through. Sykes had fought John L Gardner at

Wembley for the British title but had committed a crime in boxing terms and turned his back on his opponent. Sykes had a terrible reputation in prison, especially with the young offenders. Why a fighter was out on the piss two days before a big fight is a mystery. Sykes wrote a best selling book called *Sweet Agony*. He was a clever man but also a sadist and a lot of prisoners I have spoken too, say a brutal rapist, but I have no opinion on that.

Paul Sykes died a couple of years ago of cirrhosis of the liver. He had been a hard drinker for years. Out of all the fights that never happened, Sykes v McLean and Sykes v Field are the two I would have loved to have seen.

The abandoned McLean v Lew Yates is another 'pick em' fight. We never really saw enough of Lew to make a decision, but if he had caught Lenny flush I don't think Lenny would have got up! I knew men who have worked with Lew Yates and they all say his right hand would bring down a barn door, which just shows the punishment resistance of an in shape Roy Shaw.

Roy was taking a break and McLean was working with Joey Pyle and Alex Steen here and there. Lenny desperately had to claw his finances back after Cliff had made him a bankrupt. A replacement fight was set up with Dave Spellen but he broke his hand and pulled out as well. Lenny was going mad with rage, he had to make a living again!

At the last minute, a former light heavyweight pro called Johnny Waldron stepped in. So starts one of the strangest stories in unlicensed history. In short, the 'chaps' wanted to make a nice few quid and bet all their money on Lenny. Johnny Waldron was paid handsomely to take a dive and was happy enough with that. Waldron looked like a midget next to McLean. The fight was fixed for Lenny to win and lots of money would be won, everyone was happy.

On the bell Lenny went running and growling as ever towards Waldron. Lenny shouted: "Come on son, put it there then" and stuck his chin out. Then it happened. Waldron, with a fighter's instinct threw a medium power right hand, it caught Lenny on the chin. Lenny hit the deck and was out for the count!

The venue was silent. Lenny came round with half of London's underworld looking at him, they had all put heavy money on a

McLean victory. Waldron didn't celebrate just got out of the venue fast! It was surreal, a man who had a fight fixed for him to win had actually been knocked out!

Roy Shaw was the timekeeper and as shocked as anyone. This was not a good time for the self professed Guv'nor. Convinced that the Waldron loss was a fluke, he insisted on an instant rematch and planned a real lesson for the man who made him look stupid. This time Ilford Palais was the venue. This fight, as far as I'm aware, was straight, not hooky like the first one. So what happened? Lenny ran at Waldron straight into a right hander and was knocked spark out! It was exactly the same as the first fight, exactly the same! Again, the crowd was stunned but for different reasons, what were the chances of that happening? Two fights with a middle to light heavyweight fighter and both times knocked out in less than a minute.

Here's what Johnny Waldron had to say: "No disrespect to Lenny but he wasn't the hardest man in the world, he wasn't the best boxer in the world either but he was big. There's a bit of a funny story behind our first fight. Lenny was down for a win before the fight and all of a sudden he start's show boating and messing around. I thought, 'I'm not having any of this', so I've knocked him out in one round. Anyway a straight rematch was organised and I was right up for it and trained like mad and pulled off another win against McLean again, in round one!"

So Lenny McLean was the first boxer ever (in unlicensed anyway) to have a fight fixed in his favour ... and get knocked spark out in a few seconds!

Lenny was really gutted and went straight back to the gym and wanted a return. In the return, a straight one this time he was done in one round again ... unreal!

The job Lenny did on manufacturing his image in his book is pure genius, only the Kray twins come close in rewriting their own history. People who have read *The Guv'nor* are convinced he was unbeaten and unbeatable but it is a fact that he wasn't. Lenny was hard but not unbeatable, don't take it from me, read what his opponents say.

Nosher Powell was a pro, who had 80 fights and lost eight! He was also the MC at all the unlicensed shows and friends with all the fighters and spent a lot of time at the Thomas a' Becket training and watching others train. He was indeed an expert and great pro fighter. Nosher told me he sparred with Lenny and 'left handed him all over the ring!' Nosher also said: "On the cobbles, Roy would come out the winner as he was a very good puncher especially to the body."

The myth Lenny made of himself for a new generation was extremely clever. It's like the romantic image of Dick Turpin and the real Dick Turpin, they couldn't be more different but it's the swashbuckling myth that lives on. It's easier to be economical with the truth when there are no records. Unlike the pro game, bare knuckle has nothing except eyewitnesses. Really, it came down to who got the first book out and it was Lenny. If Roy had been the first, he might have carried the bigger myth, but Roy really only wrote his book to counter the lies in *The Guv'nor* as Roy has never been one for fame and celebrity and is still amazed when he is approached for autographs.

The decider may be whoever gets a film out first especially if it's powerful unlike *The Krays* which I thought did the twins no justice at all. The film *Charlie* I thought was good but brought me within a whisker of being nicked when the serious crime squad popped round. More of that later.

I honestly can't believe that nobody has made a film about 'Pretty Boy'. Carlton, Cass, the twins, Charlie Richardson and now Charlie Bronson have had their films made and the 'chaps' should be proud of them, not jealous, but I can't see why Pretty boy and the whole golden era of unlicensed has not been made into a film. Don't get me wrong, I'm not having a pop at Lenny I think he was an extremely clever man in the way a new generation thinks he was unbeaten, unbeatable and a lovely man. The fact is, Lenny was beaten six times. He was stopped in three rounds by Roy Shaw, knocked out twice in round one by Johnny Waldron, knocked out twice by Cliff Field in rounds two and four and outpointed by Kevin Paddock. That my friends, is the truth. If you still don't believe it, read *Through the Eyes of Others*, by my good pal Anthony Thomas. 'Big Tony' is a big fan of Lenny and runs his official website. Those losses are also recorded in a pro Lenny book! It's also a fantastic read all round about the whole era.

Lenny's next fight was with Kevin Paddock from Portsmouth. Kevin Paddock was probably the best defensive boxer on the circuit and was a very cunning counter puncher who knew his ring craft. In the ring, a good boxer will almost always beat a good slugger and this fight was no different. Lenny took this fight thinking it was an easy way to get back to winning and put his recent form behind him. He underestimated Paddock.

Kevin Paddock took every punch from McLean and most landed on his gloves or elbows. Paddock fought behind an impressive and consistent jab and double jab, Lenny carried on with the haymakers. Missing with big punches really takes it out of you and Lenny punched himself out while running into jabs. That night Lenny was given a master class in ring craft and, by the end, he could barely stand. Kevin Paddock won an easy points victory.

Val McLean, Lenny's widow, wrote in her book that Lenny never considered points losses as losses, it had to be a knockout! Of course, it was a loss and I'm sure Lenny would have claimed a win if he had had the most points. She also said that the first Shaw fight and the fight with Cliff Field (there were in fact two fights) were points losses! So the McLean books don't even match each other. Lenny said he was unbeaten (apart from the dodgy gloves fight with Roy and doesn't even mention Field, Waldron or Paddock) and Val McLean says he lost on points to Cliff and Roy and only claims one fight with Fields, a knockout that didn't count because it was a points loss ... what?

Eddie Richardson, who was well involved in the unlicensed game for a while and looked after Harry Starbuck, said: "The greatest unlicensed fighter was not Lenny McLean, although he liked to claim he was the Guv'nor. The real Guv'nor was Cliff Field. He was king of the unlicensed ring, he was a big, hard man who knocked Lenny McLean out twice."

Dave Courtney, who worked with Lenny for a long time, said: "Lenny was guilty of being a bully and I saw him take liberties with a few people and push his luck a bit more than he should have done." I have literally hundreds of quotes about Lenny and I have actually left the really bad ones out!

For example, what Dave says there is just a fact that everyone in these circles knows anyway. It's also a known fact that Lenny was a heavy steroid user and those things are not known for chilling you out and making you mellow! (Look at the size of him in the Bradshaw and Yorke fights, vitamin C doesn't do that to you!)

Lenny's next fight was with a hard nut called Johnny Clarke from South London. Clarke was a street fighter and much more suited to Lenny's style. It was a lively, exciting affair. The ref was Donny 'The Bull' Adams. At the bell, both men flew at each other. Then they started feeling each other out with Clarke throwing a few feeler jabs. Lenny, never one for hooks, started hurling the hooks as Clarke moved backwards, then held on to Lenny. These were not the tactics to use on Lenny McLean!

Lenny carried on forwards throwing hooks, with Clarke reeling back. Clarke then hit the deck after taking a huge hook to the body. But Clarke got back up (many wouldn't) and the bell went, end of round one. In round two, Clarke actually appeared to hurt Lenny with a big right hook. Lenny reeled back to the ropes and Clarke really was digging deep throwing countless hooks. Frank Warren and the Lenny team were getting worried. Then McLean rallied and a blur of hooks and uppercuts thump into each other as the two men stood toe to toe exchanging bombs. Again, unless you had a chin like Tim Witherspoon or Ray Mercer (American Pro fighters), this was not the way to fight McLean. Then ... Bang! An uppercut from the floor caught Clarke clean on the chin. Clarke hit the canvas so hard he nearly went through it! Donny Adams counted to ten and Lenny celebrated. He was back!

Clarke had to be carried back to the corner. Mixing it and going toe to toe with Lenny McLean was a foolish tactic. Paddock had it spot on, Clarke had it wrong.

Lenny then took on Ron Redrupp. Redrupp was basically over the hill or 'shot' and by now he had been in lots of wars including one with Cliffy Field which Cliff won. Redrupp, like most, looked like a midget next to Lenny. This was a very one way fight, Redrupp was way past it and simply too small. He also lacked the ring craft to defeat a much bigger man. For most of the fight, Redrupp held on to Lenny and McLean was getting fed up. Every time Redrupp got hit, he held on and wouldn't let go. Redrupp had started to gush blood and in the third round, the ref had to jump in.

As for Roy Shaw, he had got his head together and trained like a Spartan for a comeback fight with Eddie Richardson's boxer, Harry 'The Buck' Starbuck, who was a renowned doorman and hard man but also a gentleman. Harry had 14 wins and 14 knock outs. This was to be an open air show in Dartford and the place was full of people wanting to see the return of the man who started it all.

As the bell went, Roy circled Starbuck but every time he moved forward, Harry tied him up until the ref pulled them apart. This was all that happened until about a minute into the fight when Roy unleashed a savage volley of punches. Starbuck was out before he hit the canvas and it was over. The place went wild, Roy still had a lot of support. Harry was out cold for nearly ten minutes. Thankfully he was OK. Roy and Harry had a lot of respect for each other and Roy even apologised that it had to end like that.

A few years ago, I spoke to Harry Starbuck about that fight and with typical dignity, he said: "There's no shame in being knocked out by Roy Shaw, the man is a legend and far too good and strong for me." Roy holds Harry Starbuck in high esteem to this day and is the only one of his former opponents he considers a friend.

Eddie Richardson was not quite as charitable when describing his fighter: "Harry Starbuck was a big name draw and the crowd loved him, so we didn't want him beaten and we chose his opponents carefully. He was never the real thing - he was too old and unfit to get a license, but he was very popular. The guys who fought him knew what they had to do. They were being paid, usually about £600, to take a dive and Harry would get a grand. One guy fought him twice, under different names with his hair dyed! Roy Shaw wasn't paid to help Harry and he was a much harder, fitter boxer. Shaw gave him a right pasting and that was more or less the end of Harry's career." A touch harsh perhaps but then the truth is rarely ever pretty!

Roy's next fight was at Ilford Palais against Lew 'Wild Thing' Yates. Lenny McLean was in the crowd. Lew had complained that he only had six weeks to train, I don't know how long other fighters got but Lew wanted six months. He admitted that he had a hell of a lot of weight to lose but in the ring, he looked quite good.

Lew was stopped in the third round due to serious eye damage. Lew has claimed since that he is 'Britain's rightful Guv'nor'. I think there may be an argument that Cliff Field deserves that title and every single person I have spoken to has said that he was the best unlicensed fighter. A few have said Roy Shaw, purely because of the physical odds he overcame and that he started the whole thing. I may be wrong but I thought Lew only had that one fight with Roy and that was the only unlicensed fight he had.

Recently, Roy Shaw was told about Lew's book and was far from happy. Via the Internet, Roy challenged Lew to another fight to 'shut his mouth once and for all'. Lew apparently accepted the challenge but nothing has come of it since. It's amazing that all that hatred can last that many years.

I have spoken to Lew and found him a nice man but I would vote for Cliff if asked who was the best unlicensed fighter. But Lew can fight that's for sure and he's respected as a doorman and thought to be one of the best in the country.

Again, the man Roy really wanted was Lenny McLean. He challenged him repeatedly but no joy. Maybe Lenny simply thought 'we have had three fights, it's history'. Although the Roy Shaw who turned up against Starbuck and Yates was a much fitter, muscled up but leaner looking Roy than the one who turned up for McLean two and three, Lenny must have been tipping the 21 stone mark and was still a lot younger!

Roy had said if he couldn't have McLean he would definitely retire. In one article written before the Yates fight, Roy announced Yates would be his final fight. But Roy told me, if he couldn't have McLean, he would retire after beating someone who had beaten McLean. I think Waldron would have suited Roy more but he picked that slippery customer Kevin Paddock.

The final fight for the man who had come so far, through Broadmoor to starting unlicensed boxing to being the first ever Guv'nor would come on 24th November 1981, again at Ilford Palais. There were even tears in tough men's eyes that night as the man who had given them more excitement, thrills and unpredictability, the man who had given another option from the stuffy 'My Lords, ladies and gentlemen' mob at the British Boxing

Board of Control, a sport that still thrives to this day, was saying goodbye. He received a standing ovation as he came into the ring and a standing ovation at the end as he waved goodbye. The fight was predictable. Roy worked for an opening, Paddock wouldn't give it to him. It was a cat and mouse fight and Roy won easily on points.

There was an unlicensed fighter and all round hard man called Ray Hills from near my part of West London called Acton, a pretty tough place and a selection of promoters were interested in taking Ray into the pro game. He had all the right attributes but was becoming wild and getting into heavy duty crime, the downfall of many potential professional's, along with drink, clubs and pretty girls. About 90% of potential pros get to a point at about 17, 18 and 19 when they start thinking things are unfair. 'Why do I have to get up at 6.00am and do roadwork, while my mates get drunk and take a sexy girl home?' and 'There's a great all night rave on Wednesday but I have a fight on Thursday!' We nearly all go through that one, and that is one of the main reasons we don't have as many potential champions as we should. It's not lack of talent, it's getting over the wall of being one of the lads. If you want to get to the top, you simply cannot be one of the lads. It can be a lonely sport and that hurdle brings down many. I have seen so many good fighters in the gym when they are 14, 15 and 16 but as soon as they can drink, they lose interest. A lot of people don't realise the mental strength you need just to keep going to the gym let alone fighting!

In Ray Hills case, it was heavy crime instead. Armed robbery and attempted murder to be precise. Ray received 22 years and served 14 mostly like all West Londoners in the Scrubs. So when Ray eventually got out he had served up screws and cons alike and especially (instant Knighthood for Mr Hills please) nonces!

Ray, of course, had lost his pro license, so taking the advice of the well known and respected boxer Jimmy Tippett snr (not jnr), Ray made the journey to the Thomas a' Becket. On his first day he sparred with Roy Shaw and was impressed by his power and developed respect for him. From then on, Ray became a regular sparring partner for Roy, something a lot of fighters avoided. Ray joined the unlicensed circuit where he fought a draw with that master of defense and counter punching, Kevin Paddock and supplemented his income by taking bare knuckle fights.

Ray Hills also worked the door at a club in Ealing (where I also worked the door before those stupid badges!) called Crispin's, or Crispin's Wine Bar, to give it its full name. We were a bit embarrassed by the 'Wine Bar' bit but it was actually a rough old place. So much so that someone shot Ray in a drive by on the way home and nearly blew his leg off!

But Ray Hills is one of those forgotten faces of the golden era of unlicensed.

The (Ealing) Broadway Boulevard also had its fair share of claret (blood) flying about. A club in West Ealing had doormen who were just dying to fight. It used to have a window on the door that allowed you to see right down the stairs. Every week, whoever gave the doorman trouble would be kept back somehow and then locked in ... alone with eight doormen. Through the window, we used to love watching this guy who had spent the night thinking he was Charlie Richardson or Reggie Kray being forced to play the game twister but with coshes and hammers!

I don't think those guys would have passed the SIA badge course, especially after throwing the instructor in the river on a 'relaxation break'. Ray Hills would have Jimmy Tippett find hard men for him to fight. But Ray went back on the doors. You can't beat the camaraderie, loyalty and laugh you can have on the doors. And I also learned that those bouncers looking for a fight were bad at their job. I have worked with, and know of, some great doormen like Stilks, 'Big' John Bleakney, Paul Knight and Tony who I worked with at 'Big' Albert Chapman's famous Elbow Room, everyone who is anyone has heard of the Elbow Room and indeed 'Big' Albert Chapman, a man who I respect so highly words will not do it justice, and I speak for all the 'chaps' on that one! More about the doors later on.

If the title the Guv'nor is still being fought for in one hundred years from now, Roy Shaw will always be known as the first one. The original Guv'nor would not be seen in the ring again. An era was over!

Lately, I was speaking to an unlicensed fighter from that time named Phil Goodson, another unsung fighter. We spoke for a long time about what I call the golden era of unlicensed. When Phil wasn't fighting he went to all the fights. He told me that in the second Waldron v McLean fight, Waldron battered Lenny all over the ring, he said it was humiliating.

How many people reading this still won't have it that Lenny McLean was beaten six times and Bartley Gorman was NOT 'King of the Gypsies'? Now, how many of you met them? How many of you saw them fight a few times in street or ring? Lastly, How many of you know a high ranking (face) that you can ring and check with? I bet I have got the number down to nil!

An opinion is something that should be earned, earned through knowledge. When you have enough knowledge and done all your research, you are then entitled to an opinion. Otherwise, your opinion means nothing!

12
THE SHOW GOES ON!

As I mentioned before, you can't knock Lenny McLean for bottle. His next fight was against the man who had hit him so hard in the first fight - Cliff Field. The rematch was set for 12th February 1979. Lenny learned his lesson and trained like a real boxer as he did for the third Shaw fight, he was taking no chances with this lion hearted, tough nut.

Lenny came out fast but did what educated boxers do and took the middle of the ring and tried to keep Cliff at bay with a stiff jab. Cliff never threw ones or twos in any of his fights it was all threes and fours and sometimes fives and, for his size, his stamina was unreal. People would say 'he can't keep this pace up, he will drop by round four' but Cliff would keep going. He was a huge man who fought like a middleweight. Then Lenny threw a stiff one two and Cliff didn't even move. The bell went with both men giving a good account of themselves. The second round was much the same but now Lenny was starting to hold, he was getting tired and taking a lot of body punches that took his wind away. Lenny charged Cliff onto the ropes like he was losing his temper and both men exchanged bombs, end of round.

Lenny's legs wobbled and made his way slowly back to the corner while Cliff just skipped back. Round three started slowly, then both men threw a haymaker at exactly the same time but it was Lenny who wobbled back and Cliff was on top of him like a tiger, then Lenny rallied back. He caught Cliff low but they carried on until the bell.

Round four and Cliff kept throwing bombs. Lenny's stamina was going and he fell back on the ropes. The ref pulled them apart but Cliff was back in and unloading everything. Lenny's mouth was open and he was running out of air. Then an overhand right came crashing onto Lenny's chin! Lenny hit the canvas sprawled out, the ref took up the count but there really was no point. McLean was out cold and not going anywhere for a while. Cliff, checked if Lenny was okay and stayed in the ring until Lenny came round. He then had a little celebration and was off. Lenny slammed his giant fists on the canvas in anger and was then led back to the dressing rooms.

Lenny had now lost five times, been knocked out three times, stopped once and outpointed once, the Guv'nor was Cliff Field from Dunstable. Lenny McLean was left considering his future.

A lot of people wanted to see a London v the north type fight. London gets all the attention but there are some tasty blokes up north. At this time, the two they wanted most in the ring were arch enemies Viv Graham and Lee Duffy, two extremely violent men but it never came off. Both Viv and Lee lived extremely violently and died in the same way at a young age.

Viv Graham was more ring inclined than 'The Duffer' and a fight with London's Lenny was put to Viv. As I said earlier about Lenny, he deserved respect because he would fight anyone in the ring. There's overwhelming evidence to conclude that Lenny didn't want to fight Roy Shaw on the cobbles, bare knuckle and 'all in' like Roy was dying to do, but in the ring, anybody would do. It is said Viv Graham wanted to see Lenny fight before he made a decision but that Viv's father and others had watched a video of McLean in action and had warned Viv to stay well away from him. In Newcastle, Viv Graham's name has passed into legend and it would have been a great fight. As would Lenny, Roy or Cliff against 'The Taxman' Brian Cockerill or Ernie Bewick who was known as the Rocky Marciano of Sunderland but it's all fantasy. My great, late friend Harry Marsden who I miss every day, spoke very highly of these guys especially Ernie Bewick, a man named Stuart Watson and of course his closest pal, Mario Cunningham. I have already mentioned Rich Horsley and these are a few of the North East hard men. I will tell you a lot more about my friend Harry in future chapters.

In 1986 Lenny McLean was involved in probably the most violent and famous outburst of brutality ever seen in a boxing ring to this day. The Yorkshire Grey in Eltham was the venue and what followed would be shown and re shown on TV clips forever more.

Lenny was going to fight a man called Bryan 'Mad Gypsy' Bradshaw. Also on the bill was a man who became a very good pro named Rocky Kelly. Gary Heart and Del Boy Paul were also on the undercard.

Lenny was in an aggressive mood for this one, it was written all over his face and he threatened that he would smash Bradshaw's head in. The venue was small and intimate giving it a real electric atmosphere. Roy Shaw turned up to watch and so did Harry Starbuck. Lenny had told the doorman not to let Shaw in and to give Starbuck a hard time. I can imagine the doorman going "Oh, thanks very much Len!"

Roy was very, very close to losing the plot and smashing into the doorman. I think it was only the fact that Roy (and Harry) was a doorman himself that stopped him out of mutual respect, otherwise it would have been mayhem. Harry had gone to watch, Roy to challenge McLean and get him back in the ring once and for all. It's not all glamour being a doorman, I have done the doors for years and it has its dodgy moments. But in those days, before the security badge came in, you had to be able to really fight anyway. Now, you just have to be good at exams. More of that later.

Bradshaw was unbeaten but a relative novice. Between 5-600 fans packed the place out. Bradshaw made his entrance, then a massive and pumped looking Lenny climbed in the ring, he really did look huge by now. And at that size, I don't think he would have got anywhere near a fighter like Kevin Paddock, he would have been far too slow and muscle bound. Lenny must have weighed over 20 stone and looked like he had 'Roid Rage' (steroid induced rage) as he walked up to Bradshaw, bent his knees and started growling at him like a wild animal. As I say, Lenny in this mood would have been perfect for a jab and move boxer but Bradshaw was far from that. The promoter of this fight was the late Reg Parker, a friend of top doorman Stilks and many more of the 'chaps'. The ref Roy York called them to the center of the ring. As he gave the instructions Bradshaw did something amazing that's been shown on TV a hundred times. Whether he was an extremely brave man or simply panicking we don't know, but he leant back for leverage, lunged forward and WHACK! He head butted Lenny hard right above the eye!

Lenny was knocked back by the power and shock but slowly ambled back to the middle then BANG! One big right hand from Lenny and Bradshaw hit the deck, looking like he's out already. Lenny then grabbed Bradshaw round the throat with his left arm while smashing him full on with another right hook and then stamped straight down on Bradshaw's head. The ref looked like he didn't want to know and stood dumbstruck watching as Lenny repeatedly kicked Bradshaw in the head and face. Bradshaw, with his arms neatly tucked into his body and lying out cold on his back, looked like he'd been tucked nicely into bed, if only!

Corner men and officials quickly climbed into the ring and pulled Lenny away, but he slipped away from them and came running back and got some more kicks to the head in. Bradshaw, just like Adams against Roy Shaw, actually looked as if he was dead. Nick Netley and Reg Parker bravely steamed into Lenny and pinned him to the ropes. McLean, like a trapped wild animal, looked to the heavens and let out a primal roar!

At that moment, Lenny was insane but they managed to calm him down eventually. Bradshaw was put into the recovery position and the ref got his gum shieldout and made sure he hadn't swallowed his tongue (or Lenny's leg!).

Lenny left the ring and the building looking happy enough with a nice lump of cash as Bradshaw was still coming round. He was extremely lucky to be doing so. The two most talked about incidents and most often shown clips on TV to display the sheer violence of unlicensed boxing are Roy Shaw v Donny Adams and Lenny McLean v Mad Gypsy Bradshaw. The only difference is that Shaw and Adams had agreed on 'all in' but Bradshaw had taken a liberty as that fight was supposed to be a normal unlicensed 'straightener'. Head butting Lenny McLean has to go down in the book of the world's most stupid actions. McLean would have beaten Bradshaw anyway but by nutting him, Bradshaw very nearly got himself killed!

How Bradshaw came out of that with no lasting damage is a miracle, 20 odd stone of muscle from one of the world's greatest, and certainly most aggressive, unlicensed fighters stamping on your head is not something aspirin can fix in ten minutes!

'Big' Lenny was now at Legend status in the unlicensed ring and was, like Roy before him, starting of thinking of retirement but couldn't get it completely out of his system. He was still bringing money in, like most good unlicensed fighters, by working the doors at places like the Hippodrome and doing a bit of debt collecting, later with men such as 'Dodgy' Dave Courtney who included Lenny in a Courtney documentary called *Bermondsey Boy*. Dave was not the big name he would later become in this documentary. Lenny had made a small fortune from his unlicensed fights and these extras. He really didn't need to fight for money anymore but wanted to fight once more for himself.

Lenny had one more unlicensed fight when he took a challenge from a bloke from Tottenham called David York, his fighting name was 'Man Mountain York'. York was actually bigger than McLean. He was 24 years old, 24 stone and not far off seven feet tall!

The fight would be held in an open air stadium, echoing Shaw's mullering of Harry Starbuck at Dartford. This fight would be held on 7th September 1986 at Woodford Town Football Club. The posters had York saying 'Lenny has had his day' with Lenny responding 'God have mercy on his soul'. Before the fight, Jim Irwin, Lenny's stepfather who supposedly had beaten him black and blue when he was a kid, had come to make things right and the only reason Lenny didn't smash him to bits was because he had promised his mother on her deathbed that he wouldn't hurt Irwin. Never mind, Irwin used to work for my mate Ronnie Knight and when Ronnie eventually found out what Irwin had done to the young Lenny he battered him to kingdom come!

People tend not to see Ronnie as a hard man but he just doesn't boast about it and his temper is covered by that cockney charm. He is not a lover of violence like ... say ... Frankie Fraser or Roy Shaw but it's in him alright!

How Roger Cook never got really hurt is a miracle. In Spain he knocked for Ronnie and Freddie Foreman repeatedly, not clever. Did you see that first *Hell's Kitchen* when his chair broke, and he smashed his back and was carried off in agony in an ambulance? Oh my God, I nearly gave myself a hernia laughing, it was brilliant. In fact, nobody there seemed that bothered either ha ha! Classic! I also laughed when that idiot Donal MacIntyre passed out having a tattoo done. More of that snake later.

The surprise visit from the Irwin put Lenny in a complete rage and York was going to really get it now! The support bill included a young, as yet unknown, bouncer and debt collector called Dave Courtney who fought the experienced Patsy Gutteridge. Dave was good friends with Lenny at this point and they did a lot of work together. Dave has always told me that on the cobbles Roy Shaw would have beaten Lenny and I always get the feeling that Dave has a genuine affection for Roy that he never had for Lenny, he can relax and have a laugh with Roy whereas with Lenny you never knew when he would go off on one.

I asked 'Mad' Frankie Fraser the same question when Frank, Charlie Richardson and me went out to lunch at some swish gaff. Charlie is a lobster and fine wine man. Charlie, who has become like a second Dad to me after losing my own Dad, is highly sophisticated. Frank and I are er, not, and we had posh cod and chips and diet coke (I think that was still 20 quid each!).

Frank and I had finished our swish fish supper and I asked him: "Frank, who was the best in the ring and on the cobbles Roy Shaw or Lenny McLean." This small but ferocious looking man (once described as the underworld's Atom Bomb!) said without hesitation "Roy, without doubt in the ring and the cobbles because he threw one of them fights you know? And on the cobbles it would of been a massacre. Roy was in a different class all round. He was a top fighter and top armed robber. McLean was never a villain, he was as straight as a die. When they were young, Roy had the biggest touch before the 'Train' (The Great Train Robbery in 1963) and Lenny was a window cleaner. Nah, No contest. Roy was good, very good."

I liked Frankie Fraser then. Most people did I think. But when he started to offend Freddie Foreman in public (books and websites,) he put a lot of the 'chaps' in a difficult position, and I think to Frank's surprise everyone came down on Fred's side. More of that later, back to the fight ...

York was in the ring first awaiting Lenny. Lenny entered the ring and gave York a nasty stare. Lenny then did a bit of showboating for the crowd in his John L Sullivan type tight bottoms. For once, Lenny McLean looked rather small next to

'Man Mountain'. But Irwin coming to see Lenny was not good news for York. As the fighters were receiving their instructions, the bell went, very strange. They didn't even touch gloves. Anyway, once again, the boxer in Lenny McLean came out during this fight. He had matured well and took the middle of the ring using his jab to keep York off. He had matured mentally as well. You would have expected him to be the usual raging Lenny after the Irwin incident but he was patient, picking York off with stiff jabs and patiently waiting for openings. Lenny McLean was now a brawler and boxer. If he had always fought this way, he would have been almost impossible to beat. He had ideas, plan A, B and C not just plan A ... run and roar!

Lenny left hooked York into a corner but on the way in, Lenny was caught with a big one, two combination and is pushed off with ease. For those who don't know, being big doesn't always mean you have power to go with it, but York did. But Lenny kept coming forward, he'd never been a back foot fighter. York was backed into a corner and again Lenny's boxing skills were apparent as he threw bombs to the body to bring York's arms down so his face was undefended. Strangely, Lenny was fighting York like Roy Shaw fought Lenny in fight one. But York was here for a fight and replied with a few left hooks. Lenny now unloaded and York covered up and the crowd were on their feet roaring Lenny on. The way Lenny had suffered adversity and always been mentally strong enough to come back for another go, had made him very popular. The British especially, love that quality. That's what they saw in Frank Bruno. Lennox Lewis had it as well, but it fascinated me that the British crowd never gave Lennox the support he deserved. Myself and my brother-in-law Phil were real Lewis supporters and went to every one of his UK fights. We knew he was special when we saw him take apart Gary Mason, he fought like an American heavyweight, no bad thing.

But Lenny was more popular than ever. York and McLean were now having a tear up. A right, followed by two left hooks and York looked like he was going. He was only being held up by the ropes but kept throwing punches. York's huge frame was taking punishment but he was on his feet and Lenny still had the mentality of a boxer, not a street fighter, and took a split second to assess things before attacking, something he never used to do.

Lenny was getting the upper hand in a big way and York knew it. He grabbed Lenny's neck and held him down, but he didn't hold Lenny tight enough. Lenny broke loose and slammed a head butt right into York's face! York held onto Lenny and head butted him straight back! Lenny head butted him again. York then came on strong and backed Lenny into the corner with a nice combination. Both men held each other, then York slammed in another head butt. After a few punches, Lenny slammed yet another head into York. It's amazing there were no big cuts on either man. Then McLean threw a short hook and caught York sweetly on the jaw and dropped him to his knees, Lenny dropped down with him and smashed him in the stomach, Lenny was still throwing punches with York on his knees. Then York was flat on his back and Lenny clumped him a couple of times in the gut while he's lying there. Lenny's hand was raised in victory and the fight was stopped! I think with both men at the top of their game again, this would have been perfect for a final McLean v Shaw fight and a final fight for them both!

After battering York, Lenny had a quick ring celebration, then he was through the ropes and out. This was Lenny McLean's last fight in the ring. Unlike Roy Shaw, I'm sure Lenny McLean did not know that this was his last fight. Lenny had a touch of showman in him and would of made a big farewell exit and maybe even have announced something over the microphone. But it was to be his last fight, leaving a record of 15 wins and six losses.

In my opinion, by the time that Lenny fought York he was peaking, it was an impressive win even if it did have a controversial ending. By this time, Lenny McLean was not the wild, roaring, brawler he once was, relying on people being scared of him. He had developed a boxer's brain and started to respect boxing more as an art and science. McLean v York was one of the last of the classic (nearly) everything goes fights. A short time after this fight, York would have been thrown out of the ring after the first head butt because eventually unlicensed became as strict as the pro game.

So both the big players Roy Shaw and Lenny McLean had taken their bows and left the stage. Unlicensed boxing would never be the same again. But if they thought they would be forgotten, they were mistaken. What happened was just like when the Richardsons and the Krays were put away and Old Bill thought they would be forgotten forever. The opposite happened and they became legends and more famous than ever.

Roy tried one last time to get Lenny to fight him again. He tried phoning him and even going round his house but he'd moved. So he asked his mate, the boxer Billy Walker, to talk to him but he said "He won't fight you Roy, he can't get fit!"

Roy said: "I know in my heart 100% I can beat him and that's what hurts, I'm as good now as when I beat him in the first fight, he must have known I threw the second fight and something was wrong on the third, he must know it wasn't the real me ... why else would he not fight with all the advantages in his favour?

"He wouldn't even fight me on the cobbles and he's supposed to have had 30,000 bare knuckle fights and he's only 39, that's impossible isn't it? He will fight these 30,000 other geezers but he won't fight me. I just don't get it!"

13
CHANGES ALL AROUND

What happened to Johnny Owen, Michael Watson, Rod Douglas, Bradley Stone and other fighters who fired warning shots across the deck of unlicensed boxing. Have you noticed that these life threatening fights never happen to heavyweights even though they punch much harder?

Excuse me while I bore you with my theory on why this doesn't happen to heavyweights. Firstly, head guards have no effect at all. It's all down to water. The brain is protected by a thick outer jelly-like substance which is made up of water. All weights in boxing have a strict limit except heavyweights. A fighter who fights at the lighter weights can sometimes walk around between training at two or three stone over their fighting weight. So every time they fight they have to lose the weight because they always fight at well below their natural weight. They have to lose the weight fast, so very little fat is lost, it's mostly water.

Most fighters at the lighter weights wear sweat suits and spend ages in the sauna and take in minimum amounts of water so the weight doesn't go back on and therefore go in the ring completely dehydrated. That means that the protective layer of jelly that protects and actually holds the brain in place is minimised and sometimes, because of lack of water when hit, the brain just crashes against the side of the head because the protection has dried and caused bruising and sometimes bleeding to the brain. That's why it doesn't happen to heavyweights, they have no weight limit and can eat and drink as much as they like, hence their protective layer is always intact. Are you with me?

That's also what happened in the early unlicensed days because they didn't have to make a certain weight. I think there should be a three to four pound leeway in pro boxing for the lighter weights. People go on these discussion shows and rattle off all these

Left: Ray Mills, me, Roy Shaw and Chris Lambrianou. Both Ray and Chris were present the night Reg Kray killed Jack 'the hat' McVitie.

Below: Charlie Richardson, me and Chris Lambrianou. This photo proves there is no lasting malice between members of the ex-Richardson and Kray gang members.

'Big' Albert Chapman and me. There is no limit to the huge respect I have for this great man.

Above: Me and the legendary Ronnie Knight. Ronnie was married to Barbara Windsor for over 20 years. Ronnie is a fantastic man who has had utter lies written about him in the tabloids recently.

Left: A meal out with 'Mad' Frankie Fraser and his former boss Charlie Richardson. Charlie is a lobster thermedor and fine wine kind of guy, Frank and I had cod, chips and a coke!

An example of the great talent Charlie Bronson has for art.

Top right: 'Gypsy' Joe Smith, one of my closest pals.

Above: The late Johnny Nash, Charlie Richardson, Rob Davies and me.

Me, Eddie Richardson and Roy Shaw at another unlicensed fight show.

Roy Shaw, me and the late 'boss' Joey Pyle Snr.

Above: Me with the late Tony Lambrianou at one of my fight nights. Tony was part of the Kray firm and served 15 years with them.

Right: Me with Wilf Pine, the only Englishman to be embraced by the American Mafia!

Above: Me with the legendary boxer Roberto Duran.

Left: Me with Cass Pennant, who has just had a film made about his life - go on ya' big man!

Above: Me, Charlie Richardson, Roy Shaw and the late Harry Marsden. Harry was loved by us all.

Left top: Me with another legend - the great Freddie Foreman.

Left bottom: Me with Charlie Richardson. Charlie and I are like father and son and his wife Veronica is a very special lady.

Below: Dave Courtney, me, Freddie Foreman and Howard Marks.

Left: Warriors 4: the unlicensed fight show at a packed Hammersmith Palais, I put this on for Charlie Bronson

Below: A prison phone card, signed and sent by Reg Kray

The late Joey Pyle Snr (the boss), Roy Shaw, me, Alfie Hutchinson and Freddie Foreman

A cheeky joke sent to me from my friend Ronnie Biggs.

Left: Roy Shaw, Red Menzies and the great unlicensed fighter Cliff Field, who knocked out Lenny McLean twice!

My beloved late father, Tel Currie Snr and my mother Pat, I love you dearly!

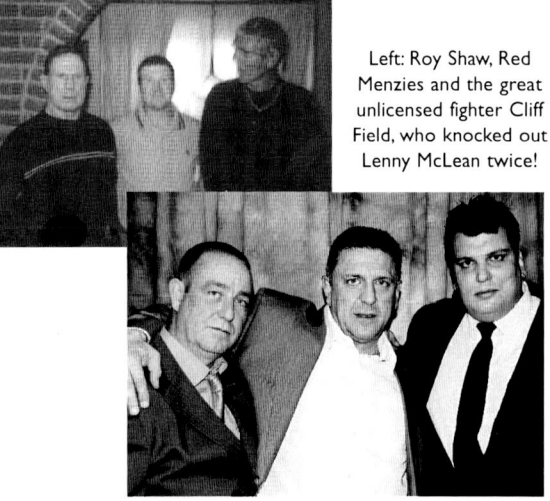

Me with Carlton Leach and Phil Gibbs. Carlton is like a brother to me and Phil is my brother-in-law.
Picture: Sean Keating (P4P Event Photography)

theories, but it's simple, to me anyway. The fighters I worry about most are men like Ricky Hatton who go on the booze between fights and of course alcohol makes you even more dehydrated.

It's amazing that nothing bad happened to fighters like Kevin Finnegan who would drink 10 to 20 pints of Guinness while IN TRAINING! Kevin actually did that every night before he fought Marvin Hagler, one of the greatest boxers the world has ever seen.

Another fighter who loved a drink was Cliff Field, now the sole legend left on the unlicensed circuit. Cliff's pro career was 11 wins with just four losses, not bad in anyone's book. People seem to judge Cliff because he lost on cuts to Richard Dunn and Muhammad Ali had humiliated Dunn, hence Cliff couldn't be that good. But Ali was the greatest heavyweight that ever lived in most people's opinion. (Out of interest, another comparison between Joey Pyle and my Dad who both died of motor neurone disease, is that they both considered Joe Louis to be the greatest heavyweight.) There's no shame in losing in five rounds to Muhammad Ali, he was 'The Greatest'. And Richard Dunn was a British, Commonwealth and European champion. He had beaten men like Danny McAlinden and Billy Aird, both legendary pro boxers. I think the criticism of Richard Dunn is harsh because he wasn't destroyed by just any fighter, this was Ali!

I think the criticism of Cliff is harsh in the pro ring because he lost on cuts. I also think things would have been very different if Lenny McLean had been nurtured as a young amateur, or even if he had a boxing mentality instead of being a bar brawler when he started. Ironically, Cliff Field, the sweetest and best unlicensed boxer of them all, actually represented the wild, heavy drinking bar brawler more than Lenny did!

Richard Dunn has been made out as the 'Eddie The Eagle' of boxing!

But his pro record is won 33 lost 12, not that bad. But there's a hell of a difference between pro fighters and unlicensed fighters. Richard Dunn would have beaten most unlicensed fighters, there's a big gap between the two. Even Roy Shaw describes Cliff as 'The real Guv'nor'.

The Guv'nor row is usually a tug of war between Roy and Lenny but all the time Roy knew that Cliff was the Guv'nor and Lenny learned the hard way twice. And just like the pro's over the years, unlicensed fighters have gradually got bigger and bigger. Men like Floyd Paterson and Henry Cooper used to fight at under 14 stone! Can you imagine a heavyweight that light now?

Cliff Field was flying high, most fighters, even the good ones, didn't want to fight Cliff. So respect to Lenny McLean for getting in the ring with him twice. Cliff had put on a boxing master class against that East End hard man, Ron Redrupp, and was finding it hard to find opponents. Then a fighter was brought over from Costa Rica to the Ilford Palais called Gilbert Acuna. Gilbert was a pro and six feet 3" so it was a great match up. But for once, Cliff found himself out of his depth in the unlicensed ring. Cliff started well but Acuna took over from about the second round on. In the fifth, Acuna simply unloaded on Cliff and the referee dived in because Cliff was not throwing anything back and was taking savage punches.

Upon his retirement, Lenny became an actor and, in the roles he was given, he was a good one. Reg Kray takes credit for setting up Lenny's new career through comedian/actor Mike Read, now sadly dead. Reg was apparently furious when Lenny refused to say a few words on the video *Epilogue of Ron Kray*, a documentary about Ron's funeral. Reg wasn't happy because, as he saw it, he was responsible for Lenny having an acting career in the first place.

Lenny was also in a crowd scene in the terrible film *The Krays* when Ron and Reg are fighting each other. According to a friend, Lenny behaved like a prima donna and insisted on being called Guv'nor right through the shoot. I later met Roy Shaw and Joey Pyle snr on the set of *Snatch*. They were completely different, they were gentlemen. On the Kray film, Lenny even threatened the cameraman and was talked out of punching his face in by Alex Steene. McLean was only a fucking extra!

At one point, the set was even going to be shut down if Lenny didn't leave but he shouted "Fuck off!" and stayed there. This had all the ingredients of 'roid rage' but the TV series *The Knock* and of course the film *Lock, Stock and Two Smoking Barrels* were great successes.

In his very next fight, Gilbert Acuna fought an up and coming

British heavyweight called Frank Bruno at the Albert Hall in 1982. Acuna was knocked spark out by Bruno in round one! It could be said that this was Acuna's last fight and he was very much past his best, but really it just proves the tremendous gulf between pro and unlicensed fighters (even though Cliff was an ex pro). As I said before, it's a completely different world. But it did give other unlicensed fighters some confidence in terms of fighting Cliff.

As was, and is no secret, Cliff does love a drink. One day, Cliff got a late call to fight a guy from Islington, London named Tshaka on Thursday 29th November 1979 at the Rainbow, Finsbury Park and Cliff was already pissed. But it was money and he took the fight. Tshaka was a Frank Warren fighter who had gone from Lenny McLean's little cousin to a real power house in boxing.

Frank was ringside for this fight. Amazingly, Cliff jabbed Tshaka's head off and won nearly every round. He was so used to booze, it didn't effect him and it was a real one way street. But the sweet was about to become sour. At the end of a one sided fight, Cliff approached the ref to raise his hand. The ref looked at Frank Warren who as clear as day nodded his head towards Tshaka. The ref, ignored Cliff, walked past him, walked up to the hardly standing Tshaka ... and raised his hand in victory!

Shouts of 'fix, fix, fix' rang around the venue and Frank Warren was gone. Cliff's corner man 'Buddy' Cooper was going absolutely mental. This was an early display of the power of Frank Warren and he was to become much more powerful than this. One nod of the head and a whole night's work, sweat and blood had been wiped out!

After this, Tshaka was not a popular fighter but you can't blame the boxer if the winner is already set. As for Cliff, he never got over this and his hatred for Frank Warren is immense. Even in 2004 when myself and Roy Shaw visited Cliff at Red Menzies' house, Cliff would still not have Warren's name mentioned. He had knocked out much better men than Tshaka. Gilbert Acuna was different, that was a loss and it happens, especially if you are in with a pro but this was not a loss. Still, Tshaka and Gilbert Acuna remain the only black marks on the record of the best unlicensed fighter of them all. Everyone in the game knows Cliff beat Tshaka and Acuna is his only real loss because of 'Warren's

Nod' to the ref and judges was seen by everyone and it was one of Cliff's easiest fights. Boxing is a ruthless sport, unlicensed is even more so but the real Guv'nor' should never have been treated like that.

In that golden age of unlicensed boxing, I have spoke to everyone from Roy Shaw down. Fighters, trainers, MCs and refs. And the result on who was the greatest is split between Roy Shaw and Cliff Fields with Lenny third. The main thing I heard was, if Roy had been a heavyweight, he would have been unbeatable.

In mid 2008, Valerie McLean, who Lenny doted on so much passed away from throat cancer. Let's hope they are reunited forever.

14
WHERE ARE WE NOW?

In the 1990s, unlicensed faded from people's minds slightly. I think this is because stars like Roy, Lenny and Cliff were not replaced and we were extremely spoilt by the pro game in this period. This was a great era for pro boxing. Cast your mind back - Nigel Benn v Chris Eubank twice, Chris Eubank v Michael Watson twice, Herol 'Bomber' Graham (in my opinion, the most difficult to fight out of all of them, Benn was made for his style!), Nigel Benn v The G man Gerald Mclellan, Steve Collins v Benn and Eubank and that's just the British middle and light middle weights!

At this time we also saw the incredible rise of a man who never received the credit or support he deserved, the Great Lennox Lewis. Who will ever forget his destruction of Razor Ruddock at Earls Court? I won't, I was there, it was electric! Frank Bruno was making a comeback and a clash between the two was inevitable and eventually took place at Cardiff Arms Park in 1993 with Lennox knocking Frank out. Bruno would eventually beat Oliver Mcall and win the world title, only to lose it again to a hungry ex con called Mike Tyson. That's just a taste, yep, we were really spoilt in the '90s and it's not until you look back now that you realise how thrilling that period really was AND it was mostly on normal TV! Remember those Saturday nights with the big build up actually getting nervous?

One of my worst experiences came in November 1993. I went to a Muhammad Ali book signing and actually got to meet 'The Greatest'. We spoke to each other and even shaped up. My girlfriend Cheryl took two photos of myself and the great man. He slurred, "you're a good looking kid ... but nothing on me!" We even embraced before parting. I couldn't wait until the day the photos were developed and was outside the shop before it opened.

As I flicked through, to my horror, I realised the pictures had NOT come out! All I got was a picture of Ali with someone else I had taken to check the camera. What a nightmare! I don't mind telling you, I actually cried! It was Ali for Christ's sake!

I do have a great framed photo with Lennox though, that man was so underrated, probably because he was a winner and the British don't like a winning sportsman, they prefer Bruno and Henry Cooper but Lennox was a true winner, that makes you unpopular straightaway over here. You have to have the 'aaahhh bless 'im' quality to be popular in the UK. Sir Henry Cooper. Why?

Frank Bruno had a lovely gentleman in his corner called Johnny Bloomfield. Myself, Joe Smith, Jimmy Stockin and the other lads had the pleasure of being trained by Johnny in our gym. Johnny told me I was the best pad man he had ever seen apart from Jimmy Tibbs what a gee! (Jimmy Tibbs is one of, if not the best trainer this country has seen. He is also from a very naughty and well respected family. Like many of my friends, Chris Lambrianou and Alan Mortlock to name just two, Jimmy is now a Christian).

Johnny told us about the second Tyson fight. Joe asked: "Was their any time in the build up that you thought Frank might win this?"

Johnny said "Never! His mind had lost that fight before we got in the ring."

"What about all those times he made the sign of the cross on the way to the ring?" I said.

"That's nothing," Johnny replied, "He did it over 30 times in the changing room! We wanted him to be a warrior and laugh in Tyson's face like Evander Holyfield, but Frank is just not made like that. If someone nutted Evander, he would nut them right back and laugh, that's how we wanted Frank to be."

Later I asked him about Frank's breakdown and told him I thought the press headlines were disgusting when the man clearly needed help, will they not be happy until people are dead?

Johnny explained: "It was coming for a long time. All the stuff with Laura (Bruno's wife) and drugs but the main thing was the suicide of George (Francis, his head trainer). We all felt guilty about George but Frank I think sort of said to himself 'what's the point in going through hell in fights to make money when I can't even help a friend?'

He added "Cass was a diamond throughout that dark period." Of course, he meant our mutual friend Cass Pennant and Frank's friend for years. We were lucky to be learning and training with a man who had been in the corner at endless world title fights. I'm surprised in a way that Joe Smith didn't team up with Johnny and dump me but he didn't. On the other hand, I'm not surprised because Joe is a very loyal man to his pals and we had started this little 'fight club' together and watched it grow.

Johnny Bloomfield passed away about four years ago, shame on me for not remembering the date. He had a heart attack. I remarked that his heart was simply too big for this world. Rest in peace Johnny.

Paul Edmunds was the promoter who brought Charles Bronson to the unlicensed ring. It was Paul that suggested the fighting name of Charles Bronson because he thought it had more of a sting than Mickey Peterson (his real name). All that rubbish about Mickey changing it to Charles Bronson because he wanted to be like the *Death Wish* character is nonsense. To this day, Charlie has not even seen *Death Wish*! Charlie just used it as a ring name, like so many people, and it stuck.

Charlie was an entertainer, calling his opponent on and sinking into the Lenny McLean squat and roaring in his opponent's face. It was in fact Reggie Kray who suggested that Mickey (as he was then) repeated this because he saw something more than just the aggression, he saw an all round winning prize fighter. I know Charlie very well, we even wrote a book together *Heroes and Villains* about all the 'faces' we have known, but the book received zero promotion. If Charlie Bronson was going to take advice from any man, or men, they would be Reg and Ron Kray and the late, great Joey Pyle snr. Joe's death was really hard on everyone, the man was loved by all. Even the WPC 'Lucy' who was put in his studio at Pinewood to stitch him up thought he was lovely!

So in a period of freedom, Mickey increased the training that he has always done. He was, and is, a fine physical specimen who still trains. Charlie's (Paul had now changed his fighting name) first fight was bare knuckle above an East End pub. He totally savaged the guy and picked up the easiest monkey (£500) of his life. Charlie was 35 years old and only 14 stone but I have seen Charlie shadow box and put on a little display close up ... and he is fast, extremely fast!

Next Charlie fought the notorious 'Bermondsey Bear' not a pretty man, covered in black body hair, loads of tattoos and no teeth. But like Roy Shaw before him, Charlie was used to screws hitting him with riot sticks ten handed and putting their size 11s into his ribs, one on one was not going to worry him after that. Charlie had years of anger and raw hatred inside him, it was now finding an outlet ... on somebody's face!

Charlie shot out at the bell and smashed a right straight into the Bear's face, he wasn't bothering with jabs. He wanted to give someone a taste of the pain he had suffered all those years. He just unloaded on the guy body and head, then he felt the pain, the Bear had kneed Charlie with all his power right in the nuts!

And he wasn't finished yet, the Bear smashed Charlie in the face with his head and tried to rip his eyeball out! Luckily, the bell sounded. War had been declared. In Charlie's mind, the Bear was now a bully screw and he was in Wandsworth or Brixton. First chance he got, Charlie nutted the Bear and splattered his nose. Then fierce punches, too many to count smashed into his face, fell on him. Charlie found an angle and put his full weight on the Bear's windpipe, of course, he couldn't breathe and was going blue. The ring was suddenly full of people trying to get Charlie off his windpipe, not an easy task but they managed. Charlie was paid well and used to pain so it was a good night, but not for the hairy bloke!

Next Charlie had a nice easy win and gave ALL his purse to a young victim of Leukemia. That's the side of the 'chaps' the public don't see or refuse to see. 90% of the fight nights and dos we have are to raise money for charity, especially sick children. It's always been that way, have a look at the old fight posters, they are all in aid of charity. I put on a couple of nights for Charlie Bronson and half the money went to children's charities. I know you are not meant to talk about it, but the lads get slagged anyway so I might as well tell you. I would love all the money made by the 'bad guys' for charity ever to be added up, Christ you could buy an island!

The youngster Charlie gave his fight money too went to Disneyworld, funny, I never read these stories in the papers, only the 'most violent man' stuff. Mmmmm, funny that!

Charlie next fought a character named Romany Ron, who was rated among the gypsies. But Charlie knocked him spark out in a couple of minutes, another nice earner. In another of Charlie's fights, that appears on nearly every unlicensed video, a gun lands in the middle of the ring. I have know idea where it came from but it was certainly a one off.

Charlie also challenged Lenny McLean to a five grand each way showdown, Lenny declined and didn't want to know. But by this time, Lenny didn't have to fight for money, he had done very well out of the game and had had more than his share of wars. I think Lenny just looked at his family and thought, it's got to stop sometime. Even Charlie shares this view. As we have seen, Lenny never refused a challenge in the ring even though many witnesses say he refused to fight Roy Shaw on the cobbles and trust me, Roy would have loved to have fought Lenny bare knuckle. So who would have won a fight in the unlicensed ring between Charlie Bronson and Lenny McLean? Being only 14 stone against about 21 stone is some disadvantage to overcome but in boxing, who knows.

About this time, Charlie met up with the real Guv'nor - Cliffy Field. They met up in a pub in Dunstable and Cliff gave Chaz the benefit of his experience. Charlie and Cliff are from exactly the same Manor - Luton/Dunstable. Charlie won't mind me saying that he has great respect for Cliff and Cliff has great respect and affection for Chaz.

The next story I have heard from Charlie himself and studying the look in his eye, I knew it was true and it's actually more common than nine to five folk may think. His next opponent was barking mad ... it was a Rottweiler!

Charlie says that his arm was nearly ripped off as it was in its jaws. "I just kept punching and punching with dog froth everywhere! I knocked it right down and ripped out half its lungs and killed it." Charlie received ten grand for that. He doesn't sound too proud of it but he had nothing, so what do you do? Some people would do it, some would rather starve, but as I say, these things go on more than you think.

Charlie and I were extremely close at one time, like brothers, but things happen and we couldn't agree on certain things ... that's life, it's sad but what can you do?

Myself and Charlie Richardson wrote the forewords for Charlie's latest 500 page blockbuster *Loonyology* and I also got comments from all the big underworld names and continued to even after we fell out, why? Because what's happening to Charlie is wrong, wrong, wrong! Justice is far bigger than two men who don't see eye to eye anymore.

The book includes photos of me with Wilf Pine, Ronnie Knight, Dave Courtney, Freddie Foreman, Howard Marks, Bruce Reynolds, Frankie Fraser, Charlie Richardson, Roy Shaw, Harry Marsden, Carlton Leach, all the gypsy boys including Johnny Frankham, Johnny Nash and a poster of my fight night I put on for Charlie but most importantly, two photos of my late Dad with kind comments from Charlie saying how much he will miss him – 'a top man ... respect'. My whole family had tears in their eyes when they read that and I would like to say here thank you to Charlie, despite our differences, because he didn't just dump Dad because he fell out with me like many would, he was man enough to see us as individuals and man enough to write those words ... Charlie thank you sincerely.

He also wrote in the book 'even though we fell out, we still respect each other and I would never slag him off. We just can't see eye to eye on a certain problem'. And that's exactly it, you won't catch me slagging off Charlie Bronson either and not a day goes by when I don't think about the rascal!

And I miss Eira (his dear Mum) one of the most lovely ladies, and I mean a REAL lady, to walk the planet. I used to call her Mum number two ha! Even now, I swear if anyone dare hurt or con Eira or Charlie's cousin Lorraine ... I would kill them, that's not hard man bullshit, I WOULD KILL THEM! so don't even think about it!

I will always respect him and support his case, I have always felt strongly about the injustice and was trying to raise public awareness when there were not many of us. We have both helped each other and there I shall leave it, if I'm honest, with a strong sense of sadness!

That other eccentric of the underworld was also boxing and started training at the famous Thomas a' Becket gym which had been used by Roy Shaw, Lenny McLean, Colombo, Brian Hall, Stevie Earlwood, Harry Starbuck, Jimmy Batten and, the man Roy had a tear up with in Broadmoor, Fred the 'Head' and almost every unlicensed fighter was 'Dodgy' Dave Courtney.

Fred the 'Head' was in the Roy Shaw, Frankie Fraser, Jimmy Boyle and 'hate 'em all' Harry Johnson mould, he was a legendary con who would attack anything that moved. There is a story about 'hate 'em all' in every prison book. Before that the Becket had been the training ground of Henry Cooper and others. Dave claimed five pro fights undefeated and then moved to where his real heroes were, in the unlicensed game. Here Dave found the gloves were not worth wearing and a middleweight could be fighting a heavyweight. It was at the Thomas a' Becket gym that Dave Courtney sparred with Lenny McLean. Lenny ran and roared at Dave and threw a punch at him so hard, it hit Dave's right guarding hand, hit him in the face and knocked him out!

It's a funny story when Dave tells it but in the close knit brotherhood of a boxing stable it would be considered a liberty. Sparring doesn't involve trying to take a far smaller man's head off I'm afraid!

Dave claims he had 17 unlicensed fights (which is more than both Roy and Lenny) and was disqualified in five. Dave claims this is because he had no ring craft. He states: "I would go berserk for a round and if I hadn't knocked them out by the third, I would be so knackered I would rather be disqualified than be knocked out in front of my mates."

If Dave was a pro, I would have thought he would have learnt more ring craft than that but Dave has never done things by the book as we know. Like most things in his life, Dave boxed for attention and having a crowd to entertain, he's still an entertainer. Dave was on the undercard of the McLean v York fight. Here he fought a near 50 year old Patsy Gutteridge, who was extremely experienced on the circuit. Dave was getting a belting so tried his head butt and get disqualified technique, but the veteran was so hard, Dave ended up splitting his own head open while Patsy just glared at him!

Dave had a good man in his corner though, a regular at my shows Harry Holland but he still didn't win. Dave has a large framed photo of himself fighting Patsy on his wall. He also has a fantastic huge, pencil sketch of Reggie Kray, it's lovely. I'm hoping he will give it to me one day! Ha! Some hope.

Dave said: "I had fights all over the place. The Grey's Inn, Crystal Palace, The Queens Hotel, Football Grounds and Luton car plant."

One fight, Dave's opponent pulled out only to be ready to fight again a couple of hours later. By then Dave was full of lager, hot dogs and crisps. The fight went ahead, only for Dave to vomit all over his opponent in the second round!

In the end Dave's mates and Patsy's mob had a mass free for all in the car park with the two fighters Patsy and Dave trying to stop it!

The '80s saw bad times for Roy, Lenny and Cliff and later on in the early '90s Joey Pyle. Cliff was a good doorman but the world is full of idiots. Cliff was on the door in Watford when a big lump started shouting: "You ain't no Guv'nor ... I'm the Guv'nor!"

Cliff kept ignoring him but in the end, Cliff knocked the idiot spark out with (compared to Cliff's usual clumps) a bit of a slap. In this country, you are not allowed to defend yourself so Cliff ended up doing 15 months in jail. Things are even worse now with the security badges. If you punch someone back, you get statements made against you, you're on camera and off to court, it's disgusting!

Cliff Field was on the door in Luton when he was attacked by a number of tinkers (Irish gypsies). None of his 'fellow' bouncers would help, all they did was guide the fight to the car park, suddenly one ran forward out of the pack and Cliff was glassed in the face and lost his right eye! Cliff's life has been in free fall since that injury and his battle with the bottle is terrible to watch.

Because of that and the drink, Cliff has taken many falls and injured himself, sometimes ending up in hospital.

None of them would fight Cliff in a 'straightener', it was a mob handed cowardly attack. Cliff now has a glass eye. This attack sent him on a downward spiral. He was barred from every pub and would sleep on park benches. He would have nasty falls and hit his head because of the lack of vision in one eye, and what with being legless all the time, he was always injuring himself. When Roy Shaw and I went to visit him he had a huge bruise down the side of his face where he took a tumble. Red Menzies and Bill 'Buddy' Cooper have tried everything but all they can really do is make sure he doesn't pass out in the open in winter. What else can you do?

Roy and I actually visited Cliff in a mental institution, with combination locks on the doors, howling and haunting screams and a woman in a frenzy being injected with the liquid cosh whilst fighting for her life against dragons!

It was actually worse than prison. Luckily, Red was with us and it made things easier. I had also brought an original work of art from Charlie Bronson that really cheered Cliff up. Unfortunately, things have just got worse and Cliff is not a well man. I actually have three brilliant and extremely rare signed photos of Cliff knocking out Lenny but because Cliff's autobiography is being written, I promised not to use them ... as much as I want to!

As I said, Roy sent a photo back 'To the real Guv'nor' ... that says it all. On my WARRIORS shows, Roy was guest of honour at the first one and I thought it would be great to have Cliff in that role at the second show. But it was not to be, Cliff is simply too ill and unpredictable. Cliff Field, the greatest unlicensed legend of them all now resides in a private care home. Red and Bill 'Buddy' Cooper still look out for him.

Then 15 years after being released from Long Lartin, the original Guv'nor, Roy Shaw, found himself back in jail. Another driver made the mistake of calling Roy a 'wanker'. NOT clever! In Roy's words, "I ripped his face off!"

Roy received six months in Pentonville and vowed he would never be an inmate again!

On the day Roy was nicked, a live TV interview was set up. Joey Pyle snr and Lenny McLean were sitting there with an empty chair where Roy should have been sitting. Joe told the interviewer: "Roy is not here due to a miscarriage of justice!"

What an interview that would have been if it had taken place with Roy and Lenny face to face and Joe as ever the diplomat. On this occasion, Roy and Len were due to be on the same side, as the argument was about banning boxing. It would have been amazing to see Roy and Lenny together. Throughout the show, Lenny smoked constantly while talking about training and keeping fit drawing comments from the audience. One old guy said to Len: "Who's heard of a champion constantly smoking?" Lenny just had another drag and took it with a pinch of salt.

Lenny McLean was working the door at the Hippodrome when a bloke called Garry Humphries, exposed himself and started masturbating over the girls in the club. Lenny and his fellow doorman gave the bloke a deserved back hander and threw him out, making sure that he was decent first. Next day, Lenny got a phone call saying Humphries was dead!

Lenny found himself on a murder charge. It was said at the trial that Humphries was more likely killed by forcefully compressed neck arteries caused by the police. While in Brixton prison, the official doctors report said Lenny was 'extremely depressed and prone to outbursts of tears'. Other reports from psychiatrists stated that Lenny was 'tearful and suicidal'. I think it was because he was a family man taken away from his beloved family, there's no shame in that in my opinion. But it also shows that Lenny was a very different man than Roy Shaw, Frankie Fraser, Jimmy Boyle and Charlie Bronson.

I have spoken to many people who were in with Lenny and got some very extreme stories but you never know who's got a vendetta and makes it up or was a good mate so glams it up, so I may have missed some gems but I'm not willing to slag a man on rumours, I would rather miss the gems. And every man is different, sometimes I think Frankie actually liked prison and was gutted when released!

But Lenny did give the impression that he was the 'Daddy' of the prison, from the people I know who were inside with him, it simply isn't true. But again, he's not going to write he was 'suicidal' is he? After all, unlike the others, he was innocent!

So Lenny McLean spent time on remand but was finally acquitted ... It was a close one. Then, for Roy and Lenny at least, things brightened up for a while. Lenny through Reg Kray and Mike Read got some acting work, starring in *The Knock* and playing Barry the Baptist in *Lock, Stock and Two Smoking Barrels*.

Then suddenly, Lenny found himself getting out of breath easily. Even picking up suitcases and climbing the stairs were exhausting him, how could it be?

Sadly, Lenny was diagnosed with cancer of the lungs and brain. He made a moving appearance on the Richard Littlejohn show where he said: "I won't give up and I shall go out like the Guv'nor!" There was not a hint of self pity, just dignity and Churchill spirit. It was a moving and inspiring interview, one that makes you go 'what am I complaining about?' Lenny said the greatest days in his life were meeting Val, the birth of his kids, beating Roy Shaw and his 'not guilty' at the Bailey. Even Roy was moved to say to me that they were just fights but if Lenny saw them as that important maybe he deserved to be called 'The Guv'nor'.

Lenny died on Tuesday 28th July 1998. His funeral was as elaborate as the Krays had been. Roy was invited but politely declined out of respect for the family. "We were never friends and I'm not a hypocrite."

Out of the three legends, Roy Shaw has done the best. He is a very successful businessman and invested all his fight money into property which paid off handsomely. A couple of years ago, Roy and I would go out clubbing every Thursday, that seemed to be the main night especially at the Epping Forest country club which was a great place. You would always bump into great people like Vic Dark down there. But everywhere we go you can hear the whispers 'that's Roy Shaw', 'Hey, look, Roy Shaw' and it's still like that. Wherever we go, it's 'Christ, there's Roy Shaw, talk to him', 'No, you talk to him'.

Sometimes, it's a bit like Beatlemania - Shaweymania! You would think with his reputation he would be roaring at people to leave him alone, not a bit of it. Even in Belmarsh max security prison cons and screws alike would walk up and shake his hand! Isn't that strange, after all the screws he's served up, they want to shake his hand!

Roy drives a lovely Bentley and has done well for himself. But ask yourself, would you go through everything he went through to reach that position, I don't think many would go through that hell to be well off. Same as Jimmy Boyle. He drives a roller and has made a fortune from sculpting and vineyards but would you go through what he went through first, I doubt it. Roy Shaw today, is happy. Many, many years ago, a prison Doctor told him: "Roy, no drugs or treatment will cure you, you will mellow yourself with age." And that's what's happened, he's still a very, very dangerous man but doesn't bite as easily anymore ... I still wouldn't recommend it though!

15
DIG THE NEW BREED

Did you know that Nigel Benn's first ever competitive boxing match was an unlicensed fight? Yep, that's true. Nigel says he was nervous because the man looked like Marvin Hagler the middleweight but Nigel smashed the Granny out of him, kicked him, stamped on his face and switched him off! That my friends, was the legendary Dark Destroyer's first fight in the ring.

Unlicensed has experienced a huge revival in recent years and that's down to good, capable promoters like Alan Mortlock, Terry Sabini, Joey Pyle jnr, Ricky English and Andy Jardine - all respected men who put on good shows and I will say to a lesser extent myself and, of course, fighters like Manny Clark, Decca Simpkin, Shane Stanton, Chris Morris, 'Gypsy' Joe Smith, 'Mad' Mickey Harrison, Mark Potter, Stacy Dunn, Stevie Knock, Butch Lesley, Gary Shaw and a nice lad called 'Tiger'.

I saw Tiger fight a number of times, he was one of Alan Mortlock's fighters. He and the other fighters in the crowd were called up at one of my Warriors shows to take a bow. Tiger was still a young lad when a few years ago he was shot while working the door and died. Unlicensed boxing lost a real character that day.

On the show I had the fighters and guests in the ring, comedian Johnny Vaughan was the MC. Lined up in the ring were Joe Smith, Jimmy Stockin, Roy Shaw, Joey Pyle snr, Andy Till, Tiger, Tony Lambrianou, Freddie Foreman and loads of others. Johnny Vaughan got in the ring, put his hands up and said: "Right, who wants it first?" Everyone doubled over laughing. He's a naturally funny man Johnny and doesn't rely on jokes. Like lightning he takes the Mick out of what or who's in front of him, a bit like Billy Connelly.

By the way, 'Gypsy' Joe Smith is a professional! Think about that, the poshest most exclusive sport, the most upper class 'members only' institution and a gypsy boy made it big! This is not pitch and putt, he's a real pro and coaches as well. Joe spent half his life on the golf course and the rest in the gym, he loved training which made life easier for me.

One of the most well known on the scene, if not the most well known is Dominic Negus from the East End, a former pro with a 13 wins and five losses record. His most famous fight was on TV, a six round points loss to Audley Harrison at Wembley but Harrison decided to hit Dominic when Dom was on the deck after a slip. Dominic nutted Harrison and turned street fighter. On the cobbles, my money would be on Dominic, Audley is not a cobble fighter, Dominic certainly is. Dominic was also into naughty stuff, heavy debt collecting and he started using steroids. Dominic was once attacked in his gym, three blokes came in, one with a gun, one with a baseball bat, the other with an axe! Dominic got the axe in his head but got up and started fighting back, can you believe that? He clumped one and actually got the upper hand, his attackers run off ... now that's hard! I know for a fact Roy Shaw thinks a lot of Dominic because he told me. As a collector, he was well known as one of the very best. I have seen him fight a few times at the Circus Tavern and his downward right hand is lethal! He was also known on the doors, that's a path many of us follow.

The evening after the Harrison fight, Roy Shaw and I went into Roy's local and Dominic was in there. He had a mark or two on his face but apart from that he was 100% fine having a night out in Essex with the lads. We had a chat with him and he was a decent bloke. Like I said before most 'proper' ones usually are. Dominic was getting into heavier debt collecting and after he was attacked and hit over the head, that made him think about things. I'm sincerely glad Dom didn't get a big stretch of bird because, as I say, when I met him I thought he was a decent man who was worth more than that.

I hoped more ex pros would join the unlicensed scene because I went to his first unlicensed fight and the place was electric! Dominic Negus is a man who makes you wonder what he could have been if he had just stayed with boxing, I reckon to the top. His book is out and well worth a read. He's an exciting fighter and couldn't have a better man on his side than Alan Mortlock. Alan has been through the lot; crime, prison, drink, drugs and extreme violence. Fortunately, Alan found Jesus and his beliefs, like those of my close friend Chris Lambrianou, are real. Neither of these special men force religion down your throat and can laugh about it as well. Personally, It's not my thing and I said to Chris once: "Chris, we will just have to accept that you are Cliff Richard and I am more Johnny Lydon (AKA Johnny Rotten)." John Lydon is one of my major heroes even if he did say a few unlearned things about Ronnie Biggs.

Kate Kray is now married to a nice bloke called Leo 'Razor' O'Reilly. Myself and Roy were sitting with Leo and Kate at an Alan Mortlock show at the Circus Tavern, like all Alan's shows it was packed but we were ringside (I have no illusions, it's only because of Roy and Kate that I was in the VIP section, although Alan and I are friends and as you may have guessed, I have great respect for the man). Roy and Kate have been good friends in the platonic sense since she married Ronnie Kray. Leo had three of his boys on the bill and they all won in scorching style. There's three lads for the future!

I think Alan now has the biggest stable of fighters in the country and is putting shows on all over the UK. But don't get Alan wrong because he is a Christian, he is still a very tough man and built like a tank!

The other big London promoters are Joey Pyle jnr and Ricky English who I also worked well with. I did two shows with Alan and two shows with Joe and Rickey because they are all friends, and I didn't want to look like I was siding with anyone person or people. Apart from that, they are the best!

So, by now my little stable of fighters was growing and was ready to be tested. Myself and my pal Steve Hough didn't start small and build up slowly, we went straight for the big time - Hammersmith Palais in London ... and we filled it!

WARRIORS 1 was on the way!

West London, had not seen anything like this for many years because Alan was operating in East London and Essex and Joe and Ricky had south London sewn up, mainly Caesar's in Streatham, and still put on great shows there, they are also branching out. So West London was for the taking. West London has always been overlooked in underworld books and documentaries. Mention crime in London and the majority automatically think of the East End or South London. If you're lucky, you will get a mention of the Nashes or Adams in North London, but for the most part mention London gangsters and people think East or South. But West London has carved (literally) a formidable reputation over the years.

The first race riots in the UK took place in Notting Hill. It wasn't the trendy place of Hugh Grant and Julia Roberts then! It was one of London's toughest ghettos just as Paddington and Kensal Green were. Paddington was once Jack Spots manor and men like Ray, Brian and Billy Mills, Jimmy 'The Paddington Puncher' Smith, Johnny Hanlon, Dave Barry, Charlie Lumley, Johnny Hall, Lenny Smithers, Kenny Smith and, of course, the four Currie brothers Danny, Ronnie, Dennis and my Dad Terry, were just a few of the true hard men that smothered the area.

Many folk still remember one of the area's greatest ever street fights when my Uncle Ronnie stood toe to toe with middleweight Champion Terry Downes, Uncle 'Chirpy' Downes as they both punched each other to a complete standstill for nearly half an hour (that's a hell of a long time for a street fight!). Even Old Bill applauded as the two then shook hands and vanished into the Prince of Wales pub together, that's how it used to work. Ray Mills often used to drink in the Prince of Wales with a hard staring, big shouldered bloke who never spoke much, his name was Roy Shaw and they are still best of friends.

West London at this time was named 'The Wild West'. Drive by shootings were a regular occurrence there as early as the '50s and the Krays became fascinated by West London. The twins came into West London thinking everyone would lay down their arms and shit themselves, in fact they were sent straight back to Bethnal Green!

I used to live about half a mile from Southall in West London which of course is Asian territory. I remember Asian gangs from when I was young and, in particular, the Tooti Nung and the Holy Smokes. In 2003, a gang from Southall called 'The Fiat Bravo Boys' received 20 years for trafficking six million pounds worth of heroin over three years. It is said they planted a nail bomb in a pub and I remember the blast and shudder of that bomb like it was yesterday. There was plenty of led flying about West London at that time as well. In Hanwell, known homosexuals were being targeted and brutally battered, battered so bad that one was killed in a toilet in 1990. A wall of silence came down and nobody was ever charged for the killing. Like Notting Hill in the '50s, racial tensions have always run high in Southall resulting in the huge riots of the early '80s. Southall was of course Asian and Hanwell and Northolt were full of skinheads at one time and the clashes were lethal. Knives, dusters, coshes, bricks and even guns were everywhere for a long time. I was very young when I first saw real, raw, racial hatred!

Peter Rachman 'The Devil's Landlord' operated in Notting Hill and bounced a cheque on Ronnie Kray. Serial killer John Christie resided at 10 Rillington Place in Notting Hill and, after the war, my Grandad became his postman. Two of the Mills brothers were present when the twins went to work on Jack 'The Hat' McVitie at the Evering Road basement. Unfortunately, Alan Mills gave evidence against the twins at the old Bailey trial which shook the whole community. Johnny Hanlon also made a mistake. He and his mates started making a nuisance of themselves in a club, problem was ... the club belonged to Freddie Foreman!

Johnny Hanlon was promptly decked by Ronnie Oliffe when Fred wasn't looking. Years later in The Scrubs, Johnny Hanlon approached Freddie, Freddie said: "Do you want to step into the recess?" In fact, Johnny had come to apologise about his conduct on that night, Freddie accepted the apology and they shook hands. It sounds twee, but the truth is, there is hard, and then there is Freddie!

Years later, Johnny Hanlon made a good living by smashing up clubs in Spain and being paid a fortune to stay away!

Albert Donoghue, who was a member of the Kray firm and turned supergrass long before Bertie Smalls (Smalls is now dead. Oh dear, never mind!), said some of the toughest people he ever dealt with were the Notting Hill mob!

So next time you think crime in London was just the East and North, think again. In fact, this may be the topic of my next book

... we shall see.

Respect has always been extremely important to me, so I asked both Alan and Joe if they minded me moving into West London. They didn't mind as long as I didn't poach any of their fighters, which I wouldn't do anyway. That would show a real lack of respect.

A few of my fighters had never put on a pair of gloves before, but some showed outstanding natural talent. Some didn't want to fight but some were rearing to go. Having your first fight in a packed Hammersmith Palais with all of London's underworld watching you takes some bottle. But I needed a face that was even remotely known to top the bill. In the end I went for Richy Horsley. He had not fought or trained for a long time, it was a gamble but Richy got straight into training and lost loads of weight. Then once the posters went up and I received a phone call from an Eastern European voice who wanted a meet about a corporate deal on tickets. It sounded suspicious so I took two lads with me.

The meeting was in a warehouse and I should have sussed it then but I wanted to sell tickets. We walked in to be met by about eight of them, they were not Russian but Croatian or something close. Some were big lumps but most were sinewy with crew cuts and all had a cold, vacant look in their eyes. They were obviously tooled up because they kept having sweeping feels past their pockets and were wearing big long overcoats in sweltering heat. But we weren't stupid and had a few 'toys' on us. One bloke, who reminded me of Ivan Drago from Rocky, said flatly: "The Palais, we want it."

I said, "What do you mean you want it ?"

"Boxing, we want it instead of you!"

I said: "Well, I would love to help but we have the Palais. There are lots of other venues in London. Perhaps I can help you find one?"

He replied sternly, "The Palais, it's ours, you English fuck off!"

Now I saw the red mist but tried to hold on to my temper ... not very well!

"Listen slag, London is my home town, the Palais is in my home town, the Palais is not fucking yours ... the Palais is ours. Try and take it and you start a gang war, understand!"

One of them put his hand in his pocket. Because we were all on edge, I had a claw hammer and a duster. Both hands were armed in seconds, my pals - we shall call them Pete and John had telescopic battens (like the police use) in their waistband under long summer shirts at the back. We were on them in seconds and absolutely battered them. Head, body, limbs we savaged the lot!

And Drago was shouting: "No more, no more you mad English!"

I was proud of my boys and the way they handled it. I am a patriot, very pro British but in no way a racist. It's about love for your country NOT colour; the footballer Ian Wright is a huge patriot. And being told that London was not mine but his flicked on my nutty switch!

I know people much tougher than me but once the switch is on I really would have to be killed to be stopped. Unlike some, I don't get off on violence and would rather business took place without it but it's not a nice world, it's full of tough, blood thirsty, ambitious nutters!

Now, I didn't know who we had straightened out or how many there are of them altogether ... I didn't know ANYTHING, which is worse than knowing there are hundreds!

All the posters were up for Warriors at the Palais, everyone wanted the Palais but they were not approaching the Palais, they were approaching me! We were only putting on a show every couple of months with an eye for one every month. Surely, there was room for everyone and I'm sure the Palais would be over the moon with all the business. But more than wanting the Palais, they wanted to show their strength in London by doing us. I don't think it would have mattered which venue we had taken, we were a new firm and perfect to bolster their power. If we had been forced to go round and cancel the show and take down all the posters what would we look like? And, of course, they would let everyone know it was them that slung the new London upstarts out. It was also for the English firms, to show others you don't do that in our capital! I wouldn't do it in Paris or Athens, why should they do it here?

Part of me thought that I may have sorted a problem, another part of me thought I may have started a gang war, I didn't know which. Steve Hough was dealing with the Palais and had nothing to do with the other side of it, he was not connected ... and he went from a man who never stopped laughing to suffering a breakdown within months!

I have also tried to keep these things from our 'Royalty' like Freddie Foreman, Charlie Richardson, Joey Pyle, Roy Shaw, Wilf Pine, Albert Chapman and other high ranking men of respect. You can't call for help in your first big outing, you would look a twat! I still try not to do that to this day ... although I will if need be!

The Police station in Hammersmith is bang next door to the Palais and they insisted on seeing the proposed guest list. The officers' jaws dropping was a picture and there was a tense 24 hours while Old Bill considered stopping the show from going ahead as they thought it was a big underworld reunion! Ha! That was pretty spot on as it goes!

A couple of drug dealers I had trouble with before were putting it about that they were going to ruin the show by planting drugs everywhere and calling Old Bill. They would also cause a riot when they got in. What sort of villain tries to get somebody else nicked? Total slags.

But they were so mouthy, I knew everything way in advance including the maisonette where they lived. Myself and three of my lads, went down there. We knew they had an intercom system. We also knew that if they had any brains, they would have a password for people to get in. An hour before, we sat outside the place in the motor and saw a bloke we all knew as a smack head go to the intercom, say something, and go in. You would know he was a junkie even if you hadn't come across him before. He was about seven stone, with eyes that indicated he actually died years ago but was still walking, his face was all bruised, his clothes didn't fit, his arms were covered to disguise needle marks and he was inspecting dog ends on the floor to see if they had any life in them. He was only in there about three minutes then came shuffling out. We drove up to him as if about to ask for directions, then myself and a pal threw him in the back. Christ, he stunk! I had dealt with junkies before but this guy smelt like King Kong's vomit and crap after a vindaloo!

So we got him to the nearest alleyway and chucked him down

there. I asked him the password on the intercom and he pretended he had no idea what we were on about, so I snapped one of his fingers and gave him a slap. He still wouldn't tell. So I smashed him in the face and broke his nose ... still nothing. Then it came to me, heroin is one of the best pain killers in the world, I doubt he could barely feel it. There was a much easier way. I told my pal to go through his pockets and take his gear, which he did. Now had his gear and he started kicking and crying like a baby and immediately screamed out the password: "Zenith! The password is Zenith, now please, please give me my medicine!"

So we drove back and were about to get out of the car when a child that could of been no older than ten years old buzzed and went up. In seconds this little kid was back down stuffing something into his tiny jeans. We all looked at each other in disgust, we were silent for a few seconds and I was very nearly sick. So, we walked up to this gaff and buzzed the intercom. "What?" said a voice.

"Zenith" I said trying to put on a bit of a junkie slow slur. Come up, they said. We knocked on the door of the upper floor masionette. We heard several chains being unlocked, then my pal kicked the door open knocking the bloke who opened it spark out with a lovely left hook on the way in!

There were six in there that we could see. We made quick work of five of them with surprise on our side battering them with batons and dusters and grabbed who I knew was the top man. I told him that it was all over London that he was going to ruin the unlicensed boxing at the Palais. Of course, he denied it. I gave him a clump and asked him again. "Not me!" he said again. So I stuck a stun gun in his neck and he jumped, twisted and turned like an Olympic gymnast!

I then told the boys to hold his hands on the table and I pulled out a claw hammer. CRUNCH went the bones as I brought the hammer down, he screamed like a stuffed pig and I gave him another blast of the stun gun. "Alright it was me but I was just larging it, I would never have done anything!"

I then put the stunner to his eyeball and said: "If as much as a poster falls off the wall that night, I will blame you." Then two of this filthy mob started coming round, a left hook to one and a right hook to the other and they went straight back to la la land. I so wanted to hurt this bastard after seeing the young age of some of his clients but I just smashed the hammer right on his nose which made a noise like walking on twigs in the woods and gave his ribs a going over. Then we left. Fight night was coming up fast.

16
WARRIORS

Thursday 17th July 2003 at a packed Hammersmith Palais (there was not a seat left) and it was time for 'WARRIORS 1'. Richy Horsley was top of the bill. I didn't sleep the night before. What if the ring doesn't arrive, etc? But all went well and I met a few of the fighters in the afternoon to show them round and let them get the feel of the place. With the ring set up, it really looked fantastic and all the fighters agreed. One remarked: "Christ, it's like Las Vegas!"

Most of the boxers had done well on their ticket sales, and instead of taking a much bigger cut of earnings like pro promoters I simply split it bang in half, nobody had done a 50/50 deal with the fighters before but I had more respect for them than that. Steve Hough and I had ridiculous expenses and honestly didn't make a bean but it was all worth it. I insisted Dave Courtney got 'a drink' because I asked him to do the auction. He said yes straight away and did the job only DC can. As far as I was concerned, he was working. It's not like the old days and there are no fighters big enough to fill an arena themselves like Roy and Lenny did. Most people I noticed as I was moving around, were watching the 'chaps' in the VIP area and not watching the fights. I stayed in the VIP area for short bursts to check the boys were OK. Although, they were literally leaning on a bar, a waitress was still assigned to look after Joey Pyle snr, Roy Shaw, Freddie Foreman and Charlie Richardson on the top table. Those boys don't need to move for anyone! They also drank free champagne all night and had the best seats. The entrance to the VIP area was guarded by our best but literally hundreds wanted to get in and meet the 'chaps'. One tried ducking under the rope and sprinting ... straight into my fist! He woke up on the high street.

The fights were good but we were still learning ... fast but we did well. But as I said, without Alan Mortlock, Steve Holdsworth and

Dave Courtney we would have been in real trouble. As I say, the fights were all OK but it was the spectacle that people couldn't believe. Lots of topless dancing girls in cages, pyrotechnics and a grudge match between two people from the crowd who hated each other and also couldn't fight! It was bloody funny and went down a treat. After a lot of booze as usual, the brainless started getting rowdy and a full can of beer hit a ring girl in the face!

It was a lump of a Londoner who I saw throw it and he said: "What the fuck are you going to do?" So I knocked him out and threw him through the back doors ... without opening them ... whoops a daisy!

Then to my horror, Steve Hough, who had never put a show on before, was having a go at Alan Mortlock who er had! It turned out that the two fighters in the ring had decided to do a lot of holding and not much punching and Steve who was running on pure nervous energy, had run over and blamed Al for stitching us up! Alan, who I have always listened to because there is a lot to learn, said to me: "Tel, get that bloke away from me before I do him. From now, I only speak to you Telboy OK?" I had never seen Alan get that angry, so I know he meant it.

I pulled Steve aside had a word and reminded him that he was in a different world now, with different rules and different commanders! I told him to apologise to Alan straight away, which he did, and told him: "Right, from now, I deal with Alan the man deserves respect you have just embarrassed me and he may never work with us again now."

I had tried all the way through the build up to teach Steve the codes and dos and don'ts with the 'chaps' but what I found to be natural, Steve found hard. He was from a very straight world and when not under pressure he was a lovely bloke. But all I needed was for Steve to get stressed again and do it to Roy Shaw or Freddie Foreman! Can you imagine?

My one regret was I really didn't have enough time for anyone and some people who were pals only got a: "Hi mate, got to go!" At this time, I used to wear a little knuckle duster around my neck on a chain that one of the boys had given me as a gift. Suddenly a pissed apparition stumbled in front of me and said: "You couldn't knock me down even with a real one!"

I was getting used to saying: "I know mate, you're right." But this big foot kept repeating it and not letting me past. So I finally said: "OK, let's try it." I pulled out a real one, slipped it on and just left jabbed him. He flew down the stairs straight into the ringside seats! I told the lads to throw him out. Feel free to clump him ... and most did!

The big event was now coming and I knew it wouldn't last long. Richy accompanied his ring walk with a thumping, blaring, 'We Will Rock You' by Queen. It was electric and brought the house down (almost literally!) and it set a great atmosphere. Richy's opponent, Tony Louis, I had obviously picked just to give him a warm up. I had seen Tony fight loads of times, Joe Smith had fought and beat him twice and I knew the strength of him. But as I say, I didn't really know what to expect because Richy hadn't been in the ring for years. I had told Richy before to work his body, he doesn't like body shots. So Richy moved around flicking out the jab, then near the ropes unloaded on the body. For this fight, I was near the back and I actually heard the thuds of the body shots sinking into Tony and after a few of these he collapsed in a heap. We had a private party upstairs where I sat with Joey Pyle, Freddie Foreman, Charlie Richardson, Roy Shaw, Bruce Reynolds, Tony Lambrianou, Dave Courtney and a few others and they all said it was a fantastic night. Joe described it as 'one of the classiest shows' he had seen. Considering he had seen them ALL, and that he was the Boss, that meant a lot to me because these guys don't give compliments if they don't mean it, just like they don't slag off unless they mean it.

One bloke started giving it large (he shouldn't of been there anyway!) and approached Joe. You don't do that unless you are 'one of ours' and even then, not in that manner. I stood up to take him out, when suddenly my pal Billy Smith (Joe's cousin) who is a hard man 'escorted' him through ... er I mean out the door. Before he threw him out he said: "You have no idea how dangerous those men are have you?" Billy hit the nail on the head with that one.

Joe put his arms around me, kissed me on both cheeks, and said: "I'm proud of you Telboy." That really made my night. Joe and the 'chaps' were escorted to their various limos etc and a few of us went on to a strip club. I went home and flopped on the bed and passed out. The next day, the phone was melting but every call was giving me a compliment on a great show. But I didn't feel right, I was actually depressed. After all that build up, I must have been on a comedown.

But we got straight into booking WARRIORS 2 for Thursday 16th October 2003. The Palais had only let us use the venue on a trial basis. If we showed we could handle the first one we could put on a second show, we got the green light and we were back into putting on another bigger, better show.

What we decided was to have more fights and less rounds -say, four or five rounds per fight. This would stop boredom and keep things moving faster. An unlicensed crowd want a punch up not 12 rounds of technical fighters cancelling each other out.

WARRIORS 2, in my opinion, was the best, brutal, most action packed show we ever did and we were told that by people who go to all of them on a regular basis. If I do say so myself, it couldn't get better than that. There was not one single weak fight, they were all crackers, and the crowd mostly stood up all the way through.

The first fight was Matty Leonard v Roman Tuerdan from Russia, Matty was one of Alan's boys and well known as a good boxer. Matty simply moved well and gave the Russian a boxing lesson. The guy had a go back but would run into three punch combinations. He was hit so often Steve Holdsworth stopped the fight in the second round after the Russian's eye was cut to pieces.

The second fight was my dear friend Andy 'Pit bull' Hunter against Simon Roberts. Andy was still a novice but I sparred with him and he punched like a bulldozer! Plus he was one of those awful things called a southpaw! This was a classic, Andy would whack Simon and Simon would whack Andy. It didn't stop, it was an absolute slug fest like when a trainer calls last ten seconds and you speed up to finish off, they fought the whole fight like this!

In the third, Andy opened up with big heavy handed bombs and Simon was counted out. Andy then did something that was more in keeping with respect and what the underworld hold dear, he faced Roy Shaw and Joey Pyle (the VIP area was right next to the ring but sealed off) and bowed twice to Roy and Joe, who raised their hands in mutual respect. At last, somebody understood the code and pecking order. Andy as I told you was overweight, diabetic and had never been in the ring until I took him on. Now, he was a big name.

Fight three was another one from our camp with a huge following called Steve O'mara. Steve stopped a Russian in three rounds. The noise from the crowd, even on the DVD is like an indoor rock concert, it's deafening and made the hairs on the back of your neck stand up. Next was Roy Shaw's son Gary who I thought was winning but Steve was in the ring and had a better view. A cut left eye didn't help and Errol Horsful, Gary's opponent took a slim points decision. Then it was Richy Horsley against Gary Marcell (the fight he accused me of losing for him) even though Richy admitted that he hadn't really trained, had had flu and barely lost, he still blamed me!

The fight itself was one of the best unlicensed fights I had ever seen. It was punch for punch, both men were desperate and had that 'you will have to kill me to beat me' look. It was toe to toe, slugging 'you hit me, have two back' and there was no let up. Richy had a nose bleed but was still throwing grenades. It could have gone either way. Richy went down briefly and got back up, then took a poleaxe that would have sparked out most people but Richy just took an eight count. It was a three rounder and Richy barely lost on points but it was still one of the best fights and displays of courage I have seen. It's worth getting the DVD just for this fight. Then Johnny Vaughan and Dave Courtney went through the charity auction for children.

Fight six was Paul Summerfield v 'The Beast from the East', another of ours.

It was another punch for punch three round smash up, with both men looking wobbly. The Beast was put on the deck in round two but just got up and carried on smashing away. I don't think I had seen a jab all night, every punch on that show was thrown to take their opponent's head off! The Beast was thumped from pillar to post and lost the decision in another three rounder. Everyone was naturally (and some unnaturally!) high as a kite, it was that sort of atmosphere.

My friend Liam from gangstervideos had put together a

montage of Roy Shaw's life and fights lasting about ten minutes. It came up on all the big screens and everyone was glued to it. Roy was called into the ring and I was nearly deafened. Roy was overcome by the reception. Obviously, this generation did not know how good the original 'Guv'nor' had been, they were open mouthed!

Chants of 'Roy, Roy, Roy, Roy' filled the Palais and I got in and gave him a hug. "Thanks Telboy, you're a diamond," he said.

"Roy, without you and Joe we wouldn't be here mate!" I then introduced Joey Pyle.

'Mad' Mickey Harrison, from our camp had a nice, slick win. He was also feared on the cobbles and had a fearless reputation. He and Joe Smith ended up outside on the green flicking punches at each other one day after a few drinks but it was getting more nasty, so the lads calmed them down and reminded them they were mates. So back in the pub for a session it was!

The final fight was 'Big' Steve Clark, another from our camp, against a Russian Champion. Steve was also a southpaw and smashed his man all over the ring and back, Steve Hough and I were leaning on the canvas as the Russian got a proper beating and was knocked out in round two.

It was an amazing night. It was hugs and shaking hands all round but things were already turning sour. There was a member at the gym and we let him train the boys, while Steve Hough and I went out looking for fighters and doing the business. But this guy had created a split. He gave the fighters the idea that he did all the work and I especially took all the credit. Neither this guty nor any of these fighters apart from Andy Hunter were gym members when we started, they all joined way down the line.

When I started, I begged the top bosses for gloves, then a heavy bag, then a speedball etc etc, until it was a fully usable boxing gym. Three times a week, I would train people in my own brand of boxercise. By now we spent three minutes on the heavy bag, then top and bottom ball, then pads, then skipping, then floor work and, if it was only the hardcore guys, some sparring. I had built it up from an unused gym to a boxing gym with packed classes in no time, the members loved it. We were going a year before Steve O'mara, Steve Clark and these other guys came along.

When they were onboard, I was working on the show. But because they were not there at the start, when it was an empty hall, they took the side of the guy training them and would go barmy when my name appeared on the videos because I was a ponce that hadn't done anything!

I built that fucking gym! From a shit pot spare hall to a fully fledged gym with classes, then a stable of boxers put onto the unlicensed circuit. That's not bad by anyone's standard but that's not what was being fed. It was my baby, my little gym, it was all in place when they joined but I didn't know this 'why is he on the video' rubbish was going on. If they had done their homework and asked someone like Andy Hunter, they may have got the truth. From then on, WARRIORS was doomed because the poor trainer was not getting his fair share of exposure. In fact, he was from another country and he told me he wanted NO exposure ... there was a good reason for it, it doesn't take much working out!

When I left to do other things that I wanted to do (I was bored with all the politics by then anyway), I think they tried to continue on their own but Alan Mortlock would have nothing to do with them, and really it was the chance of meeting a REAL London Gangster that sold tickets and who was the one that filled the VIP area with known underworld legends ... me!

I got the 'chaps' there and put it on the posters. The only one who kept going was Dave Courtney but the days of meeting a Richardson or Freddie Foreman were gone and I was on to other things as the fight nights collapsed - all because of ego!

I can assure you, if it were not for me and Steve Hough there would not of been a WARRIORS 1 and that is a fact! I couldn't have done it on my own, but I didn't need fresh gym members to do it, I had Alan Mortlock, Joey Pyle jnr and others, not to mention Joey snr and Roy Shaw and they were not people I had just rung up, they were the most respected villains in Britain who were close friends. I was OK for connections thanks, still am. So if you want to know what happened to WARRIORS ... that was it. If my heart was still in the game, I would have just invested in another gym and got another venue and taken the 'chaps' there!

I have no regrets and would not change it. There were still two WARRIORS shows to come but I was by now getting into heavier things.

17
DEBTS!

By this point, I was getting a reputation. Most people still saw me as Roy Shaw's right hand man but I was doing other things as well. I was getting inundated by people who had been ripped off and wanted their money back, which I can understand, but most were from blokes who had been ripped off by another bloke. 'You're a man, go get it yourself', was my thinking. Besides, I was a boxing promoter, not a hired thug!

It was only when I started getting messages from women or old people who had been conned down to their last penny that I felt morally in the right to help these folk against scumbag bullies. These people either didn't trust the police to do anything or were scared that when the bully got a knock from Old Bill he would really turn the screw.

One such incident happened when a young woman on a council estate was being threatened by smack heads. She was told: "Pay us or you will be badly hurt!" And to show they meant it, they cut her face! All for a poxy £200 a week! That's smack addicts for you. At first, I was dubious and a bit paranoid that it was either a rival firm wanting my unlicensed set up again or a police set up. After what had happened to Joey Pyle, Charlie Kray, Kevin Lane and Ian McAteer, plus the constant hounding of Dave Courtney over the years (more on those later), I was in two minds to say the least. But in the end, the thought of it, if it was real was driving me nuts!

Me and a few of the boys went to the flat in Shepherds Bush and knocked on the door. We were greeted by a nervous wreck of a woman in about her mid 30s, no more than eight stone and with a fresh scar down her left cheek (which my instinct told me whoever had done it was right handed, but I could have been wrong). She curled up tight on her sofa and proceeded to tell us about these bastards. We made sure we wore a fresh white shirt, suit, tie and boots so we looked nothing like drug scum. We also had a look about us, different from police. A few kind words and taking care not to step into her private space and she gradually told us that these 'men' had been coming round every week for a month. She thought it was a one off but now she was at her wits end. She shook like a leaf but began to calm down and even laugh after a while. At last someone was going to help her.

This job was actually a lot easier than we thought (as is often the case but the easy looking ones can get out of hand fast!). They lived on the same estate, she knew the number and said there were about five of them and that they were violent ha ha!

We were all so wound up now, It didn't matter who they were. Problem was, for 200 quid a week, we could hardly tax her, so we went to teach them a lesson instead. As usual with smack heads, they get sloppy. Coke heads are much more alive, paranoid in fact. We just waited round the corner for a customer to go in or out. They are so laid back, they don't even look, where a coke head would be bouncing off the walls completely paranoid!

As one bloke stumbled out, we threw him out the way (in fact he nearly went over the balcony!). I had never seen so much money! We couldn't see the wood on the massive table because it was covered in notes ... well, that sorted out the doing it for nothing bit!

Then our pal (I shall call him Mick) disappeared back down to the car and returned with a jerry can of petrol and matches. "What the hell are you doing?" I said.

"I'm hungry, I fancy some Kentucky fried smack head!"

"For Christ's sake," I said, pushing him back out the door and back to the car! But the bullies had seen what they were up against and were warned that if they bullied that lady, or in fact anyone apart from their regulars, again they would be served in a bap! The bulling stopped on that estate, but as it is the way these days, if we had been caught we would have been the bullies and ended up in nick! Great system isn't it?

The debt collecting got heavier and heavier and I was now doing jobs for real top 'faces'. And the violence just felt normal now. But I wanted to be more like Alex Steen or Alan Mortlock not 'Mad' Frankie Fraser, I wanted to be a fight promoter. But I didn't anticipate all these mainly foreigners trying to take over Hammersmith, and if the Palais had known, they would have banned the boxing.

Anyway, for now at least, we had cleared the way for ourselves apart from the back stabbing going on in camp and just to think, when I was Gym manager I begged the Club Manager for some money for boxing gear because we had nothing. He was for it and the directors agreed and the next manager was with me as well. Rob Thurston and Phil Michelle were bloody good managers and we started that gym and they were good men (if it sounds like I'm sore about the lies and backstabbing ... I am!). I still remember going through boxing catalogues with Rob and Phil, buying boxing gear for the derelict gym and with no regard for budget. They were GREAT days! I wish Phil Michelle and Rob Thurston all the luck in the world.

WARRIORS 3 was set for Thursday 11th December 2003, at the Palais of course. At the time the big Saturday night prime time show was called *Gladiators* with Ulrika Johnson presenting the show, it was massive!

So we pulled off a coup when one of the most famous Gladiators Mark Smith - otherwise known as Rhino agreed to top the bill. This was his first fight and that brings problems ... you have no idea what you are up against! There are no videos and no witnesses to find out the strength of them.

On this basis, I didn't want Rhino fighting our mate Andy 'Pit bull' Hunter but I was out-voted. I had trained Andy for a lot longer than his previous trainer and knew more about what he could and could not do ... One thing Andy couldn't do was change styles. They tried to make him fight right handed (orthodox) instead of his usual, unbeaten southpaw style, but all he did was get caught square on when he tried to change. Rhino had muscle but could he punch? Most muscle men can't! But Rhino could and he could box. And he had the advantage, he had a few videos on Andy to study, Andy had nothing. Anyone with a boxing brain could have seen that ... but they didn't have boxing brains!

On this show I worked with Joey Pyle, Joey Pyle jnr and Rickey English and they all had doubts because they understood boxing. Suddenly the people I taught to stand in a basic fight stance were all experts and me, Joe snr and jnr and Rickey were all novices!

I sat next to Dave Courtney and said: "I feel really guilty Dave, because this is going to last a few seconds!"

"I think you're right Tel," said Dave, and it did. Andy was knocked out in no time. He was on his back with 'Mad' Mickey Harrison taking his gum shield out. Andy said he was hit by 'the hardest punches I have ever felt!' But he still gave his now famous bow of respect to Roy and Joe. I bought Andy into the VIP area after to meet his heroes Roy and Joe also Tony Lambrianou, Freddie Foreman and the other 'chaps'. He just kept apologising but the 'chaps' told him how brave he had been throughout all his fights ... and it was true!

Two of our boys had previously had great fights. 'Gypsy' Joe Smith fought Tony Louis twice and flattened him twice, once at York Hall and once at Milton Keynes. Joe also ripped a Russian to pieces at York Hall and so did Andy, despite suffering a broken nose in the first round, Andy stopped him in three so we knew he had plenty of courage.

At WARRIORS 3, women were not aloud in the changing rooms for obvious reasons, but I let Andy's partner in because I felt so guilty. She was very concerned and a lovely lady.

Rickey and the ever respected Pyle family did a cracking job on the night, just as Alan Mortlock and Terry Sabini had done on the first shows. By being respectful and checking it was OK with them to put the shows on, I got the best consultants in the land and, although we were close before, we were real close friends now! I made a great, close lasting friendship with another man I already knew but welded it for life, my brother in arms Mitch Pyle. Like his father Joe Pyle, I have never heard a bad word spoken against Mitch, and when there was a do on, myself, Carlton Leach and Mitch would always end up together. We have the same humour and cracked each other up. I will ALWAYS be there for the Pyle family ... and I hope they know it!

Mixed martial arts and all-in fighting which includes grappling, boxing, locks and holds was making a huge impression as well now. This was pioneered by bodies like the MMA and led by well respected fight expert and businessman Andy Jardine. Andy's first, middle and last concerns seemed to be for the safety of his fighters. Andy made it clear to some of the more 'enthusiastic' fighters on his shows that if they disobeyed the safety rules stipulated, that living the rest of their lives knowing they had put somebody in a wheelchair would not be easy. They soon lost the cocky swagger!

There were other fights on WARRIORS 3 of course and we repeated the Roy Show 'Legend' video on all the screens big and small. The funny thing was, once we had shown Shawey at his most aggressive against Adams, Mullins etc, the fights that followed became more brutal and people started stamping on each other on the floor and becoming all round more violent. It's like they suddenly thought 'Oh, THAT'S unlicensed!'

We had regulars like Brian Nicholls, 'Big' Steve Clarke and Bobby Samples but people had paid their money to see a real life Gladiator and Rhino had trained and didn't disappoint. But to me, WARRIORS 2 was the pinnacle and it was going to be hard to beat. We also wanted Joe Smith, who all the promoters considered the best fighter on the circuit, to fight but nobody would fight him, not even the 'Champions'. We decided the best fighter of the show would also take home the 'Roy Shaw' belt and Roy would present it. It was a real championship belt and looked the business. WARRIORS 3 was over but between shows, I found myself getting extremely violent and not caring.

Sometimes on the orders of the underworld elite and I would kick money upstairs as a 'tribute', sometimes I would find my own name was now enough and I was retrieving big money back for people. I was hurting people badly with no feeling. There were loads of other rackets I was getting into, all heavy duty. I was drifting away from being a promoter and trainer and becoming a gangster. Although, I honestly never got into the drug scene, I swear I just never wanted it. Unfortunately, 90% of naughty stuff now is drugs related and the class, morals and codes I always admired in my more mature friends/heroes do not exist in drugs. The old guard, men like Eddie Richardson and Tommy Wisbey had gone down for it, Charlie Wilson had been shot dead for it and Charlie Kray and Joey Pyle had been stitched up over it but I was not going down for it. What I needed was an event I believed in ... and I had the answer!

18
WARRIORS 4

For years, I had felt strongly about the treatment, or rather abuse, the system was dishing out to Charlie Bronson and Ronnie Biggs. I decided to put on an unlicensed boxing show first for Bronson on Thursday 26th February 2004 again, at The Palais. I would do something big for Biggsy after, something different, because boxing went more hand in hand with Bronson than Ronnie Biggs but it was perfect for Charlie.

We had our usual selection of fighters. We were no longer stumbling in the dark, we were solid on our feet and knew what we were doing. A while before, Charlie made a meet between myself and a man I grew to love, one of those people you think you have known for 20 years. His name was Harry Marsden, one of the original 'Geordie Mafia' and Steve Hough and I met him in a pub in North London. We exchanged gifts and just clicked, I trusted him straight away. We would speak on the phone about four times a week, every week after that. Again, I had a video tribute made up with a musical background called *Why?*

The question being of course 'why was he still in a cage?' it was a very powerful piece. I made sure Eira, Charlie's beloved Mum and cousin Lorraine and husband Andy had a table at the front of the VIP area, They were mobbed by the public and chaps alike, and I like to think I spoiled them rotten with free champagne brought to their tables. I had my motivation back, and was 100% into being a boxing promoter again. The fighters all wore 'free Charlie' T-shirts on the way to the ring.

During WARRIORS 3, something had been worrying me. My friend Tony Lambrianou had always been impeccable, he always wore lovely suits, had polished shoes, and was clean shaven with immaculate hair. Unless we were doing something casual during the day, Tony always looked like this. He was a class act. But during WARRIORS 3, he wore jeans, a brown jacket and his face was grey and sallow, his eyes sunken, he even had a fag in his ear. With most people, I wouldn't even notice but with Tony it was different. I wonder how many other people noticed it? To me, it really stood out on the video of the show shot as ever by all our great friends Liam and Yvette. Tony was the youngest of the Kray mob and the most handsome, he had kept his looks until that time. Perhaps he was just a bit under the weather?

It was fight night, and not far into my journey the mobile rang, it was Roy Shaw: "Telboy, have you heard the news about Tony Lambrianou?"

"What news Roy?"

"He's dead!" This was impossible, I had spoken to him a few days before to check he was coming, Tony was a big attraction.

"But how Roy, what happened?"

"He was gardening, went for a nap and never woke up again, it was a heart attack!" I very nearly hit a tree. I said goodbye to Roy and phoned The Palais. I was told that when Ricky English heard the news, his legs buckled and he had to be held up. He like me, was in total shock!

I thought about all those years, with weapons, guns, knives, dusters, gang wars and 15 years in maximum security prisons ... and he dies gardening!

It was Ricky who said when I got there: "We should have a minute's silence."

I was in a daze of shock, as I put out the top name labels on the top tables - Joey Pyle, Roy Shaw, Freddie Foreman, Charlie Richardson ... and Tony Lambrianou. I still have that label today. This was actually going to be the best guest line up so far. Apart from those mentioned we had confirmed all of Charlie's family, Dave Courtney, as usual performing magic, Johnny Nash, Alan Minter, Goldie, John Conteh, Charlie Breaker, Harry Marsden, Johnny Vaughan, Carlton Leach, Jimmy and Wally Stockin, Joe Smith and Johnny Frankham, Cass Pennant, Wilf Pine, Bruce Reynolds and Johnny Jacket ... a very handy friend of Dave's. It was quite a line up.

As the guests arrived, they still didn't know about Tony, except for Harry who I had rang ahead to tell the others who were all in a pub down the road. As they arrived, I can just imagine their faces changing from smiles to disbelief. As I have said, a lot of people had paid to see the Gangsters of legend. They would turn their backs on every fight just to watch the VIP area, spot someone and maybe even get a photo and autograph! Of course, some people won't understand that but the 'chaps' pulled in the crowds ... like it or not!

This really was Tony's domain. Making people feel special, like they knew him, chatting to them, then putting his arm around them for a photo (and ALWAYS accept a drink in return! Ha!). Joe and Roy were great at this as well, others were more aloof but this was Tony's manor he was like front of house manager. Carlton has never been comfortable in the limelight and when I called his name, he had found a dark corner and refused to come out ... ooops!

It was a bizarre atmosphere. It was Bronson's night but a pal of everyone had just died. Ricky English played it perfectly. We announced the news about Tony and the bell denoted a two minutes silence, after which time the bell rang again and there was a standing, roaring, round of applause, not for a gangster, not for a Kray member, but Tony ... a gentleman we all loved. Then, we rolled straight onto Bronson and the first fight. I really don't think there was another way of doing it and it worked.

Before I go on about WARRIORS 4 and Charlie Bronson, I would like to say a bit about the Lambrianou family and, in particular, Tony and Chris who were there that terrible night Jack 'The Hat' Mcvitie was killed, as was Ray Mills and Ronnie Bender. That's four people I know who were present at one of the most infamous Gangland slayings in British history. 'Good for you!' you may say but the point is, the Lambrianou's along, with the others, have had some terribly unjust abuse thrown at them over they years, for what? Doing 15 years for other people's murder? In which time, they watched half their family die. Yes, they took the body in the car over the water and no they should not have dumped it near Freddie Foreman's place, but ask yourself, what would you do?

Reggie stepped over Jack's body and said: "Get rid of that Tony." Do they leave it there and get everyone nicked including the twins? And Ronnie in his mentally ill state had gone on about the Richardsons being deadly enemies. South London was also the Richardsons' patch so it seemed a good plan. Little did they know, that most of this Richardson 'war' was in Ron's brain and they would later all become friends. Also, the car was out of petrol so it wasn't going anywhere else anyway. They're lucky they didn't leave it to Ronnie Hart and Jack Dickson. It would have been parked in Vallance Road!

All those witnesses, no warning. They could have just left the body there, but they decided to shift the evidence and clear up. Of course, I can see why Freddie was pissed off but Fred was a real pro and had an instinct for what to do in these situations, the 26 year old Tony didn't. Let's face it, there is nobody to blame but the twins. Ronnie's 'dancing boys' Trevor and Terry witnessed it as well.

Alan Mills, turned Queen's evidence and joined the prosecution as did Hart, Donoghue, Dickson and most of the rest. The Lambrianou's stood with the twins and drew 15 years for attending a party that Chris didn't even want to go to! Imagine, you reluctantly go to a party, a man is butchered and you are left to deal with it. You end up serving 15 years mostly, in category A as a high risk prisoner, and still get called a grass! What chance is there?

Chris asked the twins for help and was refused, they were not even allowed to change solicitors. They had all been sentenced anyway, The twins weren't going anywhere but the others had a chance, they had killed nobody. The twins could have said: "He wasn't there, we did it." In fact, Ronnie Hart pinned Jack's arms back so Reg could stab him.

It was Hart that shouted "Do him Reg!" Ronnie remained silent but had opened proceedings by smashing a sherry glass under Jack's eye. But Hart rolled over and blamed everyone else. The ones who had done the worst deeds were lining up to say 'it was him Sir' and one of the Barry brothers actually brought a gun from the Regency Club to 97 Evering Road ... What did he get?

Chris only got sentenced at all because he wouldn't talk. If he had done a Ronnie Hart, he would have walked. 'Nipper' Read said: "This is your last chance," and when Chris didn't say anything, Read pistol whipped Tony about the head so he hardly had concrete evidence did he?

So, with no future, Tony, Chris, Bender and the dancing boys told everyone what was already old news and the whole world knew anyway and wrote it down for the appeal. I have asked the top names of the time whether that made those men grasses or not and to a man they all said: "Of course not, not on appeal. At the trial yes but not on appeal." One of the names that confirmed this was 'Mad' Frankie Fraser and he has called a lot of people a grass, he is a purist but even he said "No".

Ronnie and Reggie went on to write that Chris, Tony and Ronnie Bender were 'grasses and lackeys', a grass that does 15 years? A lackey that gets rid of a body killed in front of a room full of people? How?

Chris was not one for the parties like Tony was, and I speak to him with just a few select friends. Myself, Chris and Andy George spent the day and night at Charlie Richardson's twice recently. Charlie is very private and I don't think he would have welcomed a 'grass' do you? The truth is, the twins could have got them all off but thought, 'No, if we are going down, you're going!' Charlie Richardson and Johnny Nash didn't treat their men like that, like dogs.

When my Dad died this year, and when I was on life support in intensive care, who was there for the family? Chris and Helen Lambrianou and Charlie and Ronnie (Veronica) Richardson. After the Kray trial, the supergrass explosion erupted. Why? Maybe people started thinking 'If I'm going to do 15 years and STILL get called a grass, what's the point?' I wouldn't do it, but it makes sense doesn't it? The same as giving the Great Train Robbers 30 years for an unarmed robbery. People thought, 'hang on, they can't give you more than 30 anyway, what's the point of not taking a shooter and increasing our chances?'

Overnight, after the Train Robbery sentences, the law invented armed robbery! Everyone took guns out then. This theory is confirmed by Freddie Foreman, well it's obvious isn't it?

I really had a burning feeling that Charlie Bronson should be not freed straight away, but allowed on the wings to prove he was not the animal the media had made him out to be. The point of this show was awareness. I still can't believe that people make their minds up without knowing all the facts. To me, opinions should be earned and earned through knowledge, only once you have done your research, do you have the right to opinion but those with the least knowledge talk loudest. As I have said, empty vessels seem to make the most noise!

So many opinions of Bronson had been fired about from sensitive poet to wild, caged animal. I visited Charlie on my own for the first few visits and that gave us a personal, relaxed relationship. I would get the train from Kings Cross to Wakefield, which took about two hours for a two hour visit, but this would be reduced to about an hour and a half after all the hold ups and checks involved in getting into the prison within a prison. I could write a whole book on Charlie, he is an intellectual and a very complicated man. I had become close to all of Charlie's family and would ring his mother once a week or so.

Wakefield is known as 'Monster Mansion'. Huntley, Whitting, Victor Miller and all the monsters were in there and they were all on open visits whilst Charlie was on closed visits, I could only shake his hand through bars. Before a visit, I would go to the cafe and get Charlie's treats; chocolates, crisps and his flask. Behind the cafe was the nonces' visiting room, all open and get this ... a children's play centre at the back of the visiting area! Now, that's true! How sick is that?

On one occasion, I had the mind to look behind me and there with two girls was Ian Huntley. I asked the lady behind the counter to fill the flask with piping hot tea. The idea was to throw it in the rotten slag's face! But the lady must have come across this before as she said in a broad knowing Yorkshire accent: "Don't bother son, they will just put more on Charlie." It was obviously an old trick, but I so would have liked to have heard him scream!

Walking across the open concrete courtyard I heard Charlie shouting: "Ere, Tel. I bet they don't make that slag Huntley wait all that time for his visitors!"

Then a voice shouted out "Hello mate!" It was Robert Maudsley, the cannibal killer who had opened a con's head like a boiled egg then scooped out the brains like a yoke! In fact, I think he killed a couple of people in similar fashion.

Charlie and I hardly talked about violence, it was mostly poetry, art and the prison system. He told me how Huntley had a birthday party and screamed when he never got his favourite sweeties ... a screw went out and got some! Even the screws told me they didn't know why Charlie was in there. A man who had never killed, never raped, never pulled off a big heist was rotting away in 'Monster Mansion' with a life sentence for taking a teacher hostage but was released unhurt. Charlie had encountered constant physical and mental torture and the public needed to know, hence the shows that were put on.

After the first visits on my own, I visited a couple of times with my late pal Harry Marsden. Harry had in fact been in prison with a lot of 'faces' but never saw them because he was always down the chokey (punishment block). Once after Harry had been beaten black and blue and was still throwing punches, one screw said to the other "We have a mini Roy Shaw here." At the time Harry had never met Roy but his reputation was so violent and so well known Harry had earned that reputation and was extremely proud of it. He felt great glee reciting the story when I introduced him to the real Roy Shaw. Harry was shocked when he did eventually meet Roy that he wasn't nine foot tall and 30 stone of muscle! People often see photos of Lenny McLean first, then see Roy and can't believe Roy beat him!

The big screen played Charlie talking about freedom with music behind, it was extremely powerful and I held Charlie Bronson's mum's hand, Eira, all the way through it. There was then about three solid minutes of 'free Charlie', 'free Charlie', the atmosphere was spine tingling. Johnny Vaughan and Dave Courtney did a joint auction and were a hilarious double act that had the crowd in fits. Dave showed he really can get on stage with anyone and stand his ground. Some of the money went towards Charlie Bronson's legal fees but as usual, the rest went to children's charities and that still makes me extremely proud and I'm talking a good few grand!

Most of the money was raised by Charlie Bronson's artwork. We would get people to bid, take the details of the highest bidder, then Charlie would design one of his 'specials', personalised to the highest bidder with their name and details on. It was a great prize and Charlie has raised God knows how much for children with his art.

The fighters at WARRIORS 4 put on a bloody and brave show that entertained the crowd, Brian Nicholls, Steve Clarke, Gary Firby, Dean Turmiotto, Gary Shaw and Dean Hodgson were among the boxers but we were all bonded by the mistreatment of Bronson and death of Tony. It was a strange atmosphere because Tony was gone. The first man since the Krays had fallen, but the Krays were not a part of the little family obviously because they were in nick. Tony was the first of those who used to ring or be rung to see if he was coming to a do, it was strange for all of us and a bloody big hole had opened up.

That day, Joe Smith and I had lost another friend called Ray, who had died of meningitis. Ray was dodgy, he won't mind me saying that. He was into everything and was what this country is not producing anymore ... a REAL Character! There was a pub at the end of the road called The Rowan Arms but it was still known by it's previous name The Cat and Fiddle. That was a rough pub, you needed an invite to walk in there! Ray had been stabbed, shot, beaten with pool cues and, on one occasion, was literally set alight. The boys in there actually put him out because he was a human fireball!

But believe it or not, everyone loved him. And those who hurt him were always avenged. One day, after he took a beating, the pub of a rival 'firm' we suspected was blown up! It was a shit hole where only dealers and rascals would go and checks were made that women and children were not in there first, we were quite a moral 'firm' really when I think about it. But violence seemed to follow Ray and he really didn't give a shit

I think that's why he was loved. He was barred about three times a week from the pub and it was a rough pub! This is where Joe Smith and 'Mad' Mickey Harrison had their nose to nose. It may have cleaned up now, but our boys were the only ones who went in there ... It had to be the worst pub in West London ha!

I did the put pool balls into a sock, tie the end and smash someone's head in trick, and their head actually bent in! Then my pal broke his legs. It was one of those pubs, where every head would turn when you walked in. You sat facing the door and it was a real violent pub but we loved it and it was only a mile from my boxing gym. Some tasty people drank in there, some real tasty people! I certainly was not the tastiest. Not in my eyes anyway. Real cobble fights took place all the time round the back with a decent fair play man. Then, it was back in the pub for a drink with each other, just like the old days. No stabbing in the back (literally!) or any of that rubbish. But when Ray was set on fire, that was taking the piss and vengeance was ours. Ray was the life, soul and spirit of that pub and that area. He wasn't a fighter but he wouldn't back down either and 'Mad' Mickey was his closest friend so he was alright. I still miss him today, he was ringside at every show and would dive in to help us out although he was about seven stone.

Yep, Ray was a legend. Now, you don't seem to get characters or eccentrics, they are dying off and when I say characters, I don't mean big mouth bullies, people who can't take their drink or trouble makers the 'Did you spill my pint?' mob, I'm not talking about them. I mean people who make you see the world differently and you have to tell them to shut up for a second because they are making you laugh so hard!

The problem was, Ray was being cremated on the same day as Tony Lambrianou's funeral. I had already been asked to do security at Tony's East End funeral. So Jimmy, Wally Stockin and I went to Tony's funeral and Joe and Billy Smith and the others from the pub went to Ray's cremation. That area has never been the same since Ray went. Rest in peace mate.

19
GOODBYE TONY!

So, the last accessible link to the Kray firm was dead. The remainder of the 'firm' do not hang around anymore or come to the boxing shows. They all lead private lives and a lot of them would not be welcome anyway. Freddie Foreman is still around, of course, but Fred was never a member of the Kray firm, in fact he was bigger than them. Chris Lambrianou and I still have our days out, like visiting Charlie and Ronnie (Veronica) Richardson with our great friend Andy George ... a REAL diamond who runs a top security firm. Ronnie Bender died about four years ago and had a very low key funeral. Billy Frost, the twins' driver, who vanished in the 1960s and was strongly believed to have been killed by the Krays, reappeared a couple of years ago and has been on documentaries and included in books about the twins. 'Frosty' is spoken of highly. The twins' cousin Ronnie Hart buggered off to Australia where he tried to kill himself but failed, and has since died. 'Mad' Teddy Smith remains a mystery. He has been missing since the '60s. According to the first 'supergrass' Albert Donoghue, who gave evidence against the Krays, they 'dropped Teddy off for a piss just behind the twins' house in Vallance Road and he was never seen again'.

Others like Connie Whitehead are doing their own thing, the rest were never on the 'firm' in the first place because I have met at least 500 people who swear they were on the Kray Firm!

So Tony was really the last member of the Kray gang that you could actually meet. Tony lived for three things; his partner Wendy, the 'chaps' and parties - that was Tony's life - and who knows how much damage the parties did because he never went half way, Tony was all or nothing, usually all. If you knew Chris but didn't know Tony and vice versa, you might assume you had an idea what the brother was like but the opposite is true. I have never known two brothers so completely different. Chris and Tony are two completely different people in every way.

Tony's funeral was huge, a real East End gangland send off and I think Tony would have loved it. The whole of Bethnal Green was rammed with people, it was like a full scale invasion. I suppose those who didn't know him all had different reasons for turning up. I was saying goodbye to a friend but I think some people wanted to see, and shake hands with, the underworld legends because they were mobbed and, apart from 'Mad' Frankie Fraser, all the legends were there. I went to say goodbye to Tony in his open coffin in the tiny Chapel of Rest which had been used for the funerals of Ronnie, Reggie and Charlie Kray, as well as Lenny McLean, and now Tony.

Tony looked impeccable again in a suit and seemed to be at peace. I slipped a photo of Tony, his brother Jimmy, Freddie Foreman and me into the coffin, kissed his forehead, said goodbye and left. I picked that photo because, although he never said it, I think of all the 'chaps', Freddie Foreman was the man he most looked up too, I'm pretty sure of that. I would go as far too say that Freddie was his hero and was who he wanted to be. Let's be honest, Tony was well respected but he wasn't as high up the respect tree as Freddie, Charlie Richardson, Wilf Pine or Joey Pyle snr.

Tony's strength was his charm, he was rare because, like I said about my pal Ray, Tony was a character and a bit of an eccentric. He could disarm you with a smile and put you off guard with his manner. The proof of his popularity was the number of people that packed into Bethnal Green that crisp, cold day. From the Chapel of Rest, I got in a car with Johnny Nash to the church to help with security.

Something Tony said in a TV interview kept going through my mind like a mantra, until Johnny Nash's raised voice having a go at someone for not wearing black pulled me out of it ... then all I could think of was 'Thank Christ I wore black!' Tony had said: "Remember, we weren't good men ... BUT we weren't bad, evil men either."

The procession went from the Chapel of Rest, down Bethnal

Green road, left at Vallance Road and where the old Kray (Fort Vallance) house used to be. Then up Chesire Street where Freddie Foreman killed Tommy (Ginger) Marks and unfortunately missed Jimmy Evans, and past the Krays' pub The Carpenters Arms and on to Saint Matthews church, which had seen the funerals of all three Kray brothers.

St Matthews Church was so full of people, they were crammed down the aisles as 'I will always love you' and 'If you don't know me by now' were played. A couple of people tried getting in who were nobodies but we sussed them and threw them out. That's why the police can't do that job, they wouldn't know who to let in and who not to. We then sped our way through a packed East End to Southgate Cemetery for the burial. The place was completely covered in flowers and the graveside packed with 'faces'.

Afterwards, Roy Shaw, Ray Mills, Alfie Hutchinson and myself went back to former boxer Charlie Magri's pub in the East End. The pub was also rammed but I found a quiet corner with Freddie Foreman and Charlie Richardson. Frankie Fraser had not turned up, probably because Freddie Foreman had a fight with him a year or so before in a cafe near Fred's house and given Frank a beating. Frank had slagged Fred off badly in a bizarre book called *Mad Frank's Diary* but had said nothing to Fred and decided to put it in a book instead. (Not exactly an underworld method. He did the same on his website to Dave Courtney.) Only on picking the book up on the way to Spain did Fred find out what Frank was saying. He was pretty much calling Fred a grass! Very dangerous talk indeed. This underworld business was getting stranger. Imagine if the St Valentine's Day massacre had consisted of Al Capone sending Bugs Moran a rather naughty letter! Look out for the forthcoming 'Text message war!'

Anyway, Frank is no longer out and about with the 'chaps'. It's a shame, a lot of people respected Frank but you simply can't say those things! If so, pull the bloke aside and do it in private. It would have to be said, the lads came down on Fred's side. One 'face' told me: "The problem is, Frank thought when the twins died, he would be number one. But then Courtney and others became more famous and Frank couldn't take it."

Another VERY strong theory is that Marilyn Wisbey, Frank's

partner had gone off and had a sexual affair with one of Dave Courtney's doorman. Frank found out and that's when the real anti Courtney campaign started - on Frank's keyboard. It's a real shame the way Frank attacked Fred, as most people had great respect for Frank before that. Harry Marsden once said: "The Police must love us, all we do is row and fight amongst ourselves!"

Tony's funeral was spectacular and the turn out incredible, the family must have been proud. I spoke to Chris at the pub and he was overwhelmed with the amount of people that turned up. A few people have had a pop at Tony for having 'Kray Gang Boss' on the cover of his book. But the point is to sell books and he certainly did that. Charlie Richardson once told me (and before that Lenny McLean) to "write for the man at the bus stop, NOT the 'Chaps." Good advice, but I find a sort of satisfaction in writing the truth, it's like therapy ha!

You only have my word, but this book is 100% true. Trust me, I have a good imagination and could have written about the bloke I killed or the rival gang boss I had shot and then given to a dodgy undertaker ... but that would make me a liar!

To be fair, publishers tend to write what they want on the cover. The comment on the front of Carlton's book is not the way Carlton talks, it's nothing like Carlton and I bet Tony never once called himself a 'Kray Gang Boss'. The book I wrote with Charlie Bronson was called *Heroes and Villains* but we never once called it that, we called it *The Good, The Bad, The Mad and The Ugly* which we both liked, but the publisher preferred *Heroes and Villains*.

So the 'Kray Gang Boss' bit is designed to sell books. Tony never swaggered about and introduced himself as a Kray gang boss! Ronnie, and to a lesser extent Reggie, were the ONLY Kray Gang Bosses and everybody knows it. In fact, I thought Tony's book was a fantastic read. I couldn't put it down.

Tony Lambrianou made a lot of people happy, feel special even. It's hard to tell a Tony story, especially when it comes to money, with his bank card that wouldn't go in the cashpoint ('lend us 50 quid, you know you will get it back'). You have to be a certain type of person to get away with that and not get clumped but with Tony you would laugh and say 'he's at it again'.

But I do remember a serious conversation with Tony. It was at

Joey Pyle's book launch in the West End. Tony warned me that my temper and violence was getting out of control. He warned me I was getting more and more vicious, I was getting more heavily involved in gang stuff and was a whisker away from prison. He was right but at the time I couldn't even see, it which is often the case. I didn't listen at the time but his words never left me.

Wendy Lambrianou, Tony's partner was completely devastated and everyone tried to comfort her, but what can you do in a situation like that. Words don't heal only time does that but I'm glad to say the last time I saw Wendy she was the pretty, bubbly lady I knew before, so I hope she carries on going forward.

We had to face the truth that the old style gangsters were fading away. In the last few years we have lost Tony, Joey Pyle, Ronnie Bender, Ronnie, Reggie and Charlie Kray and Johnny Nash. What will the future hold?

20
A COUPLE MORE FIGHT NIGHTS!

I was worried that my pal 'Gypsy' Joe Smith was taking on too much. He was still fighting, training, working and now he was promoting. The first night for Joe Smith promotions was in a place called Osterley. We were all working as a team from our camp and this tiny little venue held an electric atmosphere, filled with gypsies and gorgers alike. We only had a three fight bill but it was one of the best nights I can remember.

Whilst things were in the early stages, Joe and I popped into David Bailey's studio in London. Kate Kray had written a book called *Diamond Geezers* and David was the photographer. Before we got there, we were crossing the road when a black taxi nearly ran us down. Joe shouted after him and he reversed all the way back. A row ensued and the driver and what must of been two fellow taxi drivers all off duty, got out of the car. They came flying towards us, but each one hit the deck before anymore words were exchanged. This gave us a nice little buzz and it was off to meet the legendary Mr Bailey.

I thought that David Bailey was great. He had on an old T-shirt with food stains down it, he wore old jeans and was unshaven. He was a proper bohemian and a 'I will live and do what the fuck I want' attitude oozed out of him, we both liked him straightaway. As you might imagine, the place was rammed with old photo albums. At one point, his secretary called up: "Mick Jagger on the phone Mr Bailey."

"Tell him I will ring him back," said David. As a complete Stones freak, I nearly hit the deck harder than those cab drivers! Some people think we live in another world but this REALLY was another world. I then bombarded him with questions about the

Stones, The Who, Dylan, The Beatles and all the people I love. He was in no rush and we were there about four hours.

David also showed us Reggie Kray's photo album and another album of the twins. In one shot, Reggie had his right hand bandaged and the dates added up to just after the Mcvitie murder. "He said he did it gardening," said our new mate Dave. "I spent ages with the twins, they were evil but always OK to me thank God." Then he showed us about ten photos of the three brothers, all slight variations of the famous one of just the twins that became legendary, that original photo was in there as well. He told us loads of stories about the twins. "Reggie was as gay as Ronnie, if not worse," he said. I was shocked because I thought that came later in Reg's prison days. David was convinced they had killed more people than the ones we know about. I don't think there was anyone in his lifetime David hadn't met from poets to the Krays, he was the man!

Ronnie used to nail boys to the floorboards and bugger them, they were evil sods. It has been written that Frankie Fraser also used to do that to grasses but he would always make them eat his bodily waste first. I prefer not to believe it to be honest but remember, the people who have told me these things are not everyday Joes, they are all high ranking 'faces'. But at the same time, I was not around then so I can't really say. Some of the stories I have heard about the twins and Frank I have left out because they are just too vile and I don't want to ruin their reputations. One things for sure, Frankie Fraser was, at one time, as a 1960's gangster told me: "An evil, sadistic little bastard but only when he thought he was in the right." The Eric Mason story is tired and worn now but if he could do that once, why couldn't he do it countless times?

Frank, of course, has embellished his life story over the years and leaned more toward the Krays who everyone assumes were his deadly enemies. The East End wasn't really part of Frank's manor but his bus tour focuses mostly on the East End when he was a South Londoner. Frank also says, the police had accused him of killing 40 people!

Make of that what you will but 40 is a lot of bodies, especially as no names have come up and, as they were supposed to be fellow gangsters, it makes it hard to believe. Recently, Freddie Foreman published his book *Brown Bread Fred*. He could have really opened a can of worms on Frank but hardly mentioned him. To me, that's the mark of Fred, a proud, respected man.

My outlook on the Krays changed the day I met David Bailey. Then Pete Gillett former cellmate of Reggie went on TV and said the first person Reggie killed was not Mcvitie but a young boy. The boy was giving him 'head' and disgusted with himself, Reg blew his head off!

Then I read a story in a book about Billy Howard 'The Boss of Soho' when Ron and Reg gave a rent boy such a sexual going over, they killed him. I was hearing more and more of these stories. One 60's gang boss also told me Ronnie had killed the boxer Freddie Mills in Soho but he may have had his own motives for doing that. He was also sure Freddie was 'Jack the stripper' or 'The Tow path killer' who killed prostitutes in West London. Freddie was about to be pulled in before he was killed ... then, the killings stopped. We talked about all this stuff with David Bailey who was in no rush to get rid of us, it may have been part of his 'relaxing the client' technique. Somewhere in his studio, there is a good photo of David Bailey, Joe Smith and me. So the trip to David Bailey was more than interesting, it was a great day.

Now, it was time for Joe's fight night. It wasn't exactly an open night, it helped to be invited or connected to get in. It was a small venue full up mainly with our gypsy, boxing and other friends. Steve Holdsworth of Eurosport refereed two fights and I refereed the main event. There were only three fights but they were all real crackers!

The fights were Andy 'Pit bull' Hunter v 'Mad' Mickey Harrison. Bobby Samples v Jimmy Stockin and Joe Smith v 'Rambo' Patton, a marine from New York. Side bets were rolling in and everyone knew each other. Guests of honour were 'Gypsy' Johnny Frankham and Les Stevens, two legends of the gypsy fight world both in the ring and on the cobbles. They may not mean much to a lot of people but to us they were kings!

I looked after the front door for the first two hours so things got moving smoothly and the unwelcome would be kept out. But of course, things never run that smoothly. At one point, three big dickheads tried to get in saying Joe Smith told them they could pay on the door (Joe's name was on all the posters, so it was easy enough to blag). I called for Joe who said he had never seen them before. With that, they tried to rush past us, two straight into me and Joe's right hands that propelled them back the other way and the other into the fist of one of the gypsy boys. We took them round the back and dumped them in a puddle, they were still there when the last fight was taking place. People didn't realise how dangerous causing trouble in a place like that was. Say a stranger had been shot. The police would be left with a room full of gypsies, all from the same extended family, do you reckon anyone would say anything? Exactly!

A couple of straighteners broke out among the gypsy lads but we just got them a 'fair play man' and they went outside. It's funny, everyone thinks gypsies are troublemakers but the only trouble we got was from gorgers (non gypsies) and that happened a lot. One thought it wise to touch up a gypsy's wife and found himself with a pint glass sticking out of his face. The other doorman had let him in when I used the gents. The other doorman was called Levi and I shall tell you about him soon. The first fight between Andy and Mickey was a complete war. It was like someone had only given them 30 seconds to win. It was matched punch for punch, claret flying all over the crowd ... they loved it!

I was in Andy's corner but both boys were from our camp. It was that thrilling, my voice went completely in the second round, so I had to use hand signals. By the third, both lads were wobbling all over the ring still throwing punches. At the final bell, they collapsed into one another's arms and slid down each other ... bloody hell, what a war that was! The result ... a draw.

Half hour later, Mickey and Andy were sharing a joke and a pint at the bar, now THAT'S how it should be done, none of this gobbing off. The next fight was the crowd puller. Jimmy Stockin is a local legend but he had retired years ago and turned to pubs instead. After constant begging from cousin Joe, Jimmy agreed to fight. I bet he was pissed when he said yes and woke up next day groaning 'Nooo, what have I done?' Jimmy did minimum training but still got gloved up ready. I said, "Ain't ya' gonna take your vest off Jim?"

"No Tel, it hides me Derby a bit!" ('Derby Kelly' = belly). On the contrary, Jimmy was fighting Bobby Samples, fit as a fiddle and a regular on the circuit. He would train with us but sometimes fight for Alan Mortlock. He was lean, sharp and fast. Jimmy's book had just come out and I didn't want to see his reputation ruined by all these people.

And it started just that way, with Bobby working behind the jab and using the ring. This time, I was in Jimmy's corner and he was getting jabbed to bits. I was screaming for Jimmy to cut the ring off then throw that famous right hander. Then, crunch! A right hand caught Bobby right on the temple and his legs wobbled like jelly as he fell against the ropes. Because he was so fit, he started moving round the ring again but he was getting tired and it was starting to go the way of the first fight with both men in the middle of the ring trying to chop each other down like a tree. This was Jimmy territory, he was a cobble fighter and toe to toe was perfect thank you very much. A flurry of jabs were too fast for Jim to see but as Bobby came back to do it again, he walked onto another Stockin right hander ... bang! Bobby was going dancing again. Bobby had realised that this man was a legendary cobble fighter, he was not going to get knocked out with gloves on. The last round (every fight was three rounds for maximum action!) was a blood fest, Jimmy was breathing through his arse but every time Bobby thought Jimmy was on the way down, bang! Another one on the chin. The last ten seconds were about who could throw the most stones at each other in super sonic speed!

The bell went and again both men slid down each other and again it was another draw, it couldn't be anything else. The crowd were up clapping, cheering and stomping their feet. I really had not seen gloved fights like it. Everyone was as high as a kite purely on the atmosphere, these were the days of Shaw, Field and McLean ... unreal!

The last fight was a bit different, this time I was referee. 'Rambo' Patton was a black tank, built like an ox and a US marine to boot, we knew nothing about him except he travelled all over the world fighting and he was unbeaten. For the first time, I had doubts for my friend. The bell went and Joe now fought how I had trained him, working behind a snapping jab. He moved around the

American, faked a jab to the stomach and like lightning brought the right hand over the top, straight onto the American's jaw ... crunch! Rambo hit the deck, I started counting. He shook his head and to be fair got back up. Joe moved and boxed, then lunged forward left, right, uppercut ... smash! He hit the deck again. He made it up at eight and indicated to me he was OK, in a BBBC fight (British Boxing Board of Control) it would of been stopped right there. He got up, Joe rushed forward with a right hand and bang! Rambo's head bounced off the canvas. This time, I didn't bother counting. He was out and the doctor was in. It had been the most thrilling night of boxing since WARRIORS 2, I was pumped with adrenalin.

All the fighters were at the bar and I sat with Johnny Frankham and Les Stevens. Now here's a thing about the reputation gypsies get. The American approached Joe for his money. Now, if Joe had said 'no', what could the guy do? He was on his own, 3,000 miles from home in a hall packed with Joe's family, all of them tasty fighters, some maybe with weapons. But Joe told him he had done well, had tons of bottle coming into a gypsy fortress to fight a gypsy and gave him nearly double the money he was owed! Now THAT'S a REAL gypsy, a man of honour and respect. As the American left, all the gypsies stood and clapped him, including Johnny Frankham. Honour is appealing, cheating someone is ugly. It had been some night, we all stayed until about three o'clock in the morning.

I was talking to Johnny Frankham and Jimmy about their knuckle fights and Joe played the fights again on the screen with everyone reliving it, clapping and cheering. It had been one of the best nights ever and me a gorger in the middle of all those gypsies. Actually, since then I have been made an honoury gypsy so I'm a bit of both now. Ha!

Two days later, myself and a pal I will call Tony, were on our way to a bare knuckle fight in Epsom. The races weren't on and the fight again was inside about half a mile from the race course. Tony was a gorger so was his opponent who just called himself 'Bear'. I always found names like that bloody funny not scary ... until I saw him! This bloke looked like Lenny McLean's big brother standing on Cliff Field's shoulders. I had met Lenny a few times and this guy was twice his size. But Tony was game and wanted the fight but he made sure everyone understood that this was not an 'all in' this was a 'straightener'. I don't blame him.

I kicked the gas canister and Bear came charging out and relevantly got Tony in a bear hug. I shouted "Oi, it's a straightener remember?" He growled and put Tony twenty feet back to the ground. I was shouting "The ribs Tone, the stomach, get his arms down!" Tony hooked away at his ribs to great effect. He brought his arms down right away, he couldn't take the body shots. Then he hit Tony a cracker right on the jaw and he hit the deck but sprung straight back up and threw a lead right to Bear's head (a leading right is pretty rare unless you're a southpaw) and he stumbled back. Tony got straight into his ribs again leaving no room for Bear to swing because he kept his head on Bear's chest. Bear was getting angry and tired, five minutes must have gone and he couldn't keep up. Then Tony threw a left hook to the jaw and a right hook to the ribs, then another one and snap! Bear's rib cracked and he yelped like a dog. "Keep punching the ribs Tone," I was shouting but Tony was getting knackered as well.

Tony found a second wind and opened up on his opponent's body. Bear's arms were literally round his waist, his head was completely open for attack and Tony threw a right, left, right hook to Bear's jaw and he fell back flat on his back. I was now gutted it wasn't an 'all in' because with him in that position, he would of been mullered!

Bear got up but you could tell his vision was dodgy and he was shaking his head. Tony then smashed him in the mouth and a loud crack echoed around the place. I thought Tony had smashed him up good but it was Tony's right hand, it had broken ... Shit! You could see Bear's confidence rise and he caught Tony with a thundering right putting him flat on his arse. Tony, fair play to him got up and threw three left hooks into the ribs and Bear yelped again, then another hook and another snap! Another rib had gone and Tony was fighting one handed. Tony just kept punching with one hand and Bear dropped to the concrete floor screaming. He couldn't get up from that no way. What happened next reminded me of the second Eubank v Watson fight. Bear, who I had written off, suddenly got up and threw an uppercut from the floor that nearly lifted Tony's head from his neck, he fell like a ton of bricks, his eyes shut before his head hit the concrete, he was out, well and truly out!

We got Tony to a doctor we knew at the time and luckily he had no lasting damage.

Meanwhile, another firm had taken over the Palais. I got a phone call to stay away and was told the Palais security had doubled their manpower in case I came back with my firm. I believe two of the other firm were stabbed that night. I had no intention of using the Palais again, it was impossible to make money there but I'm sure the WARRIORS shows will not be forgotten by those who went.

So I decided to give a straightener a go. Anyone I trained will tell you, I was extremely fast with both hands but especially feet, I could tie people in knots. We found a relevant place and I had a pal pick me an opponent. I didn't want to fight a gypsy because they were too dear to me and I didn't want a split with them, I stood with the gypsies not against them. So I fought another gorger I just knew as Burton.

Burton was sinewy, not very big and a bit cross-eyed. I have never underestimated opponents so guessed this bloke must have some hidden talent. The canister was kicked, I double shuffled my feet threw a one, two and he fell straight to the floor smacking his head on the concrete for good measure. I thought, 'that can't be it', but he didn't get up, he was out. I mean, I'm no Jimmy Stockin but that was ridiculous!

Then I received a challenge, Bear had taken a dislike of my very biased support for Tony. I think he expected me to say no but I took up the challenge, I honestly would rather have not, but saying no is harder than saying sorry in that situation. We met at the same place as before and having been training well, I was far fitter. When the canister was kicked, I danced out working behind a poleaxe of a left jab, stamping my lead foot as the jab landed for extra power. Bear threw a wild left hook that should have been read out by Michael Fish whoosh! It missed by a mile. I threw a faint to his jaw, stepped forward, leaned to my right and brought my right fist up under his ribs and he groaned. I had not forgotten that he didn't like body punches. I rested my head on his hairy chest and swung from side to side opening an assault on his ribs. Then I threw one into the pit of his stomach and he doubled over, I straightened him up with an uppercut and he hit the deck. He got the right hump, foaming at the mouth, because he thought I was just Tony's cheerleader.

He come running at me and I moved right, hooking him as he went by, his timing was shot to bits. It turned him round and he was breathing through his arse again, so I covered up and let him punch and punch, he got more and more knackered. I got him in a corner and again, before he could defend his ribs, I attacked them. Then what I was waiting for happened, crack! There went a rib but before anything could be taken in, I span on my toes and let my right hand go and snap! Another one went! Over he went, face bright red, wheezing but got up.

I was so fit, I was straight back onto him and started unloading on his jaw and face. Crack! I broke his nose, claret was pouring from his snout and his legs were doing a funny dance. I landed again straight in his eyeball, he covered his eye and moved back, I pulled his hairy arm down and moved forward, slipping punches all the way, I punched the other eye ... now he could barely see. But his chin wasn't bad, so I threw a double hook to his ribs and there was another snap! Christ! Why didn't he just call best (submit) the stubborn bastard? But he wouldn't, so I carried on to the ribs. Then he rushed at me screaming, I waited for the right micro second and threw my hardest right hand with him running towards it, his legs came up from under him, his head smashed on the concrete and he was well and truly out!

Don't get me wrong, I'm not a real cobble fighter. I wouldn't rank myself alongside any good knuckle fighter but in those fights, I was in another league. Don't forget, I had the advantage of watching him fight my mate and knew his weaknesses.

Then, I fell down the stairs at home and heard a loud crack! I went to bed, raised my leg and put ice on it. The next day, I couldn't walk on it. It turned out I had broken both the tibia and fibia of my left leg. It was a freak accident because your ankle can only go right or left at one time, so it's hard to break the main bone on BOTH sides. It was a nasty injury that required pins, screws and other metal plates. Even worse, they gave me a bandage that was supposed to stay on for a couple of days instead of a full cast ... it was left on for six weeks! The bandage was filthy and loose, it also hurt more than when I broke it originally. Because of the wound getting dirty, I had developed MRSA and was in agony. The breaks have never healed properly. My footwork was my pride and joy and I could move around a ring like a ballerina on speed, now I have to plant my feet. I also put on loads of weight. I had trained since the age of 11, my body was used to it. So even with diet, the weight piled on as no way could I run and even upper body work was agony! You can actually tell in photographs, the difference before and after the injury. Before the injury, I am slim and muscular, after the breaks I am much bigger and less muscled, even around the face ... I was pig sick! I don't drink and very rarely eat rubbish but because my body was so used to minimum food and maximum training, I still piled on the pounds.

The injury is still agony, especially when it's cold, I can hardly walk. I can't tell you how depressing it is when you have been in shape all your life!

So that was my cobbles days over, not much to write home about I know.

21
MASSIVE RIGHT HANDERS AND MASS MURDERERS!

The next venture was another of Joe's. The venue was in a hotel opposite our boxing gym right next to Heathrow Airport. It was extremely plush with a meal included, Joe was top of the bill fighting some mean looking Russian we knew nothing about. I was in Joe's corner as well as Gary Shaw who was fighting 'Mad' Mickey Harrison who was still unbeaten in the unlicensed circuit. Gary was fighting in front of his legendary Dad who was guest of honour. Joey Pyle snr was supposed to be joint guest of honour but he phoned me to say he was ill. I was looking forward to seeing 'The Boss' but Joe was, in fact, more ill than any of us thought.

Gary Shaw is a durable fighter with a style similar to his Dad's. I always admired Gary for being an unlicensed fighter, it was obvious people were going to constantly compare him to his Dad. You would think unlicensed would be the last thing he would want to do but Gary never cared what people thought and did what he wanted. He had his fair share of battles and lately he had been plagued by a series of injuries. He had taken the fight with Mickey carrying an extremely painful shoulder injury that needed surgery but he was fighting and nothing was going to stop him.

As a man, Gary is a diamond, a proper friend and a gentleman. You might think that the son of Roy Shaw would be a swaggering big mouth, giving it large, barking and bullying people (some sons of famous 'faces' are like that) but nothing could be further from the truth. Gary is a gentleman and an extremely quiet family man who keeps himself to himself. Gary has always been a good friend to me. There have been a lot of parasites around Roy over the years but Gary has told me I am a true friend of his Dad's and he knows I have no ulterior motives which I found a real compliment.

First on the fight bill was Andy 'pit bull' Hunter who was fighting a Russian. Andy's punching power made easy work of his opponent and he stopped him in two rounds. It was a class performance.

I took the small break to nip over to a room Joe had rented out to relax in before the fight, I took Roy with me to give Joe some motivation because Joe had always thought highly of Roy. I tapped on the door gently, in case Joe was asleep ... no chance! Joe's room was packed tight with people, some were family but some Joe didn't even know. This was not the way to prepare for a fight and I told Joe this, who knew it anyway but was too much of a gentleman to chuck people out. But we started asking people to leave, some were so pissed they could barely walk.

Now, there was just Joe, Jimmy and Wally Stockin, Joe's brothers John and Aaron, me and the Guv'nor - Roy. Roy asked Joe if he had been doing his fitness work, always the number one factor in Roy's priority table and they had a general chat. I left Joe to rest for a bit and put the 'Do Not Disturb' sign up. At least I knew he was with good people now. I don't wish to offend anyone but ten people completely pissed, each one telling you a different way you should fight your fight is not a great help. But with Jimmy, Aaron who was a very tasty boxer and big John in there with Joe, I felt OK. Joe's opponent was a guy called Steve Yorath. Steve was recommended to me by a fighter who had fought on my shows, he was a Welshman ... and BIG!! I mean BIGGGG!!!

He made Joe look small and not many people do that. Gary Shaw had driven down on his own, so he had no corner men or anything. Gary asked me if I would work his corner which I proudly agreed to do. Gary was on next, so we got the pads out and warmed him up with a little move around. We got the 'five minutes to go' call from what is called 'the whip' (the whip works between the fighters in the changing room and the referee, judges and officials at the ring area. It sounds an easy job but it's not. If a fighter is perfectly warmed up and mentally ready and the whip calls five minutes when in fact it's fifteen, you could have just lost that fighter his bout!). Thankfully, I have never worked with a bad whip or referee that I can recall. A light coating of sweat is what you are aiming for on a fighter when he's called out.

I got Gary greased up (Vaseline around the eyes etc) checked I had all my kit, then the whip was back to check that we were ready. Not officially, but by word of mouth, Mickey had become the favourite. I knew with a seasoned fighter like Gary, this would make him even more determined. With a novice, I wouldn't have told them ... you HAVE to know your fighter, they are ALL different!

We walked through to the announcement of "Garrrrry Shawwww!!" I glanced over at Roy, his eyes had widened and he looked like he was going into the ring, I must say, this worried me a little bit as Roy Shaw is still a very capable man. But I had a job to do, it was strange guiding one of my friends through to beat another one of my friends but, as I say, I had a job to do. Mickey had actually wanted to fight Gary for over a year on a WARRIORS show. I don't know if it was the idea of fighting and maybe beating a Shaw but Mickey was over the moon when this fight finally came off. The first time around, Gary had injured himself badly in training and both men were gutted to say the least, especially Mickey!

Don't get me wrong though, Mickey had the deepest respect for Gary as a fighter and thought him a diamond as a man, it wasn't a grudge match in a nasty sense. I know Mickey had trained as hard as a pro for this fight, he really wanted it. Gary also respected Mickey but was carrying that agonising right shoulder injury. This was a real disadvantage because watching Mickey, I had seen he was every now and then, square on and open to a big right hand. We were going to have to use the right hand sparingly and only when Gary was sure it was going to land. In short, Gary's timing was the key, if he missed, his shoulder could come out. The bell went for round one and Mickey was moving nicely, circling the ring, throwing solid jabs but making sure his glove got straight back to defend, his gloves were nice and high. Gary always takes a round to get going, so I wasn't overly worried. But Gary was getting caught a bit much for my liking, I could tell the right hand was on his mind. The concentration on Mickey's face was intense as he worked from behind that ram rod jab.

The bell went, first round to Mickey. I asked Gary if he was OK: "Fine" he replied. Round two started where we had left off in round one. Everyone knew Gary had a great chin and I think Mickey was going for a points win. Then Gary threw the right hand but I could see it coming and Mickey slipped it and Gary grimaced. 'Oh shit' I thought 'His shoulder's gone' Gary fought that round with one hand. The bell went and Gary came back to the corner. I took out Gary's gumshield and he grimaced as he was in real pain. My job was to make sure my fighter won but more importantly, that he wasn't a cripple for the rest of his life, my priority was my fighter's safety. I said to him "Gaz, it's all on this round Bruv, if you can't use the right hand, I'm stopping the fight!"

"No you're not!" Gary replied, "If you stop this Tel, you will lose a friend ... for good!"

I said: "In that case Gaz, you HAVE to knock him out in this round. You have to let the right hand go a few times but only when you're 100% sure it will land, open gaps with your jab. I will shout out NOW, then you let the right go with everything you have OK?" He nodded and I put his shield back in his mouth. "This is the round Gaz, you're going to have to get in the trenches!" He nodded again and the expression on his face changed, he knew time was not on his side.

Round three, Mickey took the middle of the ring, hands still high, jab still robotic - his fitness training had paid off. Then, I saw it, that move that Mickey makes when he's chasing and for a fraction of a second he was square on, I shouted over the crowd "NOW!" Gary threw it but missed by micro inches. 'Shit', I thought, that chance won't come again', that square on position of Mickey's was like his hunting switch of position, it only came up when he saw the chance to chase, problem was, Gary Shaw only fights going one way ... forward, the same as Roy used to.

I could see on Gary's face he was in agony. I could see the muscles in his face as he bit hard into his gum shield. I put the towel in my right hand ready to throw it. I know Gary really wouldn't talk to me maybe forever but I wasn't having him with long term damage, he had a wife and kids for Christ sake. I pulled me arm back to throw the towel. Gary took another shot, I bent my knees to get the power needed to get the towel in the ring. Then Mickey threw a massive punch almost square on. "FU**ING NOW!" I screamed. It felt like I was puking my heart up. All Mickey's weight went forward as Gary threw a right hand like a mortar attack! As Mickey put all his weight forward, Gary put all his weight forward, they met in the middle and CRACK! Gary caught Mickey right on the chin as they were both going forward doubling the power! Mickey's legs went, then he just fell so hard on the canvas it was unreal, he tried to sit up, he shook his head but there was no point in counting. Mickey was NOT going to get up!

The doctor was in the ring fast as lightning. Mickey was being attended to for what seemed like an eternity. The fight was over, we were not on different sides anymore. Both Gary and myself stayed in the ring until we both knew Mickey would be OK because (Mickey is a gentleman and sportsman, I'm sure he won't mind me saying this) that was one of the hardest one punch knockouts I have ever seen in the unlicensed boxing ring. I honestly don't think even a pro would have got up from that. I'm not going over the top here and of course the scale of everything was a lot smaller, but do you remember the final right hand Lennox Lewis threw against Mike Tyson, when Tyson was coming forward and so was Lewis, and Tyson went forward right onto Lennox right hand and Tyson just hit the deck. That was what that punch was like but in unlicensed terms!

Only when Gary had spoken to Mickey and given him a sporting hug did he leave the ring, that's what sort of man Gary is, that's the way it should be. Gary then said goodbye to his Dad and Joe Smith, he gave me a hug and off he went into the night. I was over the moon that I had sussed Mickey's little chink in the armour and Gary had exploited it, but mostly I was pleased Mickey was OK. Mickey is a good friend of mine and I have ample respect for him. Let's not forget, that was his only unlicensed defeat. Before that, nobody even got close to beating him and also Gary had been unlicensed boxing for a lot longer than Mickey. Two good fighters, two people with the courage of ten men, two gentlemen as long as liberties are not taken and most of all two good friends. I must admit, I prefer the fights when you don't know or, even better, don't like the opposition.

I have always thought that Mickey like Roy Shaw and countless others were even better with no gloves and no rules. In his prime, as long as he was stone cold sober a street fight with Roy Shaw was not something you wanted brought upon you. I can imagine it happened often, with some pissed up, muscle pumped 'hard nut' not knowing who Roy was, or even more stupid if they did know who he was, but drugs, drink or both had made them feel invincible ... until when they woke up in intensive care!

I have a little fantasy (no not that type!). I so wish they had put on a championship competition like the one for the Guv'nor but bare knuckle, 'all in' or a 'straightener', it doesn't matter, who wouldn't pay to see that? Roy Shaw, Cliff Field, Johnny Frankham, Jimmy Stockin, Paul Sykes, Mark Ripley, Vic Dark, Lenny McLean, Fred 'The Head', Charlie Bronson, John Bindon, Johnny Waldron, Bertie Coster, Bill 'The Bomb' Williams, Andy Till, Brian Hall and, some may not know, but the young Freddie Foreman and Joey Pyle snr were extremely tasty on the cobbles and the ring. I know the ages don't match up but it's only a fantasy ... Could you put those guys in order if they had all fought each other at their primes?

So back to the Hotel and I am warming up 'Gypsy' Joe Smith. Actually, Joe's real fighting alias is Joe 'Bugner' Smith. This is because Joe's Dad Aaron always called him Bugner as Joe was born in 1971, the year of the infamous Joe Bugner v Henry Cooper fight. Henry Cooper was the darling of the nation and the whole country thought that Cooper had retained his British, European and Commonwealth titles easily but after 15 rounds, referee Harry Gibbs walked towards Cooper who was preparing to celebrate, straight past him and lifted the hand of Joe Bugner instead!

It literally shocked the nation, it was a genuine national scandal and is still one of the most talked about jaw dropping moments in British Boxing history. Commentator Harry Carpenter went nuts: "How can you take away the man's three titles LIKE THAT!" Referee Harry Gibbs was a national hate figure. Actually, if you watch the fight now, there's not much in it. But anyway, on most posters Joe is Joe 'Bugner' Smith but given the choice, I think

'Gypsy' Joe Smith is much better.

Joe took care of Yorath easily, I don't think Joe got hit. Yorath was a performer, he would pretend his legs were shaking, yawn and really play to the crowd but at this time, we didn't know this and thought he was taking the piss and as he was fighting Joe and the place was full of gypsies it didn't go down well to say the least. We didn't know he messed about like this with every opponent and thought he was doing it because the place was full of gypsies, can you imagine?

So the roar that went up when Joe knocked him spark out in three rounds was ear piercing. I think he got out of their pretty quick. In fact, Steve Yorath turned out to be good value. I saw him fight a few times and he would always do the performing which really got the rival fans going. But if you didn't know that was his party piece, things could go very wrong, very fast!

With all that was going on, I was finding it difficult to sleep. Remember the Levi bloke I mentioned earlier? I happened to mention it to him and he said: "Come round, I will sort you out." He gave me a pot of some stinking, gooey paste. I only took a teaspoon and threw my guts up and really thought I was going to die!

"What was that shit? I asked him.

"Rohypnol," he replied casually, "It's used for rape."

"Oh charming, what the hell have you got a pot of rape drug in your cupboard for? Does Emma (his partner and mother of his kids) know you have that shit?"

"Yeah, she doesn't mind," he replied like I was talking about aspirin. 'Each to their own' I thought, who knows what couples get up to? Emma was a very pretty girl with lovely kids and none of us could understand what she was doing with Levi a fat, ugly, weird, alcoholic and pervert. He would boast about the girls he had sex with in the back of his white van, little did we know ... they WERE girls, school girls. He upped and left and moved to Twickenham for a while before returning to West Drayton to live again. The reason he was on 'The Firm' (if you want to put it that way) is because he would do really shitty jobs that nobody else would do, but he wasn't a pal. He seemed more like a fan, especially of me, Joe and Jimmy because he fantasised about being a gangster and he thought us three WERE gangsters. He would tell these little girls that he was a gangster! I would come out from seeing Joe and a young girl would walk up to me and ask: "Is Levi a real gangster? He said you were all gangsters and you, Joe and Jimmy were the gang bosses?"

I pulled him on that and told him, "we are not gangsters Levi, I'm a promoter and Joe's a fighter, sometimes we collect debts or sort out bullies but only if they are taking money for smack off old and weak people ... got it!" And that was about right. But he had this gangster thing in his head and really thought he was a 'face'.

If he was there and I got a call from Freddie Foreman or Charlie Richardson, he would start walking round in circles with his hands on his head going, "I can't believe it, I just can't believe it!" If we drove anywhere, he would rock back and forwards like the real loons, while we where driving, back and forward like a mental case.

"Levi, can you stop that, it's getting annoying."

"It's my nerves Tel, I can't help it," he would say.

"Well, what's making you that nervous?"

"Oh, everything." Emma always seemed happy enough, she never gave anything away although I'm sure she knew about his girls. He did weird things. Once Joe had a fight in Essex, Levi drove the whole way on the hard shoulder while reading a porno mag. Then I was told he started sticking names up to get into places for nothing, usually Dave Courtney. That's a big no, you DO NOT, repeat DO NOT stick names up! I rang Dave and told him right away, he said he was used to it. He was lucky that time.

In the back of this van once, I noticed a load of hammers but thought nothing of it, I just thought he was a nut, but if I went round for a day with my pal Joe, he would be there. Joe would just roll his eyes. He used to make everyone think he was a hard nut bouncer and asked me to teach him how to box. In one photo of the 'chaps' in the ring at one of my shows, whose big face should pop up covering Tony Lambrianou? Yep, Levi Bellfield, gangster number one! But he was like a kid when I tried to teach him how to box. He would turn away and put one knee up to cover himself, some bouncer, I had big pads on as well, he was a coward except when it came to women. Joe, me and all the 'chaps' looked up to women Levi looked down on them, I won't repeat some of the filth he said. Then he became a clamper (he knew how to get hated that prick!).

Then one day, I went round Joe's and Jimmy was there. They said go and have a look at Levi's gaff. It was a couple of streets away, so I went down and the place had literally been pulled down. Men in white and masks, the forensic guys were swarming all over the place and there was a tent set up. I said to Joe and Jim: "What the hell's happened?"

"Old Bill have been round here asking about Levi. He's been charged for rape and maybe murder!"

"Murder of who?" I asked.

"Some girls," they replied, 'SOME girls!' Then it all started coming together, the date rape drugs, hammers, the nerves, the girls, the never ending talk about sex and gangsters. Billy Smith, Joe's cousin and a good man, came in.

"I will tell you one thing," he said, "if he has done any of it, that dinlow (gypsy word) is safer in there than out here!" We all felt the same. You can use your imagination as to what we would have done to him if we saw him and the way the law works, he would have got off and we would have got seven years.

It started to be a big national press story. They had caught him on CCTV in his white van, but he wouldn't tell them where the van was and the police couldn't find it. It turned out that the murders took place near Twickenham when Levi Bellfield had moved there. But what clinched it for me was that while on remand in Belmarsh, he tried too kill himself. Now, I know one thing, if I had been accused of killing girls or anyone and I was innocent, I would NOT try and kill myself, to me he was guilty as soon as he did that. If you were innocent of such a disgusting crime, you would fight and fight until your name was cleared. Otherwise, you are going to your grave guilty, the passion of proving your innocence would keep you alive. None of the Guildford four or Birmingham six, or my mate Kevin Lane tried to kill themselves did they? Suicide is an acceptance of guilt like Fred West and Harold Shipman.

In the end, this gangster wannabe, Levi Bellfield, was 'lifed off' for killing student Amelie Delagrange and schoolgirl Milly Dowler.

There were also many rapes talked about. It turned out that he was even raping Emma, the mother of his kids, but telling me about their great sex life ... until I could shut him up! The girls that died, he bravely smashed their skulls from behind with a hammer on the common. I so wish we had known this before the police got the bastard. I sincerely apologise to the parents that we didn't. The papers couldn't get enough of the nobody, a wannabe. He was on the front of all the tabloids and all over the TV. I really can't see him as a doorman, he was a man-child, a little boy in a man's body. Putting up the only CCTV camera in the street, wasn't the cleverest idea either and none of his neighbours liked him. They described him as "a bully" but he couldn't bully a butterfly!

One thing is for sure, if you ever come out Bellfield, I swear you will not last a day you slag! And don't get mouthy in there either, between us, we know as many people in there as out here. Your time will come, keep looking over your shoulder. What goes around comes around you useless bastard and I'm one of the least angry ones!

I regret the fact that we ever let him near us but he was so in awe of Joe, Jimmy and me he would do ANYTHING we told him to, he was our lackey and gofer. People must ask: "How did you not see what he was?" We simply didn't. We were so busy leading our own lives; new babies, boxing promotions, training, Joe's golf ... you simply don't look for serial killers.

I sincerely feel for those parents and I think I can speak for all of us. We also know Levi Bellfield is better where he is! Do you know what a REAL gangster would do if he got his hands on him! I hope every single second of his worm's life is pain and depression.

22
BIG NIGHT FOR THE 'BOSS'

One of the biggest occasions of 2006 or indeed any other year came on Sunday 19th February at Caesars in Streatham. It was billed as a 'Lifetime achievement award' night in honour of the great Joey Pyle snr. The purpose of the evening was twofold. One reason was for all those who owed Joe for his help and support in the past to have the chance to say thank you. These people were not just 'gangsters' but those from the world of music like Jocelyn Brown, the world of film and TV like Billy Murray, Ray Winstone and Jamie Foreman, stars of sport like Jimmy White, Ronnie O'sullivan, Alan Minter and John H Stracey and every other walk of life, Joe has helped them all.

The other reason was that Joe was very ill with motor neurone disease. We needed to raise funds for Joe's treatment fast and also raise awareness for the disease. Joe was always a big man in body and mind and had a very special aura. He was still a mental giant but the illness had robbed him of much of his physical presence. At first, only a handful of us knew of Joe's illness and Joe being a proud man wanted it that way. As time went on, it was obvious that if the night was going to be given every chance of success everyone would need to know exactly why we were doing it.

From the very beginning, it was Dave Courtney who was the main driving force behind getting this event off the ground. Through those dark days a few years back when Dave was being called everything under the sun by everyone under the sun, Joey Pyle snr stood by Dave in public and made no secret that he stood with him all the way and that all the accusations were complete shit. When it was all the rage to slag Dave Courtney, even by some respected underworld figures, Joe would have none of it. This of course meant the world to DC and he will never forget. Joey Pyle jnr was obviously working away on his father's behalf but I had more contact with Dave throughout the planning and Joe jnr had enough to do just dealing with his father's illness and all the powerful emotions that go with it, he didn't need us ringing every five minutes about things we could just get on with.

Dave left it to me to invite most of the chaps and I was straight on the phone to our usual bunch of rascals. The list included Roy Shaw, Charlie Richardson, Ronnie Knight, Freddie Foreman, Wilf Pine, Bruce Reynolds, 'Big H' Mackenny, Carlton Leach, Howard Marks, Jimmy and Wally Stockin, Mike Biggs, Terry Smith, Vic Dark, Charlie Bronson's family and the man who would be invaluable to myself and Dave throughout the planning... Johnny Nash.

John and his brothers have long been one of London's most respected families and Joe's oldest and closest friends. When certain people knew John was working closely with us and knew that if liberties were taken they would be dealing with him, they soon changed their ideas. Sure we can handle things pretty well ourselves but with Johnny Nash with us we had a real edge. To those on the outside, the name Johnny Nash may not mean as much as Reg Kray or Ronnie Biggs but trust me, to us he is at the very top. Dave also asked me to get a few words from the top chaps to go in the official programme which I did.

With about three weeks to go, I collapsed with an attack of pancreatitis and was taken to hospital by ambulance. These days, you can use mobile phones in hospitals so I continued my round of phone calls with tubes coming out of everywhere, hooked to a drip and a morphine machine. When I told Dave Courtney I had suffered a pancreas attack, his response was: "Well, tell me where this fucking pancreas bloke lives and I will have him done, nobody attacks my mate."

It was painful to laugh but I had no choice with that one. Dave of course spent months in hospital after his so called car 'accident' so he knew exactly how boring it was.

What with me in a bad way in hospital and some of the boys threatening to do so and so, if so and so turned up, one of the chaps said: "Fuck me, the way this is going, everyone is going to be dead and the only one still alive to go to the funerals will be Joe!"

After about a week, I was out of hospital. I was feeling extremely rough but determined to get on with it. Now most of us were doing our bit and most of the people we wanted there were going. A few of the lads were tied into previous engagements they just could not break but these people had always been solid and we knew they were supporting the night. It was inevitable that with the amount of people attending, serious rivalries and hatred would come to the surface. As I was phoning all the chaps nearly every day I had a lot of smoothing over to do and tried to turn myself into Mr diplomat (some would say that me being diplomatic is totally impossible). A few feuds going back decades were reignited and I mean real deep, heavy duty differences. Some of these really annoyed me because the allegations being thrown about were totally false 'so and so is a grass' is a real classic, the amount of grasses around is unbelievable!

Other disagreements were born from some of Britain's biggest ever robberies. In the end, only a very few stayed away for personal reasons. I was full of admiration for some of the men who put grudges behind them, because on this night Joe was far more important. For example, it's no secret that there is no love lost between Freddie Foreman and Chris Lambrianou, Freddie has made that fact public. This goes back years to the days of the Krays and Fred has written about it himself in his own books. On the night though, both men turned up for Joe and their individual dignity and sense of occasion and duty to their friends was an inspiration. Chris walked over to me, gave me a hug and said: "I bet you didn't think I would turn up did you?"

Actually, I did expect him to turn up because he had never struck me as one to avoid a difficult situation. Chris said: "Joe was there to support us when Tony died so it's only proper we now support Joe."

I can't speak for the Chris of the '60s but I know the man today to be one of great character. I saw this first hand when we spent a day together and he took me to meet the staff and residents of the Ley community in Oxford where Chris had done much good work. The residents had respect for him because they knew he had turned his life around. Doing 15 years in prison for something you didn't do and having family members die while you are in there is certainly suffering.

There were many potential flashpoints but out of everyone's respect for Joe there was not one incident. Some of these hot spots could have been EXTREMELY nasty with very dangerous men bumping into someone everyone knew they hated. It took every ounce of negotiation skill I had to work through some of these. I had previously had a big fall out with a bloke called Steve Wraith from Newcastle who called himself 'The Geordie Connection' and I had given him a clump and challenged him on the cobbles but at Joe's do there was none of this, everyone was on the same side. There are very, very few people who could cast a spell of unity and peace over so many fiery characters in one place but Joe is one of those few. I don't think as many well respected faces will be together again in one place as they were on this night either.

One problem we encountered when we got to Caesars on the night is that all the seating had been changed. This was a disaster for me because I had been assured that there would be no top table as such but one long table with Joe at the head, his closest friends near him with lesser friends towards the end. In turn, I had promised all the top players that this would be the case and assured them every one of Joe's friends would be near him and not off on another table somewhere. There would be other tables around for paying customers but Joe's closest pals would be within chatting distance. Obviously, if you make a promise you have to stick by it especially with men whose word is their bond. So imagine my horror when I arrived at Caesars and saw everything had been broken up into individual sets of tables!

Of course, I had promised the seating so now I had to explain it even though I didn't have a clue when and why the original plan had been changed. You don't expect the people in charge of the floor plan to change the whole concept on the same day of the event. So now I found myself apologising to well respected men for something I knew nothing about. I just got on with it, what else can you do?

Now suddenly, there was a top table. Those on the main table were Roy Shaw, Alfie Hutchinson, Johnny Nash, Charlie and Ronnie Richardson and of course Joe Pyle snr and his wife Julie. There was a space next to Charlie and he and Roy insisted I sit there with them on the top table. I politely declined. I couldn't plonk myself on the top table like Jack the biscuit when all the great seats I had promised many people who really should have been on that table with the others hadn't materialised, I think they call that taking the piss.

My friend Wilf Pine found a seat over by the bar, I had to get the floor managers to move tables so the Lambrianou family were together, Freddie Foreman was on a good table but not as close as it should have been to Joe and Charlie Bronson's family were up in the balcony!

Wilf had a right go at a few people, the Gucci walking stick that the Mafia Don Joe Pagano had given him being ever present. In fact Joe Pagano and Wilf were like father and son for many, many years.

The orchestrater of this almighty balls up was a guy called Chris Bartholomew aka 'Chris The Greek.' How this guy got so involved I will never know, you just had to speak to him once to know he was not to be trusted. Dave Courtney, Joey Pyle jnr, myself and a few others worked their nuts off to arrange that evening's events. For us, It was actually a pleasure to work hard on this because we knew what we could achieve and for who. It's very rare anyone gets a chance to actually do something constructive when someone close to you is ill. As I have said, the love and respect for Joey Pyle snr that we all had and of course still have was more than enough motivation for all of us... All of us, except Chris the Greek. I suspected straight away that his motives came from a darker place than love and respect for a great man and friend.

I mainly conferred with Dave Courtney during the weeks of build up and had never heard of the Greek before. Then suddenly, with about a week and a half to go he popped up from nowhere. Top 'faces' were phoning me up and asking: "Who the hell is this Chris the Greek?"

I had to be honest and say I didn't have a clue, he was nothing to do with me. I suspect he was sticking names up all over the place without blessing, this is one of the big no nos.

Once the Greek said to me: "How is Charlie Bronson? Please tell him I apologise for not visiting him for a while but I will come and see him again soon." I relayed this to Charlie in a letter then thought no more about it. When Charlie's reply came through it read 'I don't know what this guy's game is but he has NEVER visited me... ever!'

Charlie's memory is crystal clear so there was no chance he had just forgotten. Charlie can tell you everything that happened in a visit with someone in 1975!

I thought what a bizarre story to make up. He must have known he would be found out because he actually asked me to contact Charlie and apologise for him not visiting. He was obviously the most dangerous type of liar ... those who really believe their own lies.

Some items had gone 'missing' from the auction on the night. One item was a huge photo of Joe in a gold frame taken from the cover of Joe's book *Notorious*. It was an extremely striking picture that dominated the stage. A few day's later my pal 'Mad' Mark Fish phoned me in a rage. The Greek had actually phoned Mark and all but accused him of stealing it... It was Mark who donated and took the picture down to London in the first place! Would it have not been easier to leave the piece at home?

According to the Greek, Mark came to the conclusion that it would be far easier to load it into the car, drive all the way to London, heave the huge picture onto the stage, display it in front of every top 'face' in England, put it back in (or on) the car and drive all the way up north and put it back in the garage! So when Mark hit the roof upon this accusation, I'm sure you can understand why.

This guy was really starting to piss people off... but more was to come.

We found out that the night before the Boss's do, the Greek had run up a massive bill at China White's club in London. As between the proper 'chaps', there is not one club owner in Britain and New York we don't know, this information was easy to come by. Where did he get all that ready cash from the night before the show? Far be it from me to say it may have been ticket money.

Then weeks later, it got about as low as it can possibly get. The

Greek was staying the night at Dave's house (Christ knows why?). In the early hours, he decided to walk into a room where Dave's new girlfriend was asleep and molest her. He screamed at her: "Don't you dare scream you little cunt!"

What a charmer this little turd turned out to be!

After smashing that common decency rule he went on to smash a top underworld rule 'do not stick names up' especially if you hardly know the person whose name you are using. Dave Courtney phoned and informed me that the Greek was now phoning selected people saying that he never molested the girl.

Then came the real clincher. The Greek was telling people that his good friend Charlie Richardson was on his side and would take his side against Dave! I told Dave that it was all bollocks and that I would ring Charlie straight away. This I did... and Charlie hit the roof!

Charlie told me he had only met the Greek three times and didn't like him then. Charlie Richardson is an extremely interesting and intelligent man. He would never bother with someone like the Greek. I told Charlie about his wondering into girls' bedrooms at night and this obviously did nothing to pacify him. I asked Charlie if he would mind ringing Dave and reassuring him, this he did. I appreciated him doing that because he and Frankie Fraser have a lot of history together and go back many years and Dave and Frank had a massive, very public fall out ... Another little gangland problem smoothed over by uncle Tel!

Charlie Richardson hates the Greek, even more now that he knows the idiot has been telling people that Charlie rushed to his aide by declaring war on Dave Courtney (I still can't believe he did that. I bet the Greek really has convinced himself that this is the case). All he has done is improve and strengthen Charlie and Dave's relationship and broadcast what a low life he is to those who didn't know already.

Chris the Greek is currently on bail. It should come as no big surprise now that the reason for this is that he attacked and nearly killed his wife with a knuckleduster. What a lovely fella. Attacking a woman is bad enough but feeling you need a knuckleduster to do it properly is unbelievable. And this was the guy left in charge to totally destroy my seating arrangements at the Boss's show.

As luck would have it, the balcony was actually the best view and you could move around up there but that wasn't the point. I was now pretty much on my own in terms of the lads I had been working with because Dave was due on stage and Joe Pyle jnr was looking after his dad and everyone else around him.

Anyway, that aside and about 200 apologies to Wilf later, myself and Howard Marks (who is more effective than any anti depressant) went upstairs and sat with Charlie Bronson's lovely mum Eira, Charlie's cousin Lorraine and her husband Andy and had a laugh. We were joined up there by 'Welsh' Bernie Davies another good, staunch and solid man... his arms are also twice the size of my car! Bernie has carried out jobs for most of the top faces and is trusted beyond question.

Filming the event for Joe was the man that films nearly all of our functions, Liam Galvin. Liam who runs gangstervideos.co.uk is not just a camera man/film maker but a close personal friend of all of ours. He is completely trusted with everything that goes on and is a man with a heart of gold and proper values. I personally think Liam, like most trusted, loyal and reliable people is sometimes taken for granted and not given the credit he deserves, it is just assumed he will always be there. I certainly hope he will be, we would all be lost without him.

Looking down I spotted my brother in arms Carlton Leach. He wasn't hard to spot as he had about 20 members of his firm with him all with biceps like baseballs. As I said before, never underestimate Mr Leach. From up there, I could see the huge queue forming from 'fans' lining up to meet and get autographs from all the underworld legends. I can fully understand why some people don't believe me when I tell them that wherever the legendary chaps are, it's like Beatlemania!

Other stars of stage and screen will be around signing the odd autograph or two but for some reason everyone wants a minute with Charlie R, Roy, Fred, Joe etc. They are all popular but the men associated with the '50s and '60s era are treated like superstars. If only Justice Lawton and Justice Melford Stephenson could see it ha!

There really must be a deep rooted love for rascals because it happens wherever they go and some handle it better than others.

I have also been to a few boxing dos where 'Nipper' Read has been present and on display but no sod asks for his autograph!

You know for a fact that if, for example, Ronnie Biggs and Jack Slipper were at the same do the people would not be lining up to see the slippered one. Despite the fact that His Slipperness is supposed to represent everything that's good, no bugger would give a toss but they would be fighting to see Biggsy.

Everyone has heard of Bonnie and Clyde but can you name one of those who shot them dead? Centuries later, people still talk about Dick Turpin but who caught him? Who hanged him? I for one don't have a clue. Makes you think doesn't it?

As I was talking to Wilf Pine a beautiful lady approached us, to our delight we saw that it was Wendy Lambrianou, Tony's widow. Of course, everyone takes the death of a loved one extremely hard and Wendy was certainly no exception. In fact, it was never actually said but at one point we all feared that maybe she wouldn't get through it. I had spoken to her a month or so before and she had said for the first time she felt able to mix with Tony's (and her) pals again. Now here she was smiling and looking fantastic. Wilf gave her a huge loving hug and his face suggested he was extremely proud of her. It was great to see her looking so well and we admired her fighting spirit.

You see, being tough doesn't always mean six foot lumps throwing people out of clubs all night. Being tough is reaching your very, very lowest and most painful form of living hell and having the spirit and character to fight back over months and years. People perhaps don't realise what a close bunch we are, I don't mean just villains but certain actors, singers and sportsmen who are always with us too. This meant that everywhere Wendy looked and everything she heard reminded her of Tony, so it was even more courageous.

My mind went back to a private barbecue party at Joey Pyle's house a few months before when the keyboard player had played Tony's favorite song *Strangers in the Night* for 'absent friends'.

On the stage there were star turns from Joe's friend of many years; Jocelyn Brown belting out *Somebody Else's Guy,* a great performance by Dave's young lady Storm, an appearance by Bill Murray and a quality bit from Dave (he purposely kept his part to a minimum so not to be accused of using the show for his own means. This accusation had been leveled at him a number of times despite the fact that if it wasn't for Dave there would have been no show in the first place - fact!).

My favorite performance of the night came from 'Narco Polo' himself, Howard Marks. He too edited his set down but was hilarious none the less. Howard is a real natural performer. Still, I suppose he would have to be... he had about 40 different IDs at one time!

He is also a man of huge intellect. His association with cannabis is not just one of indulgence, he campaigns religiously for it's legalisation in the political arena and his beliefs are backed up by years of study and research into the history of what is fundamentally a naturally occurring substance, how can something nature provides be made illegal by man? Howard has many supporters in this belief, many of them not even cannabis users. I support him all the way because taxing nature surely cannot be a good thing.

Howard also made a respectful address to Joe himself from the stage. The most emotional moment came when Joe took the microphone and made his own speech thanking everyone for their support, it was extremely moving.

There was also a huge auction of all types of memorabilia.

Typically, there was a complete ban on the press reporting of the event, a ban that came from the top. We know this because a lot of our pals are press people and many of them were there on the night and they told us the day after. As far as the authorities were concerned, this event never happened. I can assure you though, that it did.

It seems that as far as the law is concerned, Joey Pyle is still the bloke that embarrassed them way back in 1960 when Selwyn Cooney was shot dead in the East End's Pen Club. On that night, Joe, Jimmy Nash and John Read had walked into the club, shots were fired and Cooney lay dead. As I said at the start of the book, Joe and Jimmy narrowly escaped the noose and the police never forgot it. In 1992, Joe was arrested for 'offering' to supply drugs NOT supplying but offering, no drugs were found on Joe. As a result he received 14 years, an unbelievable sentence for nothing more than intent. Anyone with half a brain would see that as a revenge sentence. Even if you are found not guilty you cannot embarrass the system.

Many people consider Joe to be the 'Boss' and all have different reasons for it. On 17th February 2007, I got the call telling me that one of the most highly respected and indeed loved underworld figures of the last 50 years had passed away peacefully. It seems that, even when you expect these things, it's still a shock. I don't mind admitting, I shed a few tears as we all did that day and the next.

Joe couldn't have asked for better people to be with him at the end. His son young Joe, Mitch Pyle, wife Julie, fight promoter Greg Steene, the son of Joe's beloved late friend Alex Steene, another much loved, respected and missed man, and Charlie and Veronica Richardson. Roy Shaw, Freddie Foreman and Johnny Nash had all been up to see him the night before. The show of affection and respect was mind blowing with at least 100 people arriving to pay their last respects.

The following afternoon, Joe asked if Charlie (Richardson) was in the room. At that point, around 1pm, Charlie and Veronica walked in, sat down, gently held Joe's hand and informed him they were right there with him. Julie tenderly held his other hand. Knowing that almost everyone he loved was with him, he smiled... and then passed away. The man who was always there for everyone, and was the first and last port of call when you had a problem, was gone. This was a void it would be foolish to even attempt to fill, there's simply no point. If people think all underworld losses are that huge, they would be wrong. Joey Pyle snr played a huge part in everybody's life and had no enemies on his own side of the law, another extremely rare feat. Motor neurone disease had taken the UK's only Don of Dons.

How could I have imagined in my worst nightmares that a year later in January, my own beloved Dad, Tel snr, would be taken by the same bastard illness - motor neurone disease! It shattered my family and I had suicidal thoughts for a long time after. My Mum and Dad had known each other since they were 11 years old, they married at 18, then Dad was called up into the army for National Service. Dad's antics in the army would make a book by themselves!

As soon as I heard the news about Joe, I rang Roy 'Pretty Boy' Shaw, who along with Joe and the great Alex Steene had kicked off unlicensed boxing. As soon as I told Roy, I could hear the emotion pouring out from the other end of the line. Roy was in pieces, in fact, we all were! My immediate worry was for Charlie Bronson in Wakefield. He would be absolutely devastated. After all, he called Joe 'Dad' and Charlie loved and trusted nobody like he did Joey Pyle snr. Charlie was in a concrete coffin. If this news was delivered in the wrong manner it would be one major problem. Both Charlie's cousin Lorraine and myself phoned Wakefield to try and get the message to Charlie. At least this way, he would receive the news from one of his own and didn't have to hear it from the TV or somebody's radio. That after all, is exactly how Reg Kray found out that his twin brother Ron had passed away. He was casually walking along the wing in Wayland nick when he heard the news that Ronnie Kray was dead from another con's radio.

Luckily, Lorraine's message got through so at least he had heard the news from one of his own. Unlike most nicks, we could trust the Wakefield screws to be humane about the whole thing. Like everyone else with even half a brain, the Wakefield screws were completely baffled as to why Charlie had to share living space with the likes of Ian Huntley and Roy Whiting.

As I have said before, the famous 'chaps' are not always the most respected. The Krays were probably the most well known but respect wise, Joey Pyle snr was above them. A few of the lads are more 'famous' than Freddie Foreman but they will admit themselves, they don't come near him in the respect stakes.

Everyone who knows the facts will tell you that Joey Pyle has done far more right than wrong, nobody has committed themselves to more charity work, mostly on the quiet, without fanfare. Joe worked tirelessly for Zoe's Place children's hospice. He was the only person to write a book or do anything for children giving every single penny to the cause. The book *Looking at Life* names all those big companies who make money from children who refused to help with the book for free (most of them).

Funny how, to the outsider, Joey Pyle was the big bad gangster yet 'ordinary' people have done far less to help those less fortunate. The amount of money Joe raised for children's charities is treble that of a lot of rock stars. Every event that Joe organised was in aid of charity. In short, Joey Pyle was a good man who is much loved and missed. His death signified the end of an era.

23
FUNERAL FOR THE DON

The day of Joey Pyle snr's funeral was wet and drizzly but, as expected, it was a huge occasion. Thousands turned out to pay their final respects to the 'Don of Dons'. Every 'face' was there and everyone was genuinely grieving. The pall bearers were Joe Pyle jnr, Roy Shaw, Ronnie Field, Freddie Foreman, Roy Nash, Mitch Pyle and Vic Dark and at one point Jamie Foreman. Joe had so many friends, it was near impossible to pick the pallbearers. Johnny Nash was supposed to be a pallbearer but had badly injured his back. All these good men were extremely close to Joe. This was no show funeral and emotions were running extremely high.

Wilf Pine oversaw all three Kray funerals and he did the same for his old pal Joe. Talking of the Kray funerals, it's incredible how many people insist they had a part in organising them or personally looked after Reggie or Charlie in their time of need, there's so much bullshit around you can choke on it! Wilf Pine actually did look after all the brothers and played a big part in the organisation of the funerals. This is a classic example of the most respected men not always being the most 'famous' although, to us, Wilf is a megastar. As Joe was lowered into the rain filled coffin, the real people grieved, the plastics tried to get in the photos and everyone was left wondering 'what the hell will happen now he's gone?'

Joe played such a huge part in everything, it was an obvious question to ask. Would there be peace or would past gangland wars now be repeated? Would people take liberties and try and get away with things they would never have tried before. Joe's road was a sea of black funeral cars and mourners were everywhere.

The 'Boss' was carried by four beautiful black plumed horses in a pristine large and ornate glass sided Victorian carriage. Behind that came two funeral cars both full to the roof of flowers! Then limos and 157 cars followed those with about 300 mourners walking by the cars. Uniquely, there were two services for Joe, the first at St Theresa's Church.

The church was overflowing with mourners, all of whom would have known Joe through his different guises including club owner and part of the Nash firm. People phoned me afterwards and told me that Dave Courtney was quiet as a mouse, he hardly said a word throughout the service. I responded: "Dave is grieving, he is a mess and if he talks about Joe, he will probably go to pieces." This was not the Dave Courtney of the live shows, this Dave Courtney wanted to cry his eyes out but knew he couldn't. I had spoken to him a couple of times before and he was torn between keeping up the Courtney act or being a genuine mourner on that day, he didn't know what people expected of him anymore. I honestly got the impression that when Joe died Dave Courtney (whether you like him or not) wanted to be locked in a room full of brandy and cigars for a week and cry until there was nothing left! That's why Dave wasn't himself, he was hurting and in pain and I know that for a fact because we spoke about it after, in his mind, he really had lost another father.

The second service was held at Sutton and Merton Cemetery and afterwards Joe was buried. There were 3,000 mourners in attendance! My mind was on Joey Pyle jnr, they were extremely close, more like brothers. But young Joe has his Dad's tenacity and fought through the pain. Then I thought about my mate Roy Shaw. Despite all you have read and his reputation, Roy is one of the most emotional men I have ever known and losing Joe crippled him for a while and this loss was agony. Then there was Johnny Nash, best pals since I don't know when and Wilf Pine, Freddie Foreman, Charlie Richardson ... the list was endless. I have never known a man to have so many sincerely love and respect him, to leave a hole in so many souls. Things will certainly never be the same.

24
JOEY PYLE SNR - FAREWELL TO A TRUE LEGEND

The day after Joe died, I wrote the following tribute for the Internet:

Since yesterday, many of the UK's toughest men have found themselves weeping uncontrollably. People with solid reputations as hard and dangerous men said goodbye while trying and failing to choke back floods of tears as they told another man they loved him. The one they had come to say their final farewells to was of course the great Joey Pyle.

Of course, we all knew Joe had been ill for a long time, but strangely, it was still a huge shock. It seems nothing can prepare you completely for bad news even if you know it's coming. The benefit show we all did for him was almost a year ago to the day. I remember having some trepidation about whether Joe would make it to see that show.

True to form though, Joe fought on for a year despite the debilitating illness he was living with, and never gave up. I have said before and will say again now, Joey Pyle did a lot more good in his eventful life than he ever did bad. Sure, he did some naughty things but he also worked tirelessly for sick and underprivileged children among many other good causes. He would frequently visit Zoe's Place children's hospice with the other 'chaps' and was so touched and inspired by these amazing kids that he wrote a book called *Looking at Life* and gave every single penny it made to Zoe's while simultaneously exposing those huge companies that had made vast fortunes from children's products but refused to give anything back.

Joe continued with this work until his strength finally deserted him. His loyalty and generosity to his friends was also huge. While others talked about it, Joe just did it and there were very successful benefit nights for Ronnie Biggs, Charlie Bronson, Wendy Lambrianou and many others. Joe was always being asked to help out somebody or something and I personally never saw him turn anyone down.

As far as the 'chaps' are concerned, I would certainly say Joe was the most popular and I truly mean that. There were many reasons for this, not least Joe's larger than life personality. Perhaps the biggest factor was that despite being close to the Nash family, Joe wasn't connected to any one firm so became friendly with all of them. For example, he was great friends with the Krays and the Richardsons so could pop down the East End and see Ronnie and Reggie or into South London for a drink with Charlie and Eddie. He was good friends with both Roy Shaw and Lenny McLean, Freddie Foreman and Jack Mcvitie.

Within the so called underworld, Joe had no enemies to speak of. He always saw the advantages in peace over mindless violence for violence sake. He would also stick up for the underdog despite the fact it may have upset some faces. For example, he always said that Jack Mcvitie deserved a far more dignified end than he got.

Roy Shaw will tell you straight that Joey Pyle literally saved his life three or four times over. It was because of Joe's involvement that Roy finally saw the light of day after barely surviving hell on earth, drugged up with the liquid cosh, hallucinating in pitch darkness in the dungeons below Broadmoor. Without Joe, would Roy have died a slow painful death in the bowels of hell, a forgotten man? Roy would answer yes!

Joe stood by Dave Courtney at a time when it would have been far easier for him just to blank Dave, Joe didn't. Many did though, only to drift back because Joe was sticking with him.

It was Joe that Charlie Bronson called Dad after his own father passed away. There was no criminal link there, it was just that Charlie looked up to Joe, learned from him and was inspired by him. Charlie is just one of those hard men that are not ashamed to have shed many tears since yesterday.

The vacuum that will be left by Joe will be impossible to fill, in fact it's not worth even trying. He was a one off, unique. He was also the glue that kept many people, who on the face of it had nothing in common, together. If you think I am over playing the importance of Joe, it's obvious you never even knew him.

I could go on and on and on but I shall leave it there.

God Bless Joe, you will NEVER be forgotten.

25

BOUNCERS - A DYING TRADE?

I have worked the doors since I was 18 years old. I have seen a lot of changes as all doorman and bouncers have mostly, I'm afraid, for the worse. The worst thing I have experienced is this badge business! Now, that has really ruined things. If you can't fight a dying rabbit but are good at exams ... you are in. That my friends, is the truth. If you have a criminal record for something like assault, you are instantly off the list. Now, in some cases that may be a good idea, but the circumstances under which you got a criminal record in the first place should be at least looked at. What good are a load of seven stone pen pushers who have never had a fight? What can they do, threaten you with algebra!

The old style bouncers were the best because they were a deterrent ... and I'm only going back ten years! Nowadays, most doormen are a joke and the system is a joke. All they tell you to do is call Old Bill and make a statement, you must be joking! I have never made a statement to get someone nicked in my life and I don't intend to start now either. Isn't it obvious that if you are a doorman, you are bound to get a clump now and then? You don't get people nicked over it, then they will really want to flatten the club because a grass works there! And quite right too.

When I did the course, they actually went through on a screen how to fill out a description for the Police. I said, "No need, they will be the ones running at you with weapons shouting grassing slag! You do know you can get shot for that very easily in the city don't you?" They all looked like I was from another planet. One prick I worked with got a little lump under his eye and got the bloke nicked! Statements, court, the whole thing. I was about to flatten this prick myself but what's the point if someone doesn't have a clue why you are clumping them?

None of these doormen today can handle themselves because they are not allowed to fight back anymore. If someone clumps a doorman and the doorman clumps him back, he usually gets nicked or loses his badge (which incidentally, costs a fortune and you have to wait about seven months for ... true!).

So now, most doorman confronted with a bunch of gypsies or whoever will usually get flattened, because all they have done is been a postman or something, got a badge, learnt how to grass and next thing they are in control of who comes in that club. True, a deterrent is better, but you have to be able to back it up. And if you have been in the nick, and you can't eat because you can't get a job if you have a record, what do you do? Go back to crime, even if you don't want to and Old Bill and Judges are going 'we knew you would be back!' Well of course they are, you cut every single option and expect them to starve to death, then moan about crime figures ... what?

The best doormen are those who can defuse a situation but still turn it on if need be and that's your 'old school' bouncer like Stilks who I have worked with in some very sticky situations. Another man I have worked with is called John Bleakney from Birmingham, there's some good people from there. If John says he's with you, you don't have to look back and check, he is right there and right in the thick of it. John's worth about ten other doormen I have worked with and is a close mate ... John, you're the business brother!

Other men I haven't worked with, but have a good reputation are, for one, Lew Yates snr. I have heard stories and know them to be true as Carlton and other lads have told me and they have never seen a punch like it except for Roy Shaw. Again 'old school' - how many piss-heads are going to fancy a go at the doorman with men like that standing there? Not many! They could stop something before it started.

One funny occasion occurred when two blokes were on the floor fighting, one was pulled off and taken the long way out. Me and a pal couldn't be bothered, so counted one, two, three and threw him out of the open patio doors. Well ... we thought they were open, in fact they were shut but you really couldn't tell. CRASH! He went straight through the window. Both at the same time, we ran up to him and said: "You OK mate, bit of a nasty tumble that, you wanna lay off the spirits here, they are heavy!" But he couldn't speak, he was out cold and an ambulance was called ... whoops a daisy!

Tony, who used to work for 'Big Albert' at the 'Elbow Room' at the same time as I did, was another man who gave you confidence and that's what you want. Paul Knight, I have not had the pleasure to work with but his reputation proceeds him as a gentleman not to be messed with, he is also an extremely good writer and *Coding of a Concrete Animal* is a classic. I can write a whole book about good and bad doormen, it could go on forever, many whose names I have forgotten. But working at the 'Elbow Room' in the roughest part of Birmingham called Aston with a West London accent was a challenge! Ha!

I honestly don't get intimidated by anyone, not because I'm hard, it's just a mental attitude I have that the worst thing you can do is kill me and being a diagnosed depressive, that really doesn't bother me. Anyway, looking across and seeing a man like Albert Chapman, knowing he is on your side gives you enough confidence for ten men, words can't express the respect I have for that man. Albert Chapman may not be one of the household names (or perhaps he is, it's hard to know being on the inside looking out!) but that man has maximum respect from every single 'face' in Britain.

Another ridiculous law, in my opinion, is the smoking ban. More than half the people who used to go clubbing just don't go out anymore. They stay at someone's house and have a good time there. This is also keeping doormen out of work. Many times recently, I have been in a club or pub that has more bouncers than customers and it will only get worse. I have never smoked in my life but I am told that people want to smoke the most when they are out drinking.

It is very difficult to make a living as a bouncer at the moment and most of it (in my opinion) is the government wanting everyone numbered and watched. 'Big Brother is watching you!'

26
FOOTBALL AND TORTURE

There have been loads of fit ups and sneaky moves by the 'good guys' to get people they want in prison, guilty or not! Mostly not!

Jason Marriner is a man we all like, he's a real character and everyone loves a character. Unlike many so called 'football hooligans' Jason Marriner is actually interested in the football and has a encyclopedic knowledge of the game. There is nothing he enjoys more than a laugh and watching a football match. Unfortunately, because of a snake called Donal MacIntyre, there is no more going to football matches. Jason, like all real Chelsea fans worshipped Peter Osgood, Charlie Cooke, Alan Hudson, 'Chopper' Harris, Kerry Dixon. Mickey Thomas and Franco Zola. He reminds me in that way of my brother-in-law, Phil Gibbs. Phil is not just family but my best mate and has stood by me through EVERYTHING!

Phil and Jason actually have a hell of a lot in common. Jason actually had the balls to appreciate other teams, players like Gazza and Kegan when he was growing up. For Phil, like me, nobody on this earth will ever come near to George Best! The word 'genius' is overused (they even use it in respect of Beckham!) but George Best was from another planet, he was the greatest and even though I'm a QPR supporter, I cried my eyes out when he died. Being a QPR fan, the 'Gods' for me were always Stan Bowles, Rodney Marsh and Tony Currie who is a relative (I thank you!).

So, how did Jason get involved with MacIntyre? Little did Jason know that the BBC had planted someone next door, a paid informer called Darren Wells who was extremely right wing with heavy contacts in Combat 18 and Searchlight. Wells, had started spreading Jason's name and put it about that he was also involved with Combat 18 which is total bullshit! Jason has never been into the racist side of things but everyone makes a racist remark at some time in their lives whether meant or not.

MacIntyre was hardly seen during this stitch up. A bloke called Paul Atkinson was doing all of MacIntyre's donkey work. Atkinson would constantly ask Jason to get him gear and Jason would always turn him down. Atkinson even offered Jason 20 grand of coke! Of course, this was all recorded with the BBC's highest tech gear.

Jason and his pal Andy Frain were filmed for 18 months, in all 344 hours of tape on Jason was filmed and condensed down to one! That works out to a solid two and a half weeks in front of your TV! And NO violence was found in all that time apart from the breaking up of the 'Bloody Sunday March' in London - 344 hours and that was ALL they had. There was one scene of Jason making a call, supposedly to organise a riot. It was a sham because the person on the other end didn't pick up! Every time Jason was on the phone, he was sorting a riot!

MacIntyre did nothing apart from try his hardest to put people in prison and take the credit. He got Jason six years in prison for nothing. MacIntyre gladly saw Jason get sent down for SIX YEARS!

You will be shocked at the amount of villainy that the 'good guys' have produced over the years, you can write a book on every single one so I will keep it short. One of the 'chaps' I'm closest to is Charlie Richardson and his lovely wife Ronnie. I'm not sticking my nose into family matters but Charlie did ask me to make sure that I write two things about his brother Eddie ... so I'm just being the messenger!

Charlie (and a lot of people) were extremely upset by Eddie's book *Freddie Foreman and Ronnie Brown* (one of the chaps) included. Also Charlie will never forget the fact that Eddie stood up in court and said: "I'm only here because my name's Richardson!) that one has hurt Charlie for many years!

I think it's a shame the brothers can't get on but this is not my business.

What is everybody's business is the farce the tabloids called the 'Torture Trial'. I, and anyone else who knows Charlie well, can tell you that there is no way Charlie wired people up, electrocuted them, pulled teeth out with pliers or any of that stuff they said to sell papers and make the authorities look good. See, the authorities looked a bit of a joke in the mid '60s because of the Profumo Scandal that brought down the government, it had to get some credibility back. Could that be why 'The Torture Trial', 'The Train Robbers', 'The Krays' and others received such ridiculous sentences? Could it have been a conscious effort to regain power and respect? Charlie Richardson received 25 years for GBH! Now that's flexing your muscles - 25 years on the day that England won the World Cup against the Germans of all days! Have you ever heard of anything like that before, lawyers have told me that today, it wouldn't have even gone to court!

It's also true that most of the prosecution witnesses were cons or ex cons, they conned Charlie out of thousands and that's why some of them got a right hander ... wouldn't you do the same? The things Charlie and the rest were accused of could easily have killed someone. How do you get your money back if your victim is dead? Doesn't add up does it?

Remember, I am talking about Charlie, not Eddie or Frank who Charlie had already warned about getting into the pinball machine game. Charlie was not a man of violence for violence sake - Frank certainly was. One important factor, Charlie Richardson was NOT a gangster, he was NOT like the twins. Charlie wanted to be the richest businessman NOT the most infamous gangster. Frank had also threatened the Judge (Judge Lawton's) father a few years before which should have made it a retrial, it didn't. Again, it would never have happened today. Think about it, the Krays received 30 years for double murder - Charlie got 25 for trying to get his money back on the evidence of convicts! Can you take that in? Chris Lambrianou says Charlie was more sinned against than sinner, that's about right.

You see if the authorities make the Richardsons and Kray's look as evil as humanly possible, then send them down, the police have saved us from these evil men who would kill innocent people and the Government are back calling the shots.

I have had some fantastic nights with Charlie and Ronnie. I remember staying up late, with Charlie telling me: "Tel, you know that trial was disgusting, I never tortured anybody ever, a few people got a right hander who stole my money but that was it!"

He then told me about the infamous 'torture box' that was meant to have been used by Charlie to wire victims up and electrocute them. "Tel, there was no box. All they had was an old field telephone they found in they scrap yard. It was a scrap yard for fuck's sake, there was different stuff everywhere. In court, they brought out this field phone, which they now called a torture box and said 'Richardson USED A BOX LIKE THIS!' Not 'this is the box he used' because they didn't have one. That fake 'torture box' is in Scotland Yard to this day."

Basically, it was all a fairy tale - the war with the Krays, the 'torture box', the whole thing was contrived. One man, who ripped Charlie off and got a clump for it from George Cornell, is now a well known name on day time TV, of course, I can't say who it is but he has a nice tan though ... and he's an annoying wanker to be honest. The Richardsons worked differently to the twins, they did their own things and made their own money. Today, Charlie will not go anywhere near Eddie and vice versa. At Joey Pyle's funeral, Charlie stayed in the car because Eddie was in the church. As, I said at one boxing show it came to a real row. Roy Shaw and I held Charlie and I think one of the Nashes and Joey Pyle held back Eddie.

Charlie and Frank are not that close anymore, although they will always be loyal to each other, and the days Charlie, Frank and me have been out for dinner have been a real laugh. But never think the Richardsons, or at least Charlie, were playing the gangster game like the twins, because they never were. Charlie was always far to clever for that. Charlie is respected from gangsters to Prime Ministers all over the world and owns a gold mine in South Africa, that's a clever man, not a brainless thug. He is a man far more highly thought of than any arse licking screw who tried to break him but never did it. Charlie Richardson is a one off! Yes, there were clumps and violence but the torture box and teeth pulling is all propaganda. I know Charlie extremely well, we have spoken for hours about everything. Charlie and Ronnie Richardson are extremely special people! And Charlie was treated like a dog by the authorities, he was the scapegoat for riots and everything else that went wrong in prison. I can't see Charlie and Eddie ever making the peace and Frank has made a lot of enemies, not least Freddie Foreman and Dave Courtney.

Since I lost my Dad, Charlie has said he would take on the job of my step Dad ha! Roy Shaw, Chris Lambrianou and others have spent a lot of time at Charlie's house and there is no way the man could ever have been a sadist or any of the other media rubbish. I have spoken to him, looked in his eyes and tried to imagine him doing the things he was accused of and apart from being a tough man at a tough time, there is no way 'torture boss' was anything but propaganda.

Charlie Richardson is a gentleman and private man who has had a tough time, in prison he was a trophy prisoner along with the Train Robbers (the Krays can't really be counted except Charlie because they were killers). Chris and I have already made plans for our next visit to a Ronnie and Charlie, two people who are always great company. Somebody should study the Richardson trial and give the man some sort of compensation! I am not trying to whitewash Charlie, of course he was a rascal but he was no 'torture gang boss'.

I have written about all the good that Joey Pyle did for Charity, especially children. Look at the very first boxing posters, even they were for children's charities. So when he died those lovely people in the press called him a 'Heroin Dealer'. Let's make one thing clear, Joe was actually sentenced for intent to supply Omnipom which is a rave club drug ... hardly Heroin! The drug came through Reg Kray's pal Pete Gillette. Prior to this a bloke called Dave had asked Joe out of the blue if he could get him some drugs, Joe had forgotten all about it when Pete Gillette turned up with this Omnipom gear, Joe thought of Dave. Joe wasn't sure about Dave and he let his guard down. Dave was an undercover copper!

They met at a Heathrow Hotel and of course the room was bugged. Joe handed over the Omnipom and some Heroin, Dave handed over the money. When they got to the passageway, Joey Pyle had been nicked for the first time since the Pen Club in 1960, it was Christmas for the Police. It's an old saying, 'if they want you they will get you in the end, guilty or not!'

Joe received 14 years, cut to nine on appeal, that's a lot more than many sex cases and nonces get BUT this was Joey Pyle. Again, the media went to work in the style of 'everyone can finally sleep safe after all these years'. No, we sleep safe when you have all the nonces and rapists. None of Joe's 30 years of charity work for children made any difference of course. Joe was found guilty of 'making an offer to supply Heroin and Omnipom' NOT supplying! No drugs were found on him, it was all about intent to supply ... Joe didn't go down for supplying, it's a big difference. And if Dave the copper had not put himself in Joe's world, Joe would not have sold him anything, surely that's entrapment? Joe was not dealing in drugs until the copper kept pushing him for it. At the time, Joe was working legit in the film industry at Pinewood Studios. Again, I'm not whitewashing anyone but Joe was not a drug dealer, if he had been it would have been different but he was working on films when this Dave approached Joey!

Can that be right? That Tel Currie has never sold coke, let's keep on and on until he gives us some one night ... then nick the bastard! Surely there is something better the police could be doing?

Then of course there was Charlie Kray. Charlie was set up by undercover police to supply drugs and died in prison because of it. Charlie being arrested also made Reg's release much tougher, that's why Reg married Roberta, he had a relative on the outside again. I don't doubt Reg and Roberta were very much in love but getting married was a good move for Reg's release. You have a much better chance of release if you have relatives outside. It wouldn't surprise me if the whole Charlie Kray thing was set up to keep Reg in ... Think about it!

My great pal Albert Chapman saw the whole sorry story unfold, because it started in his club The Elbow Room and Albert actually told Charlie they were coppers but Charlie was not a villain and did not have the radar to detect such things, instead he lapped up the champagne and compliments ... and died in prison!

Dave Courtney was named an informer in open court, which I thought was illegal? Maybe I'm wrong, but I thought an informer's name could not be read out? I'm sure they made an exception, so hopefully an underworld figure would shoot him and do the job for them.

I think that when they put the twins away, the law thought the public would forget them BUT the opposite happened, they became heroes. So the powers that be thought we better damage villain's reputations in future to stop it happening again, to stop the hero worship. So we will put it out that they are drug dealers or grasses to prevent them becoming idols. Maybe they will accuse the next big name of being a nonce to ruin their reputations? Do you think the law will not sink that low? They have tried everything else!

27
THEY DESERVE MORE RESPECT THAN THEY GET!

We all know the big names, we all know of the Krays, Freddie Foreman, 'Mad' Frankie Fraser, Dave Courtney, Roy Shaw, Howard Marks and Charlie Richardson, all of whom we have talked about in some form and I shall tell you what those people are REALLY like soon, what they are like as men.

But there are men out there who really shaped the underworld and go pretty much unheard of, usually by choice. I will try and give you a very short insight into those men and if I know them either by regular phone calls or visits. These are in no particular order and, importantly, I would like you to know where I personally stand next to these men. Truth is, I don't!

I am not trying to be a 'gangster' and I know I am many leagues below these men. This is NOT about giving it the big 'un, I am aware I will be forgotten in no time, I have no illusions of who I am. So here's a list of men who are highly respected in our circles but maybe not so in everyday life.

Vic Dark is simply one of the toughest, hardest and dangerous men in the country! Maybe, except for a young Roy Shaw, Vic is the most dangerous man I can think of and many hard men agree with me. As is always the case, Vic is also a real gentleman who despises bullies and doesn't shout his mouth off. From armed robbery to shoot outs with the police, Vic Dark is a man you want on YOUR side! I kept in regular touch with Vic during his last sentence, which had all sorts of gaps in it to be honest!

Paul Massey was named 'Mr Big' of Manchester. I wrote to Paul often during his last sentence and talked to him on the phone as well as to his dear Mum.

Paul Ferris was known as Glasgow's main man after the wiping out of the Thompson family (Arthur Thompson actually pointed the finger at Paul in the dock. Paul was found 'not guilty' for the killing of Arthur Thompson jnr. (I have spoken on the phone and communicated by email often with Paul and send good will messages through various people). Paul's rival Tam 'the Licensee' Mcgraw died of a heart attack recently ... I doubt Paul shed a tear!

We have talked a lot about Wilf Pine. He was depended on by all three Kray brothers and did most of the organising and thankless work at the funerals. Reg wrongly blamed Wilf for photos of Reggie that appeared in the papers when Reg was terminally ill, the culprit was actually Reg's lover Bradley Allerdyce. Wilf is also the only living Englishman to be embraced by the Mafia. Wilf is a close friend whom I talk to at least twice a week.

'Big' Albert Chapman - Wilf Pine described Albert as the 'Freddie Foreman of the Midlands'. Albert has helped me out many times. It was in Albert's Club the Elbow Room in Aston, Birmingham that Charlie Kray first met the fake Geordie coppers. Albert clocked them straight away, he warned Charlie and Charlie didn't listen. I had some good nights working the door at the 'Elbow' and Albert is a close friend. My respect for him I cannot put into words.

Kevin Lane is unjustly serving a severe sentence, everyone knows he's innocent. Visit www.freekevinlane.com (free Kevin Lane). I am in touch with Kevin all the time.

Joey Pyle jnr; after the crippling loss of his father (for everyone) Joe took the batten and has put on great unlicensed shows, especially at Caesars in Streatham, South London. Promoters Rickey English and Warren Banford are usually Joe's right hand men and the boys are bringing back the concept of the 'Guv'nor' ... well done lads!

Mitch Pyle is Joe snr's adopted son and I love the guy to pieces! I love his company, especially when Carlton is also in the mix, it's a laugh a second. I am always there for Mitch and he knows it!

John Knight; everyone has heard of brother Ronnie but it was John who planned the second biggest robbery on English soil, the

Security Express Robbery, that bagged six million in cash! I speak to John on a regular basis and we even do our (Bad) James Cagney impressions in pubs!

Terry Sabini is Alan Mortlock's right hand man in the boxing shows and all round top man. I communicate with Terry often.

Johnny 'Mad Dog' Adair - Former C COY Commander, Loyalist paramilitary. Johnny has now moved to Scotland after Loyalist fall outs in Ireland. I have spoken to Johnny a number of times about everything except politics. I think Johnny will be moving into the mainstream and making legitimate money now.

Adams family, right at the top, although Terry was recently jailed for handling.

Ian McAteer is another man who should be free!

John McVicar is always a better escape artiste than armed robber, he is now a journalist confusing people which side he's coming from! I have had chats with John.

Curtis 'Cocky' Warren is still caged in Holland on drug charges.

Willie Gage; his appeal is won, let the man go!

Tommy 'TC' Campbell; for 21 years they kept him in prison as a murderer. Now, they have decided he is innocent! Oh, don't worry, it's only a man's life you have stolen.

The last I heard, Terry Smith was on remand. They have been after Terry for ages! Terry, Cass Pennant and I visited Tony Bowers together, we were always in contact but they have it in for Terry ... Fight on mate!

The Smiths, Frankhams and Stockins - These fighting gypsy boys are a force of nature when allied together, I love em' all! We are all very close pals.

Joe Carrington was a rascal himself in the old days. He was in Roy Shaw's corner during the 'Golden Age' and later his manager.

Jason Marriner; A lot more than a hooligan, he was stitched up by Donal MacIntyre on TV as was Andy 'Nightmare' Frain. MacIntyre filmed 344 hours of film on Jason and spent three hundred thousand pounds making the documentary and it was shown all over the world! The whole sordid story is in Jason's book *Life as a Chelsea Headhunter: It's only a Game!* Obviously, Mr MacIntyre has not made many friends and I'm sure a snake like that had few to lose!

Jim Dawkins is an ex screw who left the system in disgust when he saw what was REALLY going on! He had the bottle to write a book exposing our corrupt prison system called *The Loose Screw* for Apex Publishing Ltd. Apex is fast becoming one of the few publishers with the balls to tell the truth with no compromise!

Paul Knight is a doorman and great author. A young man with the ways of the 'old school' a gentleman who can look after himself! Paul and I speak all the time.

Jamie Foreman, Ricky Harnett and Terry Stone - These boys especially have put British actors well and truly back on THE MAP ... keep working lads!

Carlton Leach, my bruv in arms, Carl goes from strength to strength, his film *Rise of the Foot Soldier* is a success and his live shows are sold out. A man I did and do a lot of work with and, trust me, the film is true!

Cass Pennant is, in fact, an extremely clever man who has his own publishing company and a smash film on his hands. We visited Tony Bowers together with Terry Smith and it's always a pleasure catching up with the 'Big Man'. He filmed something at one of my shows and I have never remembered to ask him what it was!

Patsy Manning was a friend of all three Kray brothers but was cut badly by Reggie when Reg was having a breakdown. Reg was convinced Patsy was trying to kill him. Patsy is in Birmingham and I would always see him while working at the 'Elbow Room'.

Jimmy Tibbs is from a well respected family, Jimmy is, in my opinion, the greatest boxing trainer this country has ever produced.

John 'Mario' Cunningham; I used to visit Mario when I had come up to Newcastle to visit my great friend Harry Marsden. Harry and Mario were the best of pals and had been through many an adventure together. Mario once escaped from Durham prison on a working party. Harry and Mario were members of the original 'Geordie Mafia'.

Nosher Powell is a former pro boxer who sparred with Joe Louis among others. Nosher was MC at all the classic fights of the 'Golden Era' of unlicensed boxing and a film stuntman. I keep in contact with Nosher - a true legend!

Walter Probyn was a renowned escape artiste in his day, he was the brains behind John Mcvicar's escape from Durham. Many years later, he was accused of sex with underage girls.

Steve Holdsworth took over where Nosher Powell left off and is the best MC in unlicensed boxing. Steve also commentates on boxing for Eurosport. I will always have time for Steve.

'Big' Joe Eagan is one of Mike Tyson's REAL friends and an extremely hard man in his own right. Joe is a man you wouldn't want to fight in the ring or the cobbles!

Jason Vella is the former Essex torturer who didn't find a friend in Paul Ferris when Paul called him a 'Fat Poof' in the nick.

The Sayers family is a well respected Newcastle family headed by John Henry Sayers. Another family my late, great pal Harry Marsden admired hugely.

Jimmy Tippett snr; a very good light heavyweight in his day but lost his license for assaulting the Police. Jimmy was at Mr Smith's when Dickie Heart (no relation to the Krays, that was Ronnie Heart, the Krays cousin!) was allegedly shot by the Richardsons. Jimmy became involved in armed robbery and drug deals but I still think of him as a good boxer in hard times.

Ian 'The Machine' Freeman put cage fighting on the map in the UK, a lovely man, Ian was the first cage fighter I had heard of!

The Johnsons are a big family from the Birmingham and Cheltenham areas who have been linked to crime for years. Lately, they have targeted stately homes, stealing paintings worth over £80 million in three years!

The Burger Bar Boys - another heavy Birmingham mob.

Billy Gentry - robber and prison legend.

Ronnie Easterbrook is a robber and prison legend, still serving his time.

Gary Bedford is one of the game's best referees!

28
EPILOGUE

I'm glad to say that unlicensed boxing is alive and well, mostly in London. When I was promoting (and will again) I could never understand why there wasn't more going on up north. Norman Parker, the author of *Parkhurst Tales,* and I once had a long talk about using bull rings in Spain to stage boxing shows in the tourist season but nothing came of it. But there are a lot of openings in unlicensed boxing and none of us who care about it want it to just die. You can thank Joey Pyle jnr, Ricky English, Warren Banford, Alan Mortlock, Terry Sabini, Steve Holdsworth, Andy Jardine, Joe Smith and maybe me from stopping it fazing out a long time ago. And, thank God, the fighters keep coming.

I think in future more and more ex-pros will turn to unlicensed after their careers are on the rocks, or they lose their licenses. It's the obvious move and any of the promoters I have mentioned above will be interested. I think there will be a lot more ex-pros like Dominic Negus moving to unlicensed and more gypsies getting in there as well. Unlicensed has a great future but it's all down to the promoters, fighters and, more importantly, the spectators. If you have not been to an unlicensed fight, go along, you will love it!

So there we have it. It's pretty clear that Cliff Field was the Guv'nor of the golden age of unlicensed boxing, but what about the most respected villain of the last fifty years? About 85% of 'faces' all say 'Brown Bread Fred' - Freddie Foreman and although retired, you still don't mess with 'Brown Bread'. From the battle of Bowe, the Krays alliance, killing and making Frank Mitchell vanish, making Jack 'The Hat' vanish, getting the Train Robbers out of the country, serving ten years for the twins, the Costa del crime, Security Express, being one of the 'famous five', along with

Ronnie Knight and, of course, an author. But real people, those who meet him for the first time, always tell me what a lovely gentleman he is and I just say: "I told ya, don't mistake that kindness for weakness though!"

One thing I have learned from icons like Freddie Foreman, Roy Shaw, Wilf Pine and all the other top 'faces' is that the REAL people are not bullies and don't go around shouting their mouths off, they don't take liberties and will show you respect if you show it to them.

Don't go on about how hard you are because you will sound like an idiot. Respect is the key especially in front of ladies. Shouting your mouth off and threatening this and that does not make you hard. Those old boys who fought in the wars and saw things every day that would make a grown man cry, they hardly talk, and they don't go on about it.

I'm not going to dump my naughty pals but I am not taking part anymore. Of course, I'm no Freddie but I have left a fair bit out of this book. I don't and have never claimed to be the hardest or the biggest villain because there are a lot of bigger ones out there and unlike the films, REAL VIOLENCE is not pretty. And for the youngsters, don't get hard men mixed up with bullies, hard men HATE bullies.

But unlicensed offers a legal way out for fighters who can't get into the pro ranks, you can make money without being Ali or turning to crime. Talking of Ali, who are my five top heavyweight pros of all time?

1) Cassius Clay (pre Army. Even Ali said 'Clay was better than Ali')
2) Larry Holmes
3) Lennox Lewis
4) Joe Louis
5) Jack Dempsey

And the greatest ever?
1) Sugar Ray Robinson
2) Jimmy Wilde
3) Cassius Clay
4) Marvin Hagler
5) Gene Tunney

By the way, Joey Pyle's number one fighter of all time was Joe Louis and Roy Shaw's is Rocky Marciano.

I'm afraid in 2008 we lost one of the most respected 'faces', a man at the top - Johnny Nash.

We also lost the best man I have ever known in my life and loved beyond words, a man I always looked up to, my Dad, TEL CURRIE snr ... LOVE YOU DAD!

Stay healthy, help the weak, sick and elderly and ALWAYS SHOW RESPECT! WITHOUT RESPECT, WE HAVE NOTHING!

OTHER BOOKS BY THE AUTHOR:

Ronnie Biggs: The Inside Story
(Co-written with Mike Gray)

Heroes and Villians
(Co-written with Charles Bronson)

Bouncers
(Co-written with Julian Davies)

COMMENTS ABOUT THE AUTHOR AND THE BOOK

JOEY PYLE SNR
THE 'DON of DONS'

I have known Telboy for about ten years now and I am proud and pleased to have a pal like him. He has total loyalty to his own and has always stood up for his principles. In the ten years I have known him he has always gone with the grain in the wood and never against it and that's the right way.

I know for sure that when he finishes this book, he will only say what he feels and never be influenced by what others may think. Good luck Telboy and always remember ... CRIME DOESN'T PAY ... BUT THE HOURS ARE GOOD!

CLIFF FIELD
UNLICENSED FIGHT LEGEND

Tel Currie has been a close friend to me for many years. I met Tel through my dear friends Red Menzies and living legend Roy Shaw, a man I have great respect for. Why? Because he would always fight anyone, usually five times the size of him, Roy was naturally only a middleweight.

Boxing, unlicensed or otherwise is not just a sport but a way of life. The successful fighter carries respect and the up and coming fighter wants that respect. There are, of course, two sides to every story and boxing is also well known for its links to the underworld ... villains!

I have boxed some great fighters and also crossed paths with some pretty mean guys with fingers in pies shall we say. I'm talking about sharing a ring with Muhammad Ali and Joe Bugner, then having a chat with Roy Shaw or Joey Pyle.

One of my old friends Charlie Kray had two brothers that used to box, and I am also friends with long time prisoner Charles Bronson who also fought unlicensed, and instead of facing real injustice inside prison, should be training kids and giving them a life!

What is it that links these so called dodgy people to the noble art?
Respect? Fear? Or just the challenge?
Well now for the first time all in one book, Tel examines all these questions and more, it's time to find out ... read on and have your eyes opened!

COMMENTS ABOUT THE AUTHOR AND THE BOOK

WILF PINE
THE ONLY ENGLISHMAN EVER TO BE ACCEPTED BY THE TOP ORGANISED CRIME BOSSES IN AMERICA

A lot of things have been said about Tel Currie; he's staunch, solid, more than capable in a row, he's always there for you, and if he's your friend, he's a friend for life, all these things are true. But for me, in these days of the so called 'young turks', he has that rare quality, which we don't see much of, respect. He gives it where he feels it's deserved, and doesn't mince his words when he feels none is warranted.
I along with a lot of others admire him for it, me personally I like him, but more than that, I "respect" him.
Good Luck Tel,
Your Pal.

RONNIE BIGGS
FORMER GREAT TRAIN ROBBER AND CURRENT POLITICAL PRISONER

I was overjoyed when I heard my good friend Tel Currie was writing another book. I was even more delighted when it became obvious that this one is the best he has done so far and that he is showing in print his support for the myself and the other lads serving outrageous sentences. I have very few visits but my son Michael, Tel, Roy Shaw and Mike Gray are my most regular visitors, and we always try and have a laugh when we are together despite the circumstances, if you don't have a laugh you will just rot away!
Tel is one of those few people who is a giver not a taker. He has the respect to ask first if he can write about the chaps and makes sure everyone benefits. There have been a few idiots who have written to me asking for visits, I turned them down flat because you can just tell they want to splatter 'Biggsy is my mate' everywhere because they think it will make them popular or will help sell their stupid products or boost their pointless websites. It's not like that with Tel Currie. We are pleased to contribute to his projects because he helps us all.
Over 40 years after the Great Train Robbery, I am still in maximum security. Here at last is the real inside story of my incarceration by the man that knows the truth.
All the best Tel.

COMMENTS ABOUT THE AUTHOR AND THE BOOK

RONNIE KNIGHT
THE ULTIMATE UNDERWORLD LEGEND AND FOLK HERO, THE ORIGINAL CELEB GANGSTER

Since coming home from my stretch for handling money from the Security Express Robbery then settling away from London, I lost touch with a lot of friends of mine. One man I am in constant touch with though is Tel Currie. We speak about two to three times a week and through Tel I get to hear about everything that's going on. It was Tel who reunited me with my old pal Roy Shaw. Roy, Tel and I went for a lovely meal and a good old chat. I consider Tel a very good friend, as do all the respected Faces. A lot of people will tell you all the time that they are there if you ever need them and it's mostly always lip service but with Tel you know he means it and you know he is fiercely loyal to his friends. Be lucky mate.
Your pal.

CHARLIE RICHARDSON
ONE OF THE MOST RESPECTED MEN EVER TO COME OUT OF LONDON. IN THE SIXTIES, THE MEDIA DUBBED HIM 'THE TORTURE GANG BOSS' AND 'THE MAN THE KRAYS FEARED'

Tel Currie is a true and trusted friend of myself and my family. We have worked together on various things and made a good team. Tel's a throwback to the old days and that's a high compliment believe me. He is a young man who conducts himself like a real man of honor, and a gentleman. In no way does he represent the young scum we have on our streets today. So much do I trust Tel that I have given him full access to all the papers of my so called 'Torture Trial', the REAL story of which he will cover in this book. Tel Currie is so much more than a journalist, the type who write so many books about our people without a clue what they are talking about and declare themselves experts.
Tel IS one of our people. He is respected, liked and trusted by the major players in the business, I would never state something like that if it were not true. He has gone well out of his way to help his friends, even men like Charlie Bronson and Ronnie Biggs who are of course locked up like animals. The heat was really on for Tel when he tried helping me on a bit of business. He could have easily rolled over and most of today's plastic gangsters would have squealed like pigs straight away when being threatened with heavy bird. Trying to get this man to turn rat though is a complete waste of time, as he once said to me "Charlie, I would rather choke to death slowly on my own blood than be a grass!"
He has experienced things that most only read about in fiction novels, he has seen it and done it ... Now he's going to tell you all about it.
Your good pal.

COMMENTS ABOUT THE AUTHOR AND THE BOOK

CARLTON LEACH
ORIGINAL MEMBER OF THE NOTORIOUS ESSEX BOYS FIRM

Telboy is family to me, I consider him my younger brother. I am an extremely private person when it comes to my home life but Tel is one of the very few who comes to my house socially. He is also the only person apart from myself who has read the script for the film about my life, I haven't shown anyone else and probably won't. I can honestly say I love Tel to bits and would trust him with my life, now there's not many people I or anyone else for that matter could say they trust 100% with their life is there?

Tel and I have also worked together many times. A good team is built on trust, loyalty, strength, bottle and staunchness. Tel has all these qualities and more. You only have to look at the standard of the men whose respect Tel has earned to know how solid he is. You don't get the unconditional trust and respect Tel Currie has from men like Roy Shaw, Charlie Richardson, Ronnie Knight, Howard Marks, Vic Dark, Charlie Bronson, Freddie Foreman and tons of others if you are not completely and utterly staunch and solid. Unlike so many, Tel has been tried and tested and been in some extremely dodgy situations but never wavered .

I'm proud to say I am always here for my mate Tel no matter what and I know he is always there for me no matter what… Now you can't ask for more than that.
Love ya' Bruv!

PAUL FERRIS
KING OF THE UNDERWORLD IN GLASGOW

I have known Tel for quite a while now and consider him as one of our own.
Very few people get to know who the real firms are but Tel Currie is one of them because he is trusted …Why?
Tel is very well connected and in this life you reap what you sow and he will tell it how it is from the people who are in the know.
Some call them faces, the 'chaps' or even gangsters … We quite simply call them Goodfellas and if you're not then Tel will expose you to the bone.
Break our code and Tel will break your balls when he has you on his hit-list …
Well done Tel a truly fantastic eyeopener!
Respect Always.